Frank and Anne Hummert's
Radio Factory

Frank and Anne Hummert's Radio Factory

The Programs and Personalities of Broadcasting's Most Prolific Producers

by JIM COX

McFarland & Company, Inc., Publishers
Jefferson, North Carolina, and London

Library of Congress Online Catalog

Cox, Jim. 1939–
    Frank and Anne Hummert's radio factory : the programs and
personalities of broadcasting's most prolific producers / by Jim Cox.
        p.   cm.
    Includes bibliographical references and index.

    ISBN 0-7864-1631-9 (softcover: 50# alkaline paper)

    1. Hummert, Frank.   2. Hummert, Anne.   3. Radio
    Programs—United States—History.   4. Radio broadcasting—
    United States—History.   I. Title.
    PN1991.3.U6C67   2003
    791.44'75'0973—dc21   2003009259

British Library cataloguing data are available

On the cover: Frank Hummert (right) with Anne Hummert
and actor Karl Swenson, star of *Mr. Chameleon* (CBS Photo Archive)

Manufactured in the United States of America

McFarland & Company, Inc., Publishers
  Box 611, Jefferson, North Carolina 28640
    www.mcfarlandpub.com

For Sharon,
the love of my life

ACKNOWLEDGMENTS

Vintage radio is a terrific hobby. As the years roll by, I'm continually reminded that it's the people who practice the craft that contribute immeasurably to the positive experiences I take from it. A project like this book constantly confirms this.

Credit for a long overdue biography of two of radio's most prominent behind-the-scenes talents must be shared with a host of good people. I'm continually amazed by the fact that there are individuals who stand ready to offer their unlimited assistance to complete a research project of this magnitude, without any prospect of recompense. Not only do they give freely of their time and material resources, they also share their vast knowledge and wide-ranging expertise on a diverse number of topics.

Without Claire Connelly this volume would be far poorer. Never have I worked with a volunteer researcher who put more effort into the task, tracking down every imaginable source in a quest to locate never-before-published details of the lives of the principal figures. Her pursuits were often fraught with leads that simply didn't pan out, but she never, ever registered any disappointment. Such disappointing results were, instead, a clarion call to redouble her resolve and pursue in alternate pathways. Without her intuitive sense of direction this work would have lost a great deal, I am convinced. I'm appreciative for Claire's commitment to a most challenging assignment and am happy to acknowledge her many triumphs.

There were others who filled in numerous blanks, too. I'm espe-

Acknowledgments

cially grateful to Jim Ashenhurst and the members of his family for providing rich anecdotes that supplement the factual material. The Ashenhurst clan was responsive to every request that was made of them, and I'm sincerely thankful for their help.

I'm also obliged to the archival staff of the American Heritage Center at the University of Wyoming — where the Hummert Collection is housed — for their extraordinary collaboration in my research. Those good people, directed by archivist Carol Bowers, obligingly accommodated every request I made in an intensive, protracted on-site investigation, and did so joyfully and eagerly.

Many others supplied useful documentation and images, recalled personal eyewitness glimpses, offered candid and discerning impressions, extended valuable suggestions, and — in some cases — provided recordings of aural features that became indispensable in ascertaining the true character of the many radio series described herein.

For all of this help I am particularly thankful for the donations, both tangible and intangible, of George Ansbro, Howard Blue, Ted Davenport, Doug Douglass, Martin Grams, Jr., Michael Henry, Al Hubin, Teri Keane, Ted Kneebone, Patti Wever Knoll, John Leasure, Dennis Lien, David Lombard, Howard Mandelbaum, Elizabeth McLeod, Ted Meland, Charles Niren, Mike Ogden, Jacqueline Reid, Sydney Roby, Nick Ryan, Chuck Schaden, Dave Siegel, Vivian Smolen and Stewart Wright. Their assistance was immediate, incalculable and invaluable. The book in its present form simply wouldn't exist without their efforts.

A special thanks to several folks who have especially encouraged me in these research and writing pursuits: Chris Chandler, Dennis Crow, Ted Kneebone, Laura Leff, Gary Mercer, Ben Ohmart, Ron Sayles, Jim Snyder, Derek Tague, Paul Urbahns and Harlan Zinck.

In preparing new books I always sense that there is a host of vintage radio publication editors standing behind me who confirm and strengthen my efforts through the printed page. At times they offer staunch support in completing daunting tasks. I'm thankful for kindred spirits like Suzanne Adamko, Jim Adams, Bob Burchett, Sue Chadwick, Jack French, Jay Hickerson, Ken Krug, Patrick Lucanio, Robert Newman, Carol Tiffany, Marilyn Wilt and others whom I may have inadvertently overlooked. They supply yeoman's (yeowoman's?)

energy to this captivating pastime for very little personal recognition, while so many are fortunate recipients of their abundant labors.

Sharon Cox has augmented my endeavors for four decades. No man has been blessed with a more devoted companion, and I shall always be deeply grateful for her cooperative support and understanding in these compelling ventures.

Finally, a word of appreciation to my readers: some of you have perused previous tomes by me, while others have collected them all! I know this because my emailbox fills up after each new release. I write for the radiophile who reads for pure enjoyment as well as the serious researcher who gains new knowledge and insights that can satisfy his or her specific interests. Plugging holes in this hobby has been an ongoing objective with me from the very start. If I've been able to accomplish such intents with some degree of success, perhaps my small efforts have made a little difference.

CONTENTS

PREFACE

Not long ago I received an email message from a total stranger who explained: "I just read a thread [on a web site] about Lorenzo Jones in which you participated. Although I am interested in getting copies of his tapes, I am primarily interested in him as a person as he is my second cousin. Do you know anything about his life or could you lead me to a source about him?"

I replied promptly: "Since Lorenzo Jones was a mythical man, who are you speaking of when you mention your second cousin? Would it perhaps be Karl Swenson, the actor who played him? If so, I have a few facts about him. If you'll clarify the individual you're wanting info on, I'll certainly do what I can to help you."

In rapid response I received this communiqué from my new acquaintance: "Hmm, now I am confused. I don't know the radio show except by reputation, but I have a second cousin of the right age, named Lorenzo Jones, who I was told was also the person on the radio. I'll have to get back to you after doing more digging."

Wouldn't Frank and Anne Hummert have loved it? It's just another indication that the fictitious characters they invented live on in the hearts and memories of people many years after the Hummerts'—including some who never heard the programs that featured them! What a testimony to the potent, far-reaching impact of those imaginary figures brought to life by Frank and Anne, and who amused so many of us for such a long spell.

More than anybody else in broadcasting — and that includes *two* mediums—the Hummerts acquainted us with colorful heroes and heroines who captivated the minds of a substantial sector of the American public. Some of those figures paid visits to our homes on a weekly basis; but, even better, most were available to us five days a week. With a flick of a dial they evoked a wide range of emotions, including pathos, pain, anxiety, encouragement, mayhem, jealousy, rage, humor, love, dissension, discord and joy. Their formulas ranged from melodrama to music, from comedy to crime, from adventure to advice. The Hummerts emphatically shaped the sounds that emanated from our radios.

Frank and Anne Hummert were an unusual couple, as the examination of their lives and business dealings reveals in the pages that follow. The pair provides an incredibly fascinating study into the behind-the-scenes maneuvers of one of the most powerful and influential enterprises that operated during radio's golden age (from the late 1920s to the early 1960s).

Telling their story is long overdue. The originators, themselves, may prove to the reader to be as captivating as the mythical creatures they only imagined so many decades ago.

As noted in my earlier texts, I make no claim of infallibility. Every human effort has been made to provide correct data and avoid perpetuating falsehoods that sometimes creep into print and are subsequently repeated by others. Still, the discerning reader may discover an inconsistency here and there. Published accounts that proved to be unreliable were simply discarded in researching this material. Be assured that any mistakes you find are mine alone and are absolutely unintentional. The possibility of error weighs on me heavily; if such instances exist, I beg the reader's indulgence.

It's probably a good idea to explain to the vintage radio neophyte that, upon its inception in 1926, the National Broadcasting System operated two networks, Red and Blue. Using a United States map, the various affiliates were designated and drawn by connecting them with red and blue lines. In the early 1940s, when the Federal Communications Commission ruled—largely for competitive reasons—that the networks no longer could be jointly owned, NBC divested itself of its Blue chain while keeping the Red one. There are references in this volume to NBC (consisting of the Red network), NBC Blue, CBS (the Columbia Broadcasting System), MBS (the Mutual Broadcasting System) and ABC (the American Broadcasting Company, which originally was the Blue chain of NBC). This primer should be of help to some in sorting out the references to the respective national webs.

Frank and Anne Hummert were as complex as the industry in which they worked. Without overstating it, the dynamic duo could be dubbed the Odd Couple. Most insiders never figured them out. They were influential and high profile by reputation yet could blend into the woodwork. There they incessantly hid behind the scenes, while simultaneously keeping constant tabs on everything and everybody in their employ. The pair dominated an entire medium, as well as the lives of the people who served in it. "They were very powerful and I was very scared of them," actress Teri Keane confided to this author. From what has been written and stated by others, there were legions in the industry that shared her sentiments.

In the world of entertainment the Hummerts' venue was *Mystery Theater*. They lived their own adventurous *Real Stories from Real Life*. Surely one would be hard pressed to discover Frank and Anne Hummert residing in a classic neighborhood as *The Couple Next Door*.

The Man I Married chose a *Modern Cinderella* as his bride. To her, he was a *Helpmate*; to him, she was a *Rich Man's Darling*, yet never, ever a *Backstage Wife*. He was her *Second Husband*; she was his *Valiant Lady*. Traversing the *Rainbow Trail*, they confirmed to one another *This Day Is Ours* while harmonizing beautifully on *Your Song and Mine*.

Their fairy tale romance simulated *Amanda of Honeymoon Hill*, while the duo pursued a *Hearthstone of the Death Squad* lifestyle. In one, an impoverished young maiden marries a powerful middle-aged aristocrat. In the other, those in their servitude who have erred or in other ways displeased them face swift, incontestable justice from a firing squad. That's theory. In practice, Frank and Anne Hummert probably dwelled somewhere between those extremes. It is certain, however, that they were anything but *Easy Aces* when matters boiled down purely to business interests.

While theirs was a *Lone Journey*, for years they rode the *Manhattan Merry-Go-Round* hand-in-hand and experienced a *Happy Landing* as their lengthy revolutions finally wound to a halt. Through it all, their *Love Song* never wavered.

The couple lived an enchanted, fabled, fanciful existence. Often they demonstrated incalculable similarities to the imaginative worlds of the mythical subjects that peopled their creative efforts. Reality was for Frank and Anne Hummert — as well as their heroes and heroines— like fantasies that no one could really experience. And among all their many characters, they were the only two who ever did.

1

Ethereal Empire

This is the story that asks the question: *Can two ordinary, everyday, run-of-the-mill types find happiness in running a mill?* (Albeit a *drama* mill.)

Frank and Anne Hummert are the most prolific creatives in eight decades of broadcast history. The production dynasty over which they presided extended far beyond the serialized melodrama that became their signature trademark. This is a fact frequently missed by those who associate their monikers with soap opera alone.

In reality, the couple originated more than six score audio network series, only about half of them installment dramas aimed primarily at housewives and other stay-at-homes. The remainder can be classified as more than a half-dozen additional breeds. They include juvenile adventures, musicals, mysteries, news, advice, game, sports and situation comedy. The Hummerts, it seemed, tried to fill niches that provided for nearly everyone's tastes and needs.

Confined to a little more than a quarter-century, the pair's collective output is a feat of stupendous proportions, never duplicated — or even approached — by other program developers in *any* medium. Nor have their contributions received proper acclaim. (For a comparison of the Hummert accomplishments with those of several other prolific radio producers, the reader is directed to the appendices at the conclusion of this volume.)

So firm was Frank and Anne Hummerts' grip on matinee programming that the duo literally instituted an agenda for network radio

5

during the sunshine hours. One wag dubbed the pair "the General Motors of daytime radio."[1] By the 1940s this twosome controlled four-and-a-half hours of national weekday broadcast schedules. Their features reportedly spawned more than five million pieces of correspondence annually from steadfast fans. Simultaneously they brought in more than half of the national radio chains' advertising revenues generated during the daylight hours. The couple broadcast 18 quarter-hour serials five times weekly, a total of 90 original episodes for 52 weeks per year, with none of those ever repeated. It took brilliance and ingenuity, allied with stanch determination, to pull off such a feat. Simply put, the Hummerts were indisputably *the moguls of melodrama*.

Among their hardiest daytime perennials were such popular dishpan dramas as *Amanda of Honeymoon Hill, Backstage Wife, Chaplain Jim U.S.A., David Harum, Easy Aces, Front Page Farrell, John's Other Wife, Just Plain Bill, The Life of Mary Sothern, Lora Lawton, Lorenzo Jones, Ma Perkins, Mrs. Wiggs of the Cabbage Patch, Our Gal Sunday, The Romance of Helen Trent, Stella Dallas, The Strange Romance of Evelyn Winters, Valiant Lady* and *Young Widder Brown*. There were dozens more that may not be as well remembered.

Beyond their dominance in matinee narratives, the duo trotted out scores of diverse series at other hours, drawn from a burgeoning, seemingly endless programming supply house. In doing so they categorically established themselves as tenacious, formidable competitors in a myriad of amusement arenas. At one point they were charged with filling between 25 and 30 hours of network broadcast time weekly. No one in radio—including entertainer Arthur Godfrey, whose combined simulcasts in dual mediums occupied 15 or more hours of CBS's agenda every week during his peak years—ventured anywhere near that phenomenal figure. And no one has done it since.

The Hummerts' massive inventory of nocturnal endeavors— which could be construed as nighttime capstones to memorable days— included *The American Album of Familiar Music; Hearthstone of the Death Squad; Manhattan Merry-Go-Round; Mr. Chameleon; Mr. Keen, Tracer of Lost Persons; Mystery Theater; Scramby Amby; Waltz Time* and so many more.

Furthermore, they aired a handful of late afternoon serials that were explicitly geared to the adolescent set. Their most widely recalled were *Jack Armstrong, the All American Boy*; *Little Orphan Annie*; *Skippy* and *Terry and the Pirates*.

Despite the triumph of consistently producing such a surfeit of fictionalized imagination for American listeners of various age levels, the true enigma of the Hummerts' exploits appears to lie simply within themselves. The incredible backstage tale of how they ascended to such powerful perches is evocative of the mythical narratives for which they are best remembered. In private life, a clearly visible bent toward reclusive, puritanical, eccentric, parsimonious, ostentatious predilections — all of which have been well documented by industry insiders — mark them as two of the most inscrutable figures in radio. A glimpse into their engrossing environment is presented in the succeeding chapter.

The Hummert radio empire grew out of the couple's ties to a prominent Chicago advertising agency, Blackett-Sample-Hummert (BSH), Inc. While Frank Hummert was never a partner in the firm, shortly after he joined it his name was added to its masthead for the prestige he conveyed as a widely celebrated copywriter.[2] He had already earned liberal notoriety among his peers for his masterful ability to turn key words and phrases into persuasive marketing pitches. For his contributions to BSH — principally, generating new ideas and directing a production unit that he instituted — Hummert received a percentage of the agency's profits.

A short time later, Anne Schumacher Ashenhurst — who would eventually become Mrs. Hummert — applied for a position as his editorial assistant. Her stunning ingenuity, insight and resolve triggered an earned respect throughout that organization, causing her stock to rise rapidly within its confines.

At about that same time, Frank Hummert had an intriguing new notion: he wondered if the American housewife might be amenable to daytime fare that was more amusing than what she was accustomed to hearing pour forth from the family radio. Cooking tips, beauty secrets and personal advice dominated the daytime airwaves. Much of it was just plain dull. Hummert would acknowledge many years later that it was merely a lucky guess when it occurred to him that radio drama — then just coming into vogue in the early 1930s— might appeal to the homemakers if it was offered as serialized fiction.

In the first half-dozen years after their entry into the medium,

Frank and Anne Hummert significantly enhanced their own bottom lines while controlling at least half of the radio serials broadcast. Concurrently, they aired 36 separate programs, by 1938 purchasing an eighth of all commercial radio time — then valued at $12 million annually. The two were responsible for reportedly churning out 6.5 million broadcast words per year,[3] the equivalent of about 65 novels. A decade later, one of the four major chains, CBS, was still receiving $3.1 million annually for carrying just five of their daytime serials.[4]

In 1938 the Hummerts moved to New York to be in the vanguard of radio network production, as well as to be situated at the operational apex of many of the nation's top advertising agencies. Formally detaching themselves in 1943 from Blackett-Sample-Hummert, Inc., they opened their own shop, christening it Air Features, Inc. (in later years often referred to as Hummert Radio Features). They also formed a talent subsidiary under the banner Featured Artist Service, Inc. In the period from 1937 to 1942 the couple introduced 22 new serials to network radio listeners. No one matched the volume of dramas they contrived in that five-year period.

By the mid–1940s, virtually the entire Hummert programming slate had transferred from the Windy City to the Big Apple. The corporate owners ostensibly expressed a desire to take full advantage of a far wider selection of artists and production talent which was available in New York. Such professional expertise was primarily drawn from the area's exposure to amplified radio and theater activity. Regrettably, many individuals — some heavily dependent for their livelihoods upon the massive Hummert organization, yet unable or unwilling to make the transition from Chicago — were left scrambling to replace the economic security they were losing. Nearly every Hummert program on the air experienced significant casting changes as a result of that extensive and at times traumatic upheaval.

Air Features, Inc. could be classified as unique by every measure and in every imaginable dimension. It routinely demonstrated a large number of idiosyncrasies that stemmed from the many peculiarities exhibited by the eccentric Hummerts themselves. The backers' personal traits and habits earmarked some of the firm's business practices as odd, atypical and even — by some standards — bizarre. (The following chapters explore some of the more flagrant Hummert peculiarities that gave rise to such radical corporate behavior. A number of those curious quirks will be examined in detail.)

When radio programming as the listeners had known it from the late 1920s to the early 1960s finally folded, many of its innovations for an aural-only audience passed with it. But without Frank and Anne Hummerts' tactical influence throughout most of that period, affectionately recalled as the golden age, the resulting void would have been filled in mixed but irrefutably different ways. The couple's impact on the medium was little short of gargantuan; their legacy provides a worthy and captivating study in American entrepreneurship.

2

THE ODD COUPLE

Frank and Anne Hummert created and produced a substantial share of the detective fare, musicals, juvenile adventure and soap opera that American ears were attuned to in the 1930s, 1940s and 1950s. And in their personal lives, the melodrama for which they were so widely known sometimes played out in similar fashion.

A paid notice of minuscule proportions appeared in *The New York Times* at the death of E. Frank Hummert, Jr. That infinitesimal write-up of the passing of a man that, together with his spouse, had controlled a major portion of what American audiences listened to over their radios for about three decades—who, at one point, presumably had been the globe's highest-paid advertising executive, also—seemed an aberration.

Yet, nearly everything about Frank Hummert and his wife, Anne Schumacher Ashenhurst Hummert—Frank's junior by a couple of decades—was alleged to be odd. Clearly among entertainment's most reclusive personalities, the pair consistently shunned the public spotlight, hiding from cameras and publicity hounds. In a supreme example, *Who's Who in America* affirmed that it couldn't validate a three-line blurb printed on Frank Hummert.[1] Typically, the furtive twosome, lunching at a favorite hotel's posh bistro near their offices in midtown Manhattan, preferred to be concealed behind bulky fern planters—all the while capable of observing others but determined not to be seen themselves.

Despite such peculiar habits, their actions often reflected two egos that were arguably ferocious. On the air—where they still could not be seen or heard—as a rule the couple took full credit for the creative

11

abilities of hordes of underlings (writers, editors, actors, directors and more). To a large extent, the individuals in their employ were directly responsible for providing a grandiose lifestyle for their superiors. Yet those minions never shared in it themselves, and most were given little or no recognition for their efforts. Indeed they were threatened with dismissal if they stepped out of line by violating well-publicized canons instituted by the Hummerts, like speaking to a journalist without permission. (There would have been few "interviews" by anybody in that outfit; even the owners shunned most of them.)

In broadcasting's original medium, Frank and Anne Hummert presided in near-regal splendor over an empire of legendary proportions, unequivocally without equal. Basking in notoriety while consumed by the accouterments of royalty, the undisputed geniuses whose business acumen matched their innovative knack left an incredible and indelible mark upon early audio entertainment. They were never to be eclipsed or duplicated by contemporaries or successors.

For over a quarter-century the couple absolutely dominated daytime broadcasting as they fostered dramatic serials that filled the weekday schedules of four major chains. Unable to rest on those laurels, however, concurrently they contributed some of the more memorable mystery and musical programming available to evening listeners. They also generated several popular juvenile adventure series for the younger set that tuned in shortly before the traditional supper hour.

Yet the true enigma of these feats appears to lie within the Hummerts' own selves. An in-depth examination of their personal lives, without doubt, will be extremely illuminating. The subsequent disclosures will help the reader gain insights into the development of an entrepreneurial empire that consistently outshone all others. The Hummerts' unique procedural applications were unique among most strategies adopted by competitive program originators within several dimensions of the golden age radio broadcast industry. The reader may anticipate an assessment that should be, intentionally, a series of fascinatingly absorbing revelations.

Edward Frank Hummert, Jr., was born in St. Louis, Missouri, on June 2, 1884.[2] His mother was French; his father, English. The latter was a mercantilist in lace manufacturing and importing, and traveled extensively for Rice, Stix & Co. As a result, the family was accustomed to moving frequently, reportedly transferring during young Frank's early life to various locales across the United States and Europe. That introduced the lad early on to a Continental lifestyle, something that was to become prevalent throughout much of his professional life and beyond. Frank Sr. eventually operated his own merchandising-exporting venture under the label Hummert Hatfield Co., and the family settled permanently in St. Louis.

Frank Jr. anticipated that one day he would trace his dad's far-flung business expeditions himself. He was primed for it as a young man — in fact, under British tutelage. Frank's preparatory studies took place at Stonyhurst College in Lancastershire, England. When he returned to his native Missouri, he enroled at St. Louis University. Both St. Louis and Stonyhurst were Jesuit-run (Catholic) institutions.

By age 20, however, he had decided against a career in his father's footsteps, intrigued and persuaded instead by the public media. Young Hummert soon landed a reporting assignment on the Pulitzer Prize–winning *St. Louis Post-Dispatch*. After getting his feet wet there and apparently liking the lifestyle of the fourth estate, later he held reportorial posts with the newsjournal of the Catholic Archdiocese of Chicago, *New World*, and the International News Syndicate of *The New York Times*.

These weren't successive ventures, however. In fact, he seemed wishy-washy concerning his permanent plans. A couple of sources suggest that he suspend his journalistic pursuits to become a Texas Ranger for a couple of years. No hard evidence substantiating that claim has been found, however.[3] We do know that in April 1910, at age 25, he revealed himself to the St. Louis census-takers as a real estate salesman, apparently interrupting his communications pursuit for a while. A year later the St. Louis city directory listed his occupation as president of Hummert Advertising Agency, Inc., then operating at 915 Olive Street. But by the time he signed the World War I draft registry in September 1918 at the age of 34 he had rejoined his father in the merchandising-exporting business, working for Hummert Hatfield Co. Thus his early work experience carried him in several directions.

During these career shifts young Frank took a wife. Several usually reliable informants profess in print that Frank Hummert was a "confirmed bachelor" during the first five decades of his life. The records simply do not support that conclusion, however. This author is convinced that Frank Hummert married in his twenties and, furthermore, that his wife died *before* his second marriage. To miss that important detail is to ignore a substantial factor in his personal life. Radio researcher Claire Connelly confessed: "Although the name of Frank Hummert became a legend in radio advertising, he obsessivly shunned any publicity for himself, keeping everyone else in ignorance of any verifiable facts about his life. To fill the vacuum, legends arose that were passed on by radio and advertising historians well into the 1970s and 1980s. However, thanks to information sources that have recently become accessible to the public, we now have a clearer picture of Frank's early life, his education, his struggle to launch a career, and his first marriage."

Edward F. Hummert, Jr., married the former Adeline E. Woodlock of St. Louis in 1908. Adeline was born in July 1884, a month after Frank, and her family resided only a few blocks from the home of Edward F. Hummert, Sr., and his wife Carrie. Frank was German Catholic and Adeline was Irish Catholic. Following their nuptials, for a few years at varying times the newlyweds lived together at the residences of each of their parents.

During this period the youthful neophyte journalist amassed a sizable sum of money by speculating in real estate. He attributed his good fortune to "sheer luck" and little more. But as fate would have it, he soon lost it all, the result of some nefarious dealings of a trusted confidante. This transpired just as the nation was entering World War I. Yet another journalist, interviewing Hummert a couple of decades later, observed: "The country called him to the business of creating slogans which helped win the war far more than any bullets he might have fired."[4] One of the mottoes for Liberty Bonds that he originated, *Bonds or Bondage*, appeared far and wide across the United States and Great Britain. That telling line was to rapidly point him toward a promising career in advertising, categorically one of his most celebrated conquests.

But before giving himself exclusively to that craft, he ventured into the entertainment arena. It would prove to be fortuitous, yet another important dimension preparing him for his ultimate life's work. Hummert was soon earning $125 a pop rewriting theatrical scripts, all the while gaining invaluable experience in scenario plotting and dialoguing. It was to stand him in good stead when he reached the apex of his professional pursuits. Simultaneously, he mingled with numerous stage producers while scrupulously observing their habits and actions. From his dealings with them he made mental notes that would prove invaluable to him one day.

At the same time, he applied some of his ingenuity to a sideline venture, founding an institution for aspiring writers. By sharing the techniques and insights he himself had gained, he prepared prospects for similar occupations in scripting film and stage productions.

Hummert's eventual concentration in advertising was the result of yet another fluke. When he turned a friend's faltering commercial endeavor into a profitable enterprise through sheer promotional ingenuity, it occurred to him that there was plenty of opportunities to perform that same feat for others. Maintaining his current remunerative pursuits in the daytime, Hummert accepted copywriting assignments at night for a fledgling advertising firm. But when another working associate's poor business judgment left him liable for $900 in unpaid bills, he threw in the towel. Disgusted, he quit and moved away to New York.

Yet, of all the people he should encounter there, Hummert soon crossed paths with the very man who had bilked him out of $900! In the interim the reprobate had either reformed or become resourceful for, surprisingly, he paid Hummert full restitution for his past mistake. Then, ironically, he talked his old crony into teaming with him once more in the advertising trade. Hummert wrote promotional copy, his overt forte, while his partner solicited new accounts. It was a strategic maneuver that apparently satisfied both men. And as Hummert honed his skills, improving with application and age, others with substantial influence in the field began to take notice of his enormous talent.

By 1920 he was hired by Albert Lasker's Lord & Thomas agency in New York — one of the world's most prestigious firms in the business — as its chief copywriter. He became Lasker's renowned "fair-haired boy." At an acknowledged starting salary of $50,000, Hummert was earning what many would consider a small fortune, given the era. He proved that he could turn just the right word or phrase to capture the public's imagination. In a postwar, pre–Depression economy that was seemingly flush with cash, Hummert persuaded the masses to comply with simple buying ideas. On various occasions he coined slogans that were to earn him widespread respect throughout the advertising industry. One of his most memorable aphorisms, *For the Skin You Love to Touch*—created for soap manufacturer Procter & Gamble's Camay bar—gained generous exposure. Prophetically, Frank Hummert was to ultimately earn a large share of his future livelihood by way of several soapmakers.

Thus, after several setbacks and false starts, his star rose indubitably and quickly. There would be no cause for further retrenchment. He would never be comfortable with less, nor would he ever have to settle for it from that point on. Frank Hummert, Jr., had hit his stride.

In 1927 Hill Blackett and J. G. Sample, the two foremost advertising practitioners in the Midwest, made him an offer that he couldn't refuse. These two well-recognized industry professionals, who operated an esteemed, influential Chicago agency, invited Hummert to join them as vice president of the outfit. He accepted.

An increasingly pervasive notoriety, stemming from Hummert's creative capacity, impressed both Blackett and Sample. Fully understanding the significant draw that he brought to their practice through increased business and image building among some eminent advertising circles, the owners were persuaded within a few years to add his surname to the company's masthead. From then until the group's dissolution at the close of 1943 the firm was officially known as Blackett-Sample-Hummert, Inc. And while Frank Hummert wasn't a full partner in the operation, he received a percentage of the profits for his imaginative conceptions and for managing a radio production unit that he formed. By almost any measure, then, he had at last achieved the pinnacle of business enterprise success.

According to the 1930 Chicago census, Frank and Adeline Hummert were living in rented apartment number 154 at 1209 Astor Street. By that time they had been married 22 years. No children or any other relatives were acknowledged to be residing with the Hummerts. This author's exploration, in fact, never discovered *any* children born to that union. Frank's listed occupation was "vice president, advertising agency," while Adeline was unemployed.

Although Frank and Adeline didn't declare their rent to the census-takers, the adjacent apartments were then leasing for between

$425 and $450 monthly. Keep in mind that this official data was secured only a short time following the collapse of the American stock market in October 1929. The simple matter of the rent might suggest that the Hummerts experienced no serious financial hardships as a result of that most debilitating economic calamity in the nation's history.

Interesting also is the fact that the Hummerts resided in close proximity to North Chicago's fashionable Lake Shore Drive. Just around the corner, in fact, apartments were then renting for $1,000 to $1,500 monthly. Given Frank's earnings history (recall that he was making $50,000 a full decade earlier) while speculating on the prospects of his current income level, such an upscale leasing arrangement would appear to have been well within Frank and Adeline's financial grasp. The fact that the couple didn't choose — on the surface, at least — to live ostentatiously has some significance. As this account shall verify in good time, the absence of such trappings then was in marked contrast to the lifestyle Frank would embrace during his second marriage.

At a date thus far unsubstantiated, but following that 1930 census and before 1935, Adeline Hummert died.[5] The circumstances surrounding her demise are unclear. The simple fact is that at some point in the early 1930s Frank Hummert became a widower.

In the meantime, at the advertising agency that employed him during the same era, Hummert was to make an initial transition into broadcasting, the province in which he became legendary and in which he left his most enduring imprint. But he would not do it alone. He was to be aided appreciably by an equally bright and talented young woman. It was someone whom he hired as an editorial assistant, who eventually was to become not only his partner in business but also in life. We shall leave his account momentarily to pursue hers.

Anne Shumacher, who was born in Baltimore on January 19, 1905, was the daughter of a Maryland police lieutenant. As she grew up it was evident to many that she would be an overachiever for she exhibited strong motivation and superior intellect. She especially liked to write. Diminutive in stature, she would later be characterized as "super-efficient and yet — since she was petite — unfrightening."[6]

By the time she reached Goucher College, a finishing school for well-heeled, erudite young women, Schumacher was eager to apply her linguistic leanings to writing for recompense. The history major —

Baltimore native Anne Schumacher excelled at Goucher College, paying her own way as a newspaper stringer. Then she went into journalism full time. She married a year later, became a mom the next and divorced a couple of years after that. She went looking for work and found it at a Chicago advertising agency. Little could she have imagined the career that awaited! (Courtesy of Chuck Schaden Radio Collection)

who was actively engaged in the institute's dramatics club during her last three scholastic years—tested her creative abilities as college correspondent for *The Baltimore Sun.* Her father had made it perfectly clear to her earlier that higher education for women was, in his opinion, superfluous; as a consequence, he refused to underwrite her annual $200 tuition.

Showing marked determination, ingenuity and pride, for four years Anne paid her own way in school by earning a generous three cents per published line in *The Sun.* In 1925, after graduating magna cum laude, she seized the moment to practice her newly acquired skills full time: she became a full-fledged reporter for the newspaper for which she had interned during the last quadrennial. There is at least some evidence that, on the side, she penned an advice column for the lovelorn. That may have been an omen of things to come. So much of her professional occupation was to intertwine with amorous relationships, albeit of a make-believe nature.

Over the next few months, Schumacher herself was romantically linked with a fellow journalist, John Watson Ashenhurst. A native of

2. The Odd Couple

Viola, Illinois, he was an alumnus of Monmouth (Illinois) College and was by then *The Baltimore Sun's* city editor. At the tender age of 26 Ashenhurst purportedly was the youngest individual to fill that responsible post on any major U.S. metropolitan daily. A family member recalled that he was "a handsome, intelligent, charming guy" who could fluently converse in five languages. At the same time, he could be "incredibly arrogant." Editor Ashenhurst's working life would be consumed by print journalism.

In 1926 he accepted an appointment as a Hearst correspondent with that news syndicate's Paris bureau. A starry-eyed Anne Schumacher tagged along. There she gained her own reporting berth for a precursor journal of *The International Herald Tribune*.

On July 26, 1926, the star-crossed pair were wed in the French capital. The following spring they returned to the states in anticipation of the birth of their only child, John Randle Ashenhurst, who arrived on April 26, 1927. One of Anne's initial priorities— recall her resolute determination — was to secure an income to help sustain their growing family. Finding no attractive newspaper opportunities readily at hand, in time she applied for a position at Chicago's Blackett-Sample-Hummert ad agency. With her journalistic experience, plus the confidence she exuded with her can-do personality, she was hired in 1930 as editorial assistant to E. Frank Hummert. (Actually, until he met her, Hummert had been cool towards employing a young newspaperwoman. J. G. Sample nearly pushed Ashenhurst on him, so a version of the story goes, having earlier been significantly impressed when he met the ambitious, spirited applicant.) Although they didn't realize it then, it was to be a life-changing appointment for everybody concerned.

Her new employer soon discovered qualities in Anne Ashenhurst that would make her a valuable part of that firm. An observer dubbed her "captivating," noting that her superior was awed by her "tinkling voice" and found her to be "a fount of ideas and organized efficiency."[7] She worked hard and her contributions were duly noted. She wanted the pay of a man and got it. In less than two years her take-charge knack was rewarded with promotion to a vice presidency.[8] By early 1933 she was reportedly elevated to a full partnership.[9] In terms of compensation, she became the premier feminine practitioner in American advertising. (In a 1985 interview she gushed: "I was highly paid.

I was in the highest tax bracket — imagine that!"[10]) Her career had spiraled rapidly upward and she would never be content with less than top-echelon decision-making in any firm.

Unfortunately, her glowing success at the office didn't transfer into her personal life. While Anne was putting bread on the table, John W. Ashenhurst was having minimal results in finding gainful employment that could be even remotely rewarding monetarily as well as personally gratifying to himself. He soon became dejected by his plight. According to his nephew, "Anne got a job at the Hummert agency while John focused on spending her salary."[11] Ashenhurst was cited as "totally irresponsible where money was concerned and something of a boozer."[12] If he saw something and wanted it, he bought it, whether it fit comfortably into the family budget or not.

Meanwhile, what of their offspring, John R. Ashenhurst, whom John and Anne nicknamed Johnny? A great deal of the boy's early years were spent with his paternal grandparents in Monmouth, Illinois. "Neither [John nor Anne] won any parenting awards that I'm aware of," allowed the same informant.[13] Anne was focused on her developing career while John appeared to languish in a stupor much of the time. By 1929 the couple separated; in time, they divorced. Yet, surprisingly, it was John who gained the rights as the custodial parent, although it was obviously with Anne's blessing.

John W. Ashenhurst never remarried, and there were strong indications that he carried a torch for Anne all the days of his life. Decades later, while on his deathbed, he spoke with her by telephone in a prolonged call. Their dialogue appeared to bring him some resolution and peace at last. At age 64, he died on May 17, 1963, in Chicago.

It will probably come as a surprise to no one that the instability of young Johnny Ashenhurst's early life may have noticeably contributed to his becoming a "problem child" as he grew older.[14] While his daddy imbibed heavily, the little fellow was shuttled back and forth between his patriarchal kinfolk. As he advanced in age, he was dispatched to a succession of costly private prep schools, always paid for by his mother. But he often ran away from them, which frequently culminated in expulsion.

An uncle, James G. Ashenhurst, befriended the youngster while attempting to steer him into acceptable behavior. Later — after Anne resettled in the environs of New York — on several occasions, when business took him to the Big Apple, she and James met to consider some ways that he might be instrumental in guiding the troubled youth. After it became obvious to everybody that his determined efforts were accomplishing precious little, he asked that Johnny not visit in his home any more. By then the situation had become too disruptive for Ashenhurst's own family. The cordial friendship that existed between James and Anne immediately evaporated, and their strategy planning ended.

By the time Johnny was a teen, his mother was unprepared for, and unwilling to be burdened further by the frequent taxing challenges he presented. A lifelong strain that had existed between them was never resolved. There was even one report suggesting that he expressed disdain for her method of earning a livelihood.[15] Although in later years he telephoned her spasmodically, usually requesting financial assistance, he was frequently drunk at the time. Repetitiously, she advised him to call back when he was sober, then hung up on him. The two seldom completed a civil conversation. That arrangement seemed to satisify Anne, relatives acknowledged. Allegedly, she never saw her son again after his upper teen years.

Following high school, Johnny joined the Marines and was shipped off to China. While there he met a family of refugees seeking asylum in the United States. The clan included a father who had escaped from fascist Italy, a Russian mother and their older teenage daughter, Julie. Johnny and the girl were romantically attracted to one another, so much so that the lovebirds decided to wed in China. Assuring his new in-laws that he could convince his mother to sponsor them for American citizenship, Johnny and his bride carried her parents' life savings with them to the States with the avowed intention of relocating the family there.

But Johnny's mom turned thumbs down to the plan. And the cache, totaling about $8,000, soon slipped through Johnny's fingers without Julie's knowledge. Nonetheless, the young couple became parents of a daughter, Anne, before they — like Johnny's parents before them — divorced. But unlike his own father, Johnny remarried and fathered another daughter, Pamela, by his second wife.

In the years ahead Johnny Ashenhurst derived the bulk of his livelihood by working as a grill chef at several Chicago restaurants. And like his dad, he also became a heavy drinker, a factor that undoubtedly contributed to declining health much too early. Death came in Chicago in the early 1980s. His mother, then in her mid-seventies, didn't attend his funeral, so his kin observed.

Returning to Blackett-Sample-Hummert (BSH), the agency's heavy involvement in the new medium of radio so early in the game, while to some degree happenstance, was undeniably promising. Actually, it was a precipitous stroke of luck, based almost entirely upon Frank Hummert's own intuition. About 1930 he postulated that the American housewife might appreciate daytime audio fare more amusing than the cooking tips, beauty secrets and personal advice in dealing with this and that at home which dominated the airwaves during the sunlight hours. Years later Hummert would acknowledge that it was all merely an auspicious supposition on his part (he considered it "a shot in the dark"): in 1931, it occurred to him that radio drama — which was just then coming into vogue — would possibly appeal to homemakers if presented in the form of serialized fiction. (Some further analysis follows in chapter 6.)

By 1932, BSH executive Hill Blackett boasted that his firm was "handling more than 150 broadcasts a week, and have been [doing so] for some time."[16] He noted further that a year earlier (1931) NBC informed BSH that a third of the mail the chain received "was addressed to advertisers whose radio broadcasting we supervise."[17] Such acknowledgment removes any doubt that BSH was wading deep into the new medium quite early in the venture, and indicates the depth of its commitment.

During the first half-dozen years of radio soap opera, the Hummerts — married during that period (in 1935) — significantly enhanced their own bottom lines while controlling at least half of the radio serials then broadcast. Concurrently they aired 36 separate programs while purchasing an eighth of all commercial radio time by 1938, at $12 million annually. Their factory churned out 6.5 million broadcast words per year.[18] Suddenly, after facing earlier personal financial hurdles, together they had struck gold. None realized it any better than they.

Frank Hummert reached the zenith of his profession in 1937 and was duly cited as advertising's highest-paid executive.[19] "Everyone conceded his flair and his ... brilliance in his copy layout put him up there with half a dozen of the copy greats," a pundit assessed.[20] The following year the duo moved to New York to be in the vanguard of network radio headquarters, not to mention being situated among the operational powers of many of the nation's foremost advertising agencies. For a few years the couple would occupy a splendidly spacious apartment on fashionable Fifth Avenue. In time, however, they would acquire a magnificent estate set amid the aristocratic aura of nearby Greenwich, Connecticut.

They retained their identity with Blackett-Sample-Hummert through 1943, although one wag observed: "The relationship was clouded, another one of the innumerable secrecies in which Hummert seemed to delight."[21] But they formally cut the ties that bound them to the ad agency at the start of 1944 while opening their own production shop. The couple labeled it Air Features, Inc. (at times referred to interchangeably as Hummert Radio Features). They also established a subsidiary that could reward them handsomely for delivering on-air talent. They named it Featured Artist Service, Inc.

(As an aside, Blackett-Sample-Hummert dissolved entirely after 1943 when Hill Blackett refused to sell his half-interest to partner John G. Sample. Blackett then established a new agency under his own name, Hill Blackett, Inc. Sample took new partners and formed Dancer-Fitzgerald-Sample, Inc. While Frank Hummert had never been a partner in the original enterprise, most of the business had been cultivated via his creative efforts. Subsequently, Air Features, Inc. displayed no preference for the dual firms that succeeded Blackett-Sample-Hummert, making its wares available without favoritism to Hill Blackett and Dancer-Fitzgerald-Sample.)

Virtually the entire Hummert programming entourage had transferred from Chicago to New York by the mid–1940s in order to take advantage of the greater talent pool in the Big Apple. As a consequence, nearly every Hummert program on the air experienced significant casting changes at this time.

In addition to the expected daily transactions that distinguish a prospering business, Air Features could also be noted for a number of well-documented eccentricities that set it apart it in the entertainment industry. Its oddball patterns clearly stemmed from its owners. At times they flaunted stupefying behavioral traits. Both Hummerts appeared utterly heedless of the gossip that swirled about them. They retreated to their own little world instead — visibly revolving around each other — and deliberately shut out almost everybody who attempted to penetrate it.

A flagrantly callous disregard for others, at times bordering on disdain (and often surprisingly aimed at those in their employ who were helping make them wealthy) possibly overshadowed every other curious quirk they exhibited. Their seeming coldness toward the cares and concerns of others branded them as insensitive snobs and social outcasts. Yet if any of it ever bothered them, neither one let on.

The pair did, however, on at least one occasion try to mix it up in public with some business associates. It's an incredibly delicious episode that epitomizes the Hummerts as the social misfits they were. It also underscores the fact that they didn't care what impression their oddball behavior made. The tale, reported by one of the principals involved, took place in connection with the debut of the Hummerts' exclusive wartime serial *Chaplain Jim, U.S.A.* Edward Kirby, who participated in that little charade, was at the time head of a federal radio entity that linked the military with the broadcasting industry.

> The premier broadcast of *Chaplain Jim* was a memorable one for Edward Kirby and his wife Marjorie. It took place in the spring of 1942 in NBC's large studio 8H at Radio City.... The Hummerts invited them to watch it and to have dinner with them afterwards. "I wonder where they'll take us," Mrs. Kirby said to her husband shortly before the show began. "Maybe it will be to Club 21 or the Stork Club."
>
> When the show ended, the Hummerts met them at the studio exit and led them out to the street where a horse and carriage awaited them. "This is for us," Frank Hummert told them. "This way we don't have any problem with gas rationing. We hope you don't mind," he added, "if we have dinner at our place." "Our place" was an elegant apartment on Fifth Avenue....
>
> As Frank Hummert led the Kirbys through it, he turned on the lights in the room ahead while Anne turned them off in the one they were leaving. "I hope you don't mind if we eat in the

kitchen," Hummert told them. In the kitchen, he opened up a can of Campbell's vegetable soup while Anne opened a can of peaches, which she served on a bed of lettuce. Later she commented, "I hope you don't mind if the cake has been here a little while. It's still good though."[22]

It was so apropos, so typically characteristic of Frank and Anne, as shall be confirmed shortly.

There was a definite aura and mystique that constantly enveloped the Hummerts. "The couple were so secretive with everything," insisted a contemporary researcher who poked into their lives.[23] The industry periodical *Advertising Age* dubbed Hummert "a man of mystery who avoided personal publicity and co-workers."[24] Reclusive to a fault, the couple seldom made public appearances, and went out of their way to avoid being seen by nearly everybody. (The earlier mention of their hiding behind a bistro's fern planters is confirmation of that conduct.) They never turned up as mystery guests on TV's *What's My Line?* nor with a fantasy to fool the panel of *I've Got a Secret.* If they were invited to such outings they politely declined. Seeing — rather than being seen — was their forte. Not surprisingly, they were also camera shy. Very few photographs of either of them, separately or together, have been preserved. Fewer still are in circulation.

Momentarily, let us stray from the matter at hand.

On just one occasion during her professional life was Anne Hummert known to have spoken before an audience. Having only recently moved to the environs of New York, during the 1938–1939 academic year she was invited to be a guest lecturer for a survey course in broadcasting at Columbia University. Other industry well-knowns appearing separately throughout that term included orchestra conductor Howard Barlow, comedian Eddie Cantor, thespian Norman Corwin and radio executive Frank Stanton. Anne Hummert's assigned topic was daytime serials. Her visit prompted a witness to describe her as chic, petite, alert and high strung. "She spoke without notes, never hesitating. After talking for about forty minutes, she answered questions in the same brisk manner, seemingly ready for every question."[25] On that occasion she acknowledged that people seemed to like dramatic radio figures from the Midwest best. Hence, a preponderance of

Hummert serials were situated in the region, as "the speech of characters from that area wasn't identified with any particular dialect that might show partiality or distract listeners."[26]

What followed the day's exchange was particularly illuminating:

> One of the [class] members later decided to write an article on "soap operas," to be sent to *Harper's*. Wanting to quote her directly, he phoned Air Features and asked for an opportunity to check the quotation with Mrs. Hummert, to ensure its correctness. She came on the phone and said, "That's no problem. I'll send you a copy." She had apparently prepared for the lecture by writing it in full and memorizing it. Her public appearance, so unusual for the Hummerts, must have seemed crucial to her — perhaps an occasion to answer stinging criticisms."[27]

Could the reason that she gave no more known public speeches be that she didn't have time to memorize any others while outlining the plots of dozens of shows every week? It might be a proper inference.

When the Hummerts hired lead actors or other staff members for their many radio productions, they routinely dispatched a trusted attorney to perform the dirty deed. Completely loyal to their (the Hummerts') own interests, the lawyer would shove a contract under the unsuspecting eyes of the candidates the couple had selected — binding agreements that compensated the performers with absolutely negligible fees, far less than those paid by other producers. Rarely did the duo become directly involved in those exchanges. Thus, there was little opportunity to negotiate anything: an artist accepted it or rejected it. It was an impersonal method of doing business, but typical of the practices that distinguished the outfit from some other operatives in radio.

On the other hand, talent for the support roles in their dramas was normally enlisted by the Hummerts' hand-picked, closely-monitored program directors. Those actors were hired at set rates, similar to a practice pursued by nearly all other radio producers. Air Features' writers proved to be an exception to the arms-length practices, at least initially. Yet they, too, were generally kept at bay after employment. Most Hummert scribes never met with their sovereign leaders beyond the launch of their engagement, no matter how enduring or ephemeral.

(One wag dubbed the inception a "stern commission.") During that initial — and solitary — communication, Anne Hummert would wryly portend: "I shall only call you once. That will be to tell you that I no longer need your services."[28] Pensively she reminisced to a *Newsweek* journalist: "We had one writer who lasted for seven years."[29] An Air Features wordsmith seldom had a reason to report to control center. "Any contact desired with Supreme Headquarters must be made through the chain of command," an informed source elucidated matter-of-factly.[30]

Miscreant thespians also lived in fear of ringing telephones. "Any actor who was five minutes late to an Air Features rehearsal was in trouble," serial heroine Mary Jane Higby remembered. "There would be a message to 'call the office as soon as you get off the air.' When he did, the receiver would burn his ear. If it happened again, he could start looking for another source of employment."[31]

It is probably appropriate to provide some further perspective on Air Features' management before proceeding. Most enterprises have one or more ranking associates to whom the owners entrust their business while they are away or when they can't give full attention to all of its facets. In the Hummert province it might be stretching semantics to say that they put their full trust in perceived confidantes, given their consistently demonstrated penchant for playing their cards quite close to the vest. While the couple prided themselves on keeping their thumbs plugged into every hole in the dike, on occasion it certainly looked as if they had acquiesced — at least on the surface — and allowed someone else to fill the void.

There is substantial evidence among the Hummerts' personal papers that a couple of Air Features' internal auditors, Maurice (Mickey) Scopp and James A. Sauter, carried extra duties beyond the rank-and-file. Actually, Sauter was awarded the title of president of Air Features, Inc. (more will be said about his role in that capacity shortly). But his assignments may have altered or he may have left the corporation early. His influence seems to be absent after the 1940s. (It is also possible that he expired; he and Scopp both predeceased Frank Hummert.)

On the other hand, there are several documents signifying Scopp's titular control, to whatever extent it existed. An internal memorandum from Anne Hummert to Scopp and the script editors, dated

August 20, 1945, is typical: "I shall be away with Mr. Hummert for the remainder of the week. If anything comes up, please see Mr. Scopp." Notice the formality, consistent in all of her communications. There are instances of similar notes, suggesting that at least temporary authority may have been relegated to Scopp.

Among the private papers there exists a number of messages in which Anne Hummert instructs Scopp in how he is to proceed in dealing with specific issues, writers, directors and actors on several Air Features series. Each one is explicit and sometimes includes numbered steps so there can be no possible excuse for misunderstanding. Normally, carbons of such communications were dispatched to the firm's program and casting directors. In order for Scopp to be apprised of background details for matters under discussion, Anne Hummert reports conversations that she has had with individuals related to the current deliberations.

It's plain even to a casual reader that Scopp is intimately involved in informing the various personnel — drawn from an approved cache of Air Features writers, announcers, directors and actors — that they are being shifted from one show to another effective on specified dates. The Hummerts routinely transferred many of their players between dramas, purportedly to prevent anyone from becoming "too identified" with a single series, either in their own minds or in those of the audience. By relying on Scopp for such important transactions, Frank and Anne Hummert maintained arms-length distances between themselves and the vast body of minions in their employ. No confrontations there. The trait was as illustrative of their personalities as it was of their business style.

Those typewritten missives were direct and often tinged with an edge. This one concerning *Amanda of Honeymoon Hill*, dated October 20, 1944, is emblematic.[32] It was addressed to Mr. Scopp and Mr. Ludlum (a new program director whose tenure may have been brief, for his name doesn't appear in vintage radio glossaries):

> I have listened to the show today, and I think that it is in a deplorable state.
>
> From theme to theme everything is wrong with it....
>
> I believe that Mr. Ludlum and Mr. Scopp both should get in touch with Mr. [Ernest] Ricca [another Air Features direc-

tor], to have a clear understanding with him as to what is wanted. Granted that the scripts are not good, nevertheless there is no possible excuse for playing the telephone scene as Amanda did.... Furthermore, the actress who played the part of Bettina was extremely bad....

As far as [actor] Jimmy Meighan was concerned, there was no reason for a tired man to wheeze and hem and haw and blow into the mike to indicate that he is tired.

Furthermore, in the playing of the theme, "Annie Laurie," [organist] Anne Leaf is playing *off* the melody.... You don't know that it is "Annie Laurie".... A new arrangement should be worked out to ... make it sound as if something is actually going on the air. Further, I have indicated over and over, the same music of the theme should *not* be used under the lead-in....

I have instructed Mr. Ludlum that it may be advisable to re-cast Bettina ... and I have asked him to get hold of Miss Leaf at once, in an attempt to affect as much ... change as possible before Monday....

The principal thing to tell Miss [Joy] Hathaway [the heroine] is that she should play her lines with strength and fire, but not with despair and weeping....

ASH

When Anne Hummert issued a missile, there was usually enough fire to go around so that nobody felt left out.

One more instance of Mickey Scopp's seemingly pivotal role is illuminating. On one occasion a *Variety* reporter recalled being summoned to a rare interview in the private office of Frank and Anne Hummert. The journalist later complained in print:[33] "This writer demanded to know why a man, never introduced or identified, was seated on a divan in the corner, giving Hummert a witness, but not *Variety*, probably Mickey Scopp." It's evident Scopp carried some clout in the enterprise. The reporter concluded: "The whole interview ... had a cloak-and-dagger plot quality all its own." From many perspectives, that, too, was symbolic of Air Features and its principals.

In 1947 a magazine scribe offered readers some further insights into the shroud of secrecy that persistently swirled about Air Features, obscuring it from prying eyes and ears. "The Hummerts are modest to the point of silence on the nature and scope of their operation," said the reporter. "The Hummerts have developed a security system so tight as to be reminiscent of that enforced at Los Alamos. Top echelons of the Hummert hierarchy become noticeably nervous when approached for information. Like many of the characters in their plots, they suddenly develop amnesia. Even former Hummert writers (known within the corps as 'dialoguers') who have been expelled for deviationist activities ... speak only in guarded tones of their period of enlistment." [34] The outfit possessed an image of sinister-like qualities. Apparently only those on the inside knew the full implications of its bizarre organizational behavior.

Top echelon Hummert executives, including Mickey Scopp and James Sauter, and possibly the program and casting directors, were known to receive an occasional box of cookies during the Christmas season. It appeared to be more than the rest of the staff ever anticipated or got. [35] "All of them bow low to Anne Hummert's generalship and skill," a source cautioned. "An audience with Anne in her colonial office, whose blue walls exactly match the color of her eyes, is a matter of grave concern. [Her office was decorated with "disarming pastel-tinted chintzes," a newspaperman, one of the few allowed into that inner sanctum, revealed. [36]] Hummert executives have been observed to turn color merely upon being informed of an impending telephone call from Mount Olympus. On such an occasion, a secretary calls up with the following curt signal: 'Please keep your line clear. Mrs. Hummert will talk to you in ten minutes.' As H-hour approaches, the executive is likely to expel visitors, such as dialoguers with whom he has been quietly planning, say, a brain tumor, in order to brace his nerves for a few minutes before the conference begins." [37]

Yet while the Hummerts may have gained a reputation as slave drivers, there is plenty of evidence that they expected no more of their staff than they themselves were willing to give. Both were, in fact, true workaholics. There are numerous recorded instances indicating that the couple's normal business day extended to 14 hours seven days a week. The astute entrepreneurs toiled away at appointed tasks roughly 60 percent of every week, except when they were on an extended vacation. And in sparse moments during the Second World War, Anne further devoted herself to a consulting mission on radio production with both the U.S. War and Treasury departments. (This challenge is delineated in chapter 6.)

2. The Odd Couple

Their prescribed daily routine left the moguls of melodrama precious little time for sleep, exercise, leisure, social life, attending music and dramatic performances, or cultivating outside interests beyond work. In fact, they were fortunate to have dependable help to maintain their physical facilities at home and at work, for there was hardly an opportunity for them to attend to those matters themselves.

Some of the distinction between the owners and those who steadfastly labored beneath them boiled down to wealth. As tactfully as it may be acknowledged, the Hummerts maintained a perceptibly exalted inference of their own self worth. Addicted to the trappings of opulence, the couple eventually settled in an impressive French Colonial manor of ostentatious proportions in tiny Greenwich, Connecticut. The home's size was enormous, its furnishings profligate. A staff of well-groomed, assiduous, intensely loyal servants of Japanese origin maintained the mansion and its cloistered grounds. The Hummerts, meanwhile, were stealthily transported in regal splendor to and from their suburban Fairfield County estate in Greenwich and their New York offices; as needed, a chauffeured limousine could be summoned at a moment's notice.

A press writer who knew the Hummerts fairly well speculated that, among their working associates, (including those on their payroll and those who weren't), possibly only James Sauter and Mickey Scopp ever managed to see inside their fabulous estate. "Nobody else in broadcasting was ever known to penetrate its privacy," he acknowledged.[38] If the infamous duo had any social excesses, he observed, they were kept well hidden. They obviously preferred one another's company to spending time intermingling with media movers and shakers. The reporter recalled an oft-repeated legend concerning the Hummert fortress that circulated for years among industry insiders. It pictured a formal dining room with only two chairs, one at either end of a long refectory table.[39] That story is indicative of a lifestyle that was popularized by many contemporaries throughout the business.

There was never a question about their being able to afford such upscale preferences, of course. By the early 1940s it was conjectured that together they were netting at least $300,000 annually out of radio, a tidy sum for that wartime epoch.[40] They were cited as "probably the

31

highest-earning creative team in the United States, Hollywood excepted."[41] "It was clear to any of us who thought about it that if [daytime serial creators] Irna Phillips and Elaine Carrington were taking hundreds of thousands of dollars out of soap opera, the Hummerts were taking millions," a daytime actress acknowledged.[42] (One report revealed that the average doctor at that time made less than $5,000 a year, while lawyers averaged a mere $2,500.[43]) Though the Hummerts lived a bizarre existence, it's clear that their affluence shielded them very well from the have-nots who surrounded them.

Despite their incredible wealth, however, one could hardly postulate that Frank and Anne Hummert possessed such commensurate power and prestige if they were spotted on the streets of Manhattan.

"Hummert was a thin, ascetic-seeming type who [in his office] had a curious mannerism of pulling his legs up in front of himself, pressing them against the edge of his desk," making bystanders nervous "for fear the frail man would fall."[44] With features not unlike those of convicted spy Julius Rosenberg, Hummert was painted by an eyewitness as "tall, thin, solemn-looking, and he stooped slightly."[45] No less an astute observer than James Thurber declared Hummert an "extreme example" of the *cerebrotonic ectomorph* posited by Dr. William Herbert Sheldon — an individual who is fittingly characterized as thin, unmuscular, thoughtful, sensitive and quiet to the point of introversion.[46] Hummert "lives on coffee and cigarettes," John W. Ashenhurst observed.[47] Another witness confirmed that he was "a thin, cadaverous-looking chain smoker."[48]

Mrs. Hummert, on the other hand, was presented as small, slender and "cheerful-looking" by one account. "She wore no make-up except a light trace of lipstick…. There was no mink about Anne Hummert. She wore a cloth coat of fine quality. Her shoes were likely to be Cuban-heeled pumps, her hats small, dark, and unadorned. She looked like a well-to-do Quaker lady."[49] One critic, carried away with the adjectives, depicted her as "small, quiet, refined, puritanical, secretive, rather severe…, feisty, indefatigable, and high-strung."[50]

Not surprisingly, in light of a multitude of analogous documentation, it took an acquaintance of Anne Hummert, an ex-school chum, to speculate in an alumnae publication: "Anne and her husband are people for whom 'success' is a capital-letter word; yet they remain

The dynamic duo, Frank (right) and Anne Hummert, chat with one of their most prominent actors, Karl Swenson, before an airing of *Mr. Chameleon,* on which Swenson starred. Frank Hummert was variously depicted as thin, frail, quiet and a cadaverous-looking chain smoker." Anne Hummert was considered small, slender, feisty, and high-strung, with similarities to "a well-to-do Quaker lady." (Courtesy of CBS Photo Archive)

simple people leading lives far more like those of the people they write for."[51] That contemplative review was in sharp contrast with what most observers saw and stated. (This was the same misinformant who purported in a lavish puff piece on Anne Ashenhurst that, in regard to the routine followed by Hummert hacks, "There is no pressure writing against deadlines."[52] How ironic.) Another judge may have been nearer reality when he assessed, "Many saw Frank and Anne as totally wrapped up in themselves and living in an ivory tower."[53]

By every measure, Air Features, Inc. (also known as Hummert Radio Features) was unique. From their spacious digs in Greenwich the

Hummerts presided over a mammoth radio empire. A biography of William S. Paley, owner-chairman of the Columbia Broadcasting System, who was also a strong-willed, resolute, persuasive commander-in-chief, includes an alluring tale of his relationship with the predominant moguls of melodrama. Nothing was lost on the observant Paley — he was well aware that the Hummert serials "caught fire with a huge audience of housewives" and that the couple's operation supplied half of such programs broadcast on network radio. As the yarn is recalled in print, one senses the chairman's considerable personal triumphs in the art of seduction.

> "It was very important to have Frank Hummert on your side," said Paley. "He was so powerful. If he said he wanted a program to go on NBC or on CBS, that was it. We fought to get him."
>
> Twice a month, Paley dutifully met for lunch with Hummert and his wife at the Park Lane Hotel. For all his understanding of the mind of the housewife, Hummert was something of a misanthrope. He always insisted that they be shielded from the other diners by potted ferns. While Hummert picked at a plate of raw vegetables, Paley turned on his famous soft sell, plying him with questions about his programs. Paley managed to flatter Hummert and simultaneously learn a great deal about which programming formulas worked and which did not.
>
> "I think he liked my style," Paley said later. "I never pressed him hard for anything. In a paternal sort of way he would tell me what I wanted to know. I hardly ever talked business directly with him. He just placed his productions where he wanted to, and from what I got from him, I think he favored me." [54]

Interestingly, a memoir of General David Sarnoff, chairman of the Radio Corporation of America, parent firm of the National Broadcasting Company and Paley's archrival, mentions no clandestine gatherings with the Hummerts. [55] That doesn't mean they didn't transpire; it reveals only that Sarnoff's biographer wasn't aware of those summits or didn't assign them much importance.

Upon due reflection, it seems not just bizarre but incongruent that Paley, who was rather widely recognized as a flamboyant playboy-socialite and simultaneously head of one of the two largest national broadcast chains, would reserve two lunch dates every month for the ascetically sheltered Hummerts. This is especially true when one considers that the trio seemed to have maintained no real agenda on their docket. After all, the Hummerts could never be considered by anybody as social butterflies. Signifying a repressive, hang-back demeanor at all times, they probably were seldom invited to parties. On the surface, then, their meetings with Paley seem to be those of misfits. Yet the whole episode underscores just how prominent the producers were and, as Paley indicated, how valuable the Columbia Broadcasting System measured their contributions. He obviously considered it worth his time to court them heavily.

To the Hummerts alone went the credit for the concepts, plot lines and actual words uttered on the programs they produced. Laboring dutifully below them were a half-dozen editors, a score of writers and five-dozen clerical workers. Outside the Hummerts' own cloister was stationed rows and rows of typists, relentlessly knocking out stencils for mimeograph machines. These subordinates endured autocratically run assembly-line methods and sweatshop tactics. The Hummerts offered little tolerance to those who broke well-publicized codes. "The damn operation is just like General Motors," explained a network executive.[56] It was, in every sense, a radio drama factory. The names of those whose careers were launched in the "Hummert salt mines"—a phrase that caught on with many who persevered in that facility—would be virtually synonymous with the founders of the Radio Writers Guild.[57]

Air Features was renowned among industry insiders for upholding a surfeit of hard-and-fast policies that were inviolable. "There was a rule or set of rules laid down by the Hummerts to govern almost any contingency," a pair of observers reported.[58] "The Hummerts did not want their original concepts tampered with..., so they ran their shows by rules rather than inspiration," said another.[59] Those canons were well understood by all who earned a living under the Hummert regime. Other production houses had no such cardinal statutes. An actress who played in dozens of Air Features dramas shared a few of the common practices:

> The directors were not allowed to introduce "art" effects— unessential sound, background music — that might obscure one word of the dialogue.

Frank and Anne Hummert's Radio Factory

An actor needed a formidable technique to play a hysterical scene to suit the Hummerts. They demanded excitement and pace, but each vowel and consonant had to be enunciated with painful precision. For two characters to overlap speeches was absolutely forbidden.

As for the writer, he had a typed list of regulations to guide him — all aimed at insuring that the listener knew at every moment who was talking to whom and about what. This meant frequent character identification and plot "recap."[60]

At infrequent intervals Frank and Anne Hummert would make previously unannounced visits to the shows they produced, occasions that inevitably became an "intimidating presence at rehearsal," noted one wag. "If you displeased the Hummerts, you might be wise to consider a new line of work. They frowned on clowning around, late arrivals, or a breath of scandal."[61]

The Hummerts often delivered many of their commands to subordinates and received feedback without ever leaving their Greenwich domicile. A staff of messengers knew the route so well that they could probably have driven it blindfolded. In 1947 Thomas Whiteside observed: "Communications between the Park Avenue boiler room and Supreme Headquarters in Greenwich are usually in writing. Anne Hummert is undoubtedly the strategist. She manages Air Features, which she visits several times weekly."[62] There could never be any question about who was the power behind the throne.

Frank Hummert tenaciously defended their methodology devoted to mass production, low costs, standardization, and specialization. According to him, while it wasn't humanly possible for the two of them, Frank and Anne, to produce every line of the scripts broadcast in their names, the pair supplied "the initiative, the conception, the detailed synopses and essentially direction, tone, casting, and nature of the series."[63] Declared one analyst of their strategy: "The only justification for the whole system appears to be that the Hummert shows remained among the most popular. Who is to say that another procedure might not have wrecked Frank and Anne's near-perfect inventions?"[64]

Salaries became a major bone of contention among the Hummerts' underlings. By 1938 scriptwriters earned only $25 for each

36

2. The Odd Couple

Theirs was the story that asked the question: "Can two ordinary, everyday, run-of-the-mill people find happiness in running a (drama) mill?" Frank and Anne Hummert loved to surprise casts by dropping in unexpectedly on rehearsals of their radio series. Shown in the background, they appeared at the second broadcast of the crime detective drama *Mr. Chameleon*, July 21, 1948. (Courtesy of CBS Photo Archive)

11-minute episode. A decade later that figure had increased to just $35.[65] Initially, those artists received about half of what they would have made while working on competing serials. The disparities apparently grew over the years. As time went on, other producers compensated their writers from between $1,000 to $2,000 weekly for five dramatic episodes. The disparity was astonishing.

Petitioning on behalf of the Radio Writers Guild (RWG) — with whom all Air Features scribes were affiliated — president Erik Barnouw lamented: "To bring the Hummerts to a higher level was one of our main aims."[66] A characterization outline of the *Ma Perkins* series that was given prospective writers of that washboard weeper explained: "It is not money and high position that count, but what you do for others—what's in your heart."[67] The scribes must have carried that bit of cheer with them to the bank as they went to cash their paltry paychecks. Radio historiographer John Dunning assessed the remunerative tactics of the Hummerts in five succinct words: "They were not generous people."[68]

Barnouw, of the Radio Writers Guild, reported on the daunting task that stood before that body in dealing with the Hummerts. The RWG hoped to convince the Hummerts to upgrade their pay scales. Calling the couple "a difficult target," Barnouw noted that—just as everyone before him had long ago discovered—they were often sequestered at their home in Greenwich: "I found no New York writer who had met Frank Hummert; only a few had ever met Ann [sic] Hummert. The Hummerts dealt with writers largely through intermediaries and through written synopses and memoranda.... The task offered a livelihood but involved a frustrating relationship."[69]

Air Features remained a persistent thorn in the sides of those running the Radio Writers Guild. When that 1,200-member body, representing nearly every wordsmith in the business, called an industry-wide strike for October 26, 1948, its aim was to negotiate a contract that would be fair to its skilled artists. Reforming the Hummert organization was a primary goal of that endeavor. Until then, efforts to prompt any change had been futile.

But once the strike was called, the Hummerts offered a surprise response: RWG president Barnouw was suddenly summoned to a lunch gathering with the reclusive pair at the Park Avenue establishment they frequented, only a few steps from their offices at 247 Park Avenue. (Their favorite watering hole, the reader will recall, was situated in the Park Lane Hotel at 299 Park Avenue. Both 247 and 299 were razed in 1967.)

Barnouw asked Peter Lyon to accompany him. Knowledgeable about union matters, Lyon had preceded Barnouw as RWG president and was then serving as chairman of the group's strategy committee. The guests were a bit startled over the physical setting of the summit for it transpired at the Hummerts' "special table in a corner masked by potted palms, preventing others from observing them."[70] One wag observed that Frank Hummert could be comfortable on such occasions lunching on little more than a bowl of shredded wheat. He was seldom unnerved by anybody.

Barnouw characterized Anne Hummert as "stylish and a bundle of energy," while Frank was "tall, gangly, with a folksy, bucolic character ... older and ... sallow-looking." "Together they seemed to epitomize a Hummert serial formula. Could a folksy geezer from the Midwest find happiness with a svelte, dynamic secretary in suburbia?"[71]

When the quartet got down to brass tacks following the repast, Anne Hummert deferred to her husband to relate what was on their collective minds.[72] "If there is anything I hate," said he, "it's lawyers. If lawyers get involved in a thing, it poisons the whole business. Now this matter of the writers' contract, and the strike, and all that—the only people likely to gain from it are the lawyers. So that's no good."

Their lunch companions agreed, and Hummert continued: "So here's what we would like to do.... We [he and Anne] would like to join the Radio Writers Guild. We want to be able to say to our sponsors, 'We're union members. There's been this strike vote. We have to go along. We have no choice.' Is there any reason we can't join?"

Barnouw and Lyon were flabbergasted. Nothing like that had occurred to them as a potential outcome. They assured the couple that they were eligible to join and would be welcome. Lyon gave them application forms, which he took from his briefcase. Hummert said they would fill them out at once and have them delivered to RWG offices together with their membership dues.

Feeling by then as if he was on solid ground, Lyon pressed them: "Now about our contract. Could you sign it on behalf of Air Features?" Hummert responded, "That's what you'll have to take up with Air Features." Barnouw was baffled, wondering if it was some type of trap.

Hummert acknowledged, "You probably think I own Air Features. That's what everybody thinks. I don't own it. I'm just an employee. I set it up that way, on purpose. The president of Air Features is Jim Sauter. That's the fellow you'll have to talk to."

The elder statesman agreed to make the introductions with Sauter. Their table talk done, the foursome dispensed with lunch and trotted over to nearby Air Features. Crossing the full length of the clerical sector, they were promptly ushered into the private domain of "J. Sauter,

President." At Hummert's request, Sauter quickly signed the paper that covered a "large chunk" of network programming. The die for compensatory reform genuinely had been cast that day.

The fact that the opposition had caved in so readily was shocking news at RWG. Discussions at the Waldorf-Astoria Hotel involving a coalition of advertising officials and the RWG, both sides represented by legal counsel, were soon under way. A minimum basic agreement covering employment of freelance writers was hammered out by early 1949. When the National Labor Relations Board held a vote of all covered scribes in 1951, the pact was implemented. It was definitely a fateful turning point for those skilled artisans. And Frank and Anne Hummert could be credited with playing a decisive role in its victory.

Unfortunately, the tightwad tactics that the twosome practiced for so many years weren't limited to their writers alone. The co-conspirators crafted enough "Spartanizing" techniques to reach every subject in their vast domain.

A cardinal rule rigidly enforced by the Hummerts was to limit to 25 the number speaking parts appearing in a soap opera during a given week. If more than five individuals were heard on a single day, for instance, fewer than five could turn up on a subsequent day that same week. At all times the bottom line was kept in clear focus in writing, directing and performing. The fewer number of individuals required for participation in a broadcast series inversely netted greater amounts of cash for the Hummert treasure chest. Consistently, that appeared to be an overriding factor in the planning of many of their dramas.

Actors on Hummert serials were then commonly compensated at $15 per show and $5 to $6 per hour of rehearsal time. In that organization, rehearsals were kept to an absolute minimum to also reduce overhead expenses. Practice sessions could never last more than an hour (although 90 minutes was customary for some other producers' quarter-hour episodes). Hummert program directors fulfilled that expectation by relying almost exclusively upon seasoned radio thespians. Using the same individuals over and over meant calling upon a skilled, dependable corps of actors that required little instruction and was readily accessible. At the same time it significantly reduced costs while giving directors confidence in those thespians' performing abilities.

2. The Odd Couple

An active network program announcer of the period, Jackson Beck, recalled: "When you worked for Frank and Anne Hummert ... on one of their fifteen-minute daytime serials ... you took home exactly $11.88. On a thirty-minute nighttime show you'd get five bucks for a small part, maybe $35, occasionally $50 for a lead. Sometimes you'd get an additional five for a re-broadcast" (when a live program was repeated for West Coast audiences, due to three-hour time differences).[73] Beck continued: "Those figures sound ridiculous today, but if you hustled, you could make two hundred a week. With rent about $140 a month for a three-room apartment, that was pretty good money."[74]

The intense frugality carried over from the dramatic series that the Hummerts created to their musical features as well. Standard arrangements performed by dependable musicians employed at scale (the absolute minimum wage permitted by union artist contracts) were the norm. Furthermore, the invariably shrewd business operatives implemented a strategy that allowed themselves to amass commissions from the talent they hired for their various series.

The pair maintained that the salaries made the writers their employees but never their designers. Any scribe who challenged the system, adding his or her own name as creator of such material, was immediately seeking employment elsewhere. The duo dictated the outlines for each program, suggesting characterization and dialogue. One wag observed that Anne Hummert had "a photographic memory" and "was renowned in the industry for her ability to remember each intricate twist of every one of their creations."[75] Writers took the couple's ideas and fashioned action and conversation to flesh out the scripts. Said one pundit: "That the husband and wife personally and collectively plotted all ... [their] serials was hard to credit and yet impossible to refute."[76]

As a precaution and, as previously noted, to prevent dialoguers from becoming too identified with a given program the Hummerts scuttled the line-up at random, moving their scribes from show to show on sudden impulse. Scriptwriters were required to stay at least three weeks ahead at all times (some reports claim as many as six weeks). Moreover, weeks of approved episodes sitting on a shelf for future broadcast could be instantly jeopardized when Anne Hummert had a change of heart about a plot's direction. Such a whim often sent writers scrambling to revise finished chapters while keeping three to six weeks ahead.

A pair of radio chroniclers recalled the Hummert hireling who labored relentlessly "to get himself 19 scripts ahead so he could take a trip to Mexico."[77] But his plans instantly evaporated when he was abruptly told that Mrs. Hummert wanted the plot altered. So much for his siesta in the sun! Another informant allowed: "When Mrs. Hummert was dictating a change of direction, no one ventured an opinion. Vacation plans were shelved and work redone, and an errant remark might be met with instant dismissal."[78]

By her very nature, Anne Hummert had the ability to instill the fear of the Lord in her dialoguers. There is a widely circulated tale documented by numerous print sources that she once instructed one of her "nameless hacks" (Manya Starr) to "include God on every page of every script."[79] The well-intentioned scribe politely quizzed: "And who will play the part?" As the story goes, the redoubtable Ms. Hummert fired the wordsmith on the spot.

Frank, too, could display an equally mean streak, particularly when confronted at an inopportune moment. There are several recorded instances in which he demonstrably lost his temper rather suddenly. He so jealously guarded his privacy, for example, that on one occasion he canned a subordinate for directly addressing him while both occupied the men's room.[80] Seasoned staffers soon learned it was better to tiptoe around him rather than challenge Hummert with almost any topic of discussion.

There were very few exceptions to the cardinal rule that prevented scriptwriters' appellations from being mentioned on the air. Of the members of the Hummerts' huge stable of writers, Larry Klee may have been the name most familiar to radio audiences. For nearly all the many years he penned the weekly detective drama *Mr. Keen, Tracer of Lost Persons*, following the conclusion of each episode an interlocutor habitually announced: "Dialogue by Lawrence Klee." (Several internal memos among their personal papers indicate that Klee's work, in particular, earned munificent favor among the scripts of the abundant Air Features wordsmiths.)

The Hummerts' justification for not giving on-air tribute to most of those dialoguers was that, "it would spoil the illusion ... [for] our listeners believe these stories are real."[81] Radio Writers Guild agents were candidly informed that mention of a scribe's name was simply out of the question.

For whatever the reason, as the end of radio's golden age approached, the Hummerts gave evidence of thawing just a wee bit. (Could the RWG agreement possibly have influenced them?) By the 1950s a handful of names of writers, directors and actors were being revealed — people who were making the Hummerts look good with every broadcast, and some who had been doing so for years. On *Our Gal Sunday*, for instance, longtime announcer Ed Fleming was allowed to add at the end of each weekday episode (after a common spiel about the Hummerts): "Dialogue by Jean Carroll. Directed by Arthur Hanna. Vivian Smolen plays Sunday, and Karl Swenson is Lord Henry." Jean Carroll obviously became one of the Hummerts' darlings for the writer also received on-air credit as author of *Young Widder Brown* in that durable series' fading days.

There was one foible among the Hummerts' many quirks regarding giving credit, however, which will probably never be understood. When *Stella Dallas* hit the airwaves each day, not once but *twice* the announcer made reference to the fact that "This chapter in the later life of *Stella Dallas* is written by Anne Hummert." It was never explained why her name was linked to that lone drama plucked from an arsenal of similar programs, nor why she claimed to have written its scripts herself. Given the fact that the Hummerts dictated plotlines for dozens of dramas airing concurrently, it's almost unthinkable that she could have penned the dialogue for five episodes every week for any one of them. Chalk it up to another ambiguity that clouded the mysterious duo's habits. Their personal excesses and idiosyncrasies turned up in the story lines of many of their own narratives. (For a fuller interpretation, see chapter 6.)

The reader will recall that during the heyday of Air Features, Inc. the assembly-line factory was situated at 247 Park Avenue. But when the networks canceled almost all of their remaining programs in the mid–1950s, Frank and Anne scaled back, moving Air Features to 44–46 East Fifty-Third Street. By then their advertised services included packaged radio–TV programs — live, on film and transcribed. Only three shows were still airing—*Backstage Wife, Our Gal Sunday* and *The Romance of Helen Trent*. The *Radio Annual* for 1958 lists I.S. Becker as Air Features president. The *real* high command was still secretively, as well as cleverly, hiding its own undoubtedly misunderstood purposes.

Their long, profitable ride came down to a final gasp in the early 1960s with the expiration of the golden age of radio. A short while later Frank and Anne Hummert sold the rights to their vast Air Features holdings to the Columbia Broadcasting System. Continuing their luxurious lifestyle, for several years the couple traipsed the globe on the millions they had earned as shrewd businesspersons and investors across the decades.

They made only one outward change, in fact—when they sold their infamous palatial estate in Connecticut and moved to New York. But they continued to thrive in high cotton. At 1220 Park Avenue they occupied an ostentatious triplex apartment overlooking Central Park, where they took five-mile walks together almost daily. The routine persisted until illness at long last overtook Frank Hummert.

As noted already, he died the way he lived, at least in the final three decades of his life. At the insistence of his spouse, only a small paid notice appeared in a single newspaper following Frank Hummert's demise on March 12, 1966. In fact, word was suppressed for several weeks until inquiries from frustrated reporters began to mount. An obituary's headline, appearing in the April 27, 1966, issue of the entertainment bible *Variety*, characterized Hummert as being "Ever the Hermit." The accompanying article explained: "The mysterioso behavior policy of the widow was strictly in accordance with the Hummert traditions.... That a man whose mark on broadcast advertising and programming history could be obliterated from the record was, of course, preposterous, whatever the motivations of the recluse mentality. Oddly enough, as Anne Ashenhurst, the widow was a reporter on the Paris *Herald*."[82]

As for Anne herself, she confessed that she was devastated at the passing of her beloved Frank. Although the significant disparity in their ages would indicate the likelihood of such an early contingency, her reaction revealed that she was caught off guard. The widow soon downsized, moving to a smaller apartment on Fifth Avenue that was also nestled against New York's famed Central Park. Characterized all her life as a workaholic, Anne retired immediately upon her spouse's passing. "Everyone said I couldn't retire, but when Frank died I was ravaged. I was knocked for a loop. I thought I had worked enough. I didn't slow down; I simply stopped."[83]

She *did* continue to travel, however, just as she had done with Frank. She also walked three miles daily until a few months before her own demise. She read incessantly and frequently attended ballet and opera productions, something she never had time for when she was working. In 1978 Anne Hummert was named first artist-in-residence of her alma mater's communication program. She labeled the occasion "a beautiful swan song ... one of the happiest experiences of my later life."[84] She remained active in alumnae affairs at Goucher College on into the early 1980s, beyond her seventy-fifth birthday.

During some of those years following Frank's death, Anne Hummert maintained contact with former thespians Arthur and Geneva Hughes, who discreetly resided on Manhattan's West End Avenue. Hughes was the durable hero of the Hummerts' popular *Just Plain Bill* serial, the program that originally demonstrated staying power for the genre while launching their dreams of a radio empire. Although no special favoritism is known to have been shown to Hughes and his wife, an ex–Broadway actress, insiders believed that *Just Plain Bill* was the Hummerts' personal favorite among their immense body of soap opera creations.

Robert Hardy Andrews penned the early years of *Just Plain Bill*. In 1949 the same author's novel, *Legend of a Lady: The Story of Rita Martin*, was published. The mythical narrative so blatantly parallels the personal and professional achievements of Anne Hummert that Andrews felt compelled to include a disclaimer in the frontispiece: "This book and its incidents and people are all fiction from beginning to end."[85] Some of his readers have referred to the tome as a "veiled attempt" to recount the life story of Anne Hummert. Indeed, there are times when the resemblance is so striking that any disclaimer becomes moot. It's an intriguing introspective look at an incredibly fascinating character.

When, late in Anne Hummert's life, the American Heritage Center of the University of Wyoming expressed an interest in housing tens of thousands of Hummert broadcast scripts and some of their personal papers, the doyennne of daytime radio drama seemed totally dumbfounded. Wondering aloud why "anyone would want all that stuff," she nevertheless obligingly gave the institution her consent. Later she claimed it took three planeloads to carry their material to Laramie. But an archivist at the repository insisted that "three planeloads" stretched believability considerably. "Maybe one Greyhound would be more like it," she gingerly allowed.

The Hummert scripts and papers were identified, cataloged, labeled and deposited into 460 corrugated cartons, becoming an important addition to the storehouse's performing arts holdings. That collection is the largest single repository of Hummert memorabilia in existence, and on occasion draws researchers who pour intensely over the many secrets of vintage radio history held therein.

Anne Hummert died in her own bed on July 5, 1996. She was buried in Chicago's Graceland Cemetery. Two granddaughters and two great-grandchildren survived her.

In a thoughtful examination of radio drama published more than three decades ago, author Raymond William Stedman — claiming that "few radio figures were as fascinating or as widely misunderstood as the Hummerts" — apologized to his readers for his own at times deprecating assessment of their programming: "They would be flailed for their dramatic 'horrors' [Stedman, himself, had previously cited their banal-dialogued serials] but almost never praised for their more ambitious offerings. And through it all they maintained a rare personal dignity coupled with a seldom-recognized humility."[86]

He continued: "I humbly submit that I, and the body of broadcasting critics, may have missed something the Hummerts and their faithful listeners did not. This said, I shall attempt to describe the Hummert role in serial history with as much fairness as I can, trying to report or to analyze but not to condemn. If my stand is interpreted not as objectivity but as cowardice in the face of possible reprisal by all those *Helen Trent* fans, so be it."[87]

Despite possessing the quirks that labeled them as incorrigible eccentrics, the pair distinguished themselves with numerous admirable donations to the world of aural broadcasting. Several of their noteworthy achievements are spelled out in successive chapters. Suffice it to say at this juncture that radio as Americans experienced it during its golden age likely would have been vastly different had Frank and Anne Hummert not been on the scene to influence it so pervasively.

3

MERRIE MELODIES

The fact that Frank and Anne Hummert were heavily immersed in producing musical extravaganzas for radio audiences has escaped the notice of most scholars of the medium, both then and now. With their enveloping involvement in melodrama — so convincingly verified through a myriad of highly visible products in the soap opera, crime detective and juvenile adventure breeds— the little detail of the duo's involvement in a variety of musical endeavors has been almost completely overlooked. (This is probably true of all but the most thoroughly indoctrinated scholars of vintage radio melody.) By actual count, however, about 30 percent of their colossal warehouse of radio creations focused wholly on music.

Several of those tune-filled features remained on the air for many years. This attested to their owners' attempts to diversify, expanding their personal interests far beyond the territory for which they were generally acclaimed. Let it be further noted that seldom did one of their prime time concert music and musical variety series fall out of the top 10 in ratings certified by the radio pollsters.[1]

Even those who heard their musical feasts live were probably unaware of the Hummerts' involvement in the formation and production of those shows. Unlike most of the programs in their seemingly endless repertoire, the Hummerts' names were almost never mentioned over the air on most of their musical features. This was a conspicuous departure from an established style so prevalent elsewhere; routinely the twosome heard themselves credited on the numer-

47

ous shows that emanated from the Hummert drama mills. The absence of their monikers on their musicals perhaps bespoke of the appeal those programs had to a more erudite, dynamic, and influential audience than those listeners tuning in to narratives.

Nor should it come as any shock that the couple that so acutely invested themselves in washboard weepers—which for decades may have been the bane of the middle class housewife—could harbor an affinity toward programming for more sophisticate tastes. After all, Frank and Anne Hummert received quality preparation from prestigious institutions of higher learning. This could insure, presumably, some degree of exposure to refinement and culture. But some of Frank Hummert's own attraction to more urbane pursuits may have stemmed from experiences that occurred early in his professional life.

One of Hummert's notable advertising triumphs was in founding a national Brunswick New Hall of Fame for a recording label client's artists. Years later he recalled with some satisfaction that it established new voices on the operatic and concert stages. As another consequence, phonograph disk sales sharply increased, while some of the record label's obscure talent emerged for the first time to widespread public scrutiny. Simultaneously, Hummert directly benefited from the outcome of these dynamics: he was introduced to and connected with the world of classical and pop music. Doors opened that were to become invaluable to him once he entered the field of radio entertainment a short time down the road.

Even before he moved into the field of advertising, however, he spent engaged in rewriting theatrical scripts. From that practice he not only gained exposure to the various components of stage creations in several forms but to their producers as well. It surely set the stage for what was ahead while enlarging his vision for opportunities he would eventually seize.

Even though Frank and Anne Hummert apparently spent little time in their working lives indulging in any serious quests they may have harbored for opera, film and stage musical productions (although she treated herself in later life by attending such performances regularly), that doesn't necessarily mean they didn't find those pastimes stimulating. Their demanding schedules simply left them little opportunity to devote very many hours to outside interests. At home they may have participated vicariously by way of radio and recordings and eventually by television, as their routines permitted.

Beyond all that, of course, the addition of tuneful prime time radio features to their stable of aural series offered the promise of appreciably increased bottom lines. Never ones to resist any lucrative prospects, the Hummerts literally made beautiful music together for a full two decades. That genre, as a result, became a key player among the programming concepts they offered to the national chains.

Their initial attempts to introduce musical fare to radio audiences date from their very earliest entrance into the medium, in fact. While many of their musical treats were heard only briefly, listeners accepted a few of them so profoundly that they continued to air for long spells. "Hummert radio musicals tended to go on year after year, ... often for one or another American Home Products or Sterling Drug brands. These were straight orchestra and singer formula stuff, the very stuff of radio's first decade."[2] Actually, Sterling Drugs offered *all* of the Hummerts' most durable musical features on behalf of well-established brand names like Bayer, Dr. Lyons and Phillips. American Home Products *did* underwrite a fleeting [Arthur] *Hammerstein Music Hall,* lasting just over three years, principally for Kolynos. That seemed brief in relation to several of the Sterling Drugs programs.

The couple was pushing all the right buttons— not just pleasing audiences but advertisers as well, while applying their shrewd business acumen to rake in the profits. "It appears that the Hummerts were extremely astute operators in terms of giving sponsors a simple, inexpensive, unobjectionable type of program, built for long runs and cumulative network discounts. The orchestras were reliable, the arrangements standard, the wages strictly scale."[3] Scale was the absolute minimum that artists must receive for rehearsal time and performances, in compliance with union contracts. Frank and Anne Hummert earned a reputation in the industry — which they apparently wore proudly, almost like a badge of honor — for not offering their talent any recompense above scale. Money they didn't have to pay out, of course, went into their own pockets.

Straight melodies ruled their musical productions, seldom straying from ballad or waltz tempos. A critic noted that radio and classical or semi-classical music became "natural allies," and certified that many of the Hummert features in this category were deemed "distinguished."[4] The lyrics on their shows were marked by uncommon clarity, also a hallmark of their dramatic series. Complex musical arrangements that might obscure the listeners' quick recognition of a tune simply had no place on their programs. The public embraced the formula and kept a handful of those musical indulgences in the ether for 15 to 20 years.

Just as with soap opera and other genres, by introducing such a large volume of musical features, one might anticipate that many series would not survive for very long. Some simply did not find favor with listeners, while others never attracted sufficient sponsors or went head-to-head with formidable programming on competing chains and were lost on the ratings pile. Many programs were rapidly discarded and quickly forgotten, among them *Evening Melodies, Gems of Melody, Matinee Melodies, Melodiana, The Musical Revue, Showland Memories* and *Sweetest Love Songs Ever Sung*. Nondescript monikers were usually withdrawn after brief exposure to radio audiences. A few series without long-term staying power even featured the performers' names in their titles: *Abe Lyman and Movieland's Favorite Band, Don Donnie's Orchestra, French Mignon Trio, Hammerstein Music Hall* and *The Imperial Hollywood Band*.

As this author observed in an earlier tome, when the Hummerts encountered a premise that they liked they tended to beat it to death.[5] Thus they provided the fans with a plethora of French-themed shows. In addition to the *French Mignon Trio,* there was *La Gaiete Parisienne, Paris Night Life,* plus *Folies Bergere of the Air, Folies de Paree* and *Revue de Paree* (the latter trio of monikers applying to the same show).

But nothing surpassed their notion of visiting cabarets for the purpose of eavesdropping on mythical choral "performances" on a kind of whirlwind carousel marathon. Each series bore its own distinctive variation but the basic idea remained the same. Thus, listeners could tune in to *Broadway Merry-Go-Round, London Merry-Go-Round, Manhattan Merry-Go-Round* and *Monday Merry-Go-Round*.

By 1947 investigative journalist Thomas Whiteside disclosed to the public that Anne Hummert was managing Air Features, Inc. Presumably this included the task of overseeing all of the melodramatic narratives that the couple created for a multiplicity of programming species. There is hard evidence to the contrary, nonetheless.[6]

Frank Hummert persisted in riding herd over the couple's nighttime crime thrillers, in spite of Whiteside's insistence that he was "content to handle the *American Album of Familiar Music, American Melody Hour, Manhattan Merry-Go-Round* and *Waltz Time.*"[7] Actually, the quartet of shows named was undoubtedly the most timeless, resilient and celebrated of at least 37 musical offerings the Hummerts cultivated. (One pundit dubbed *Manhattan Merry-Go-Round* and *The American Album of Familiar Music* "the elevator music of its day."[8]) Make no mistake: the four series together made a profound contribution to radio harmony. Each will be examined independently.

The oldest and most durable of the foursome, *The American Album of Familiar Music*, dated from October 11, 1931. It remained a continuous and popular network feature for two decades (through June 17, 1951), with the exception of a few summers off. *Album* debuted about the time Frank Hummert and his then-assistant Anne S. Ashenhurst were attempting to prove his theory that housewives would favorably respond to fictional accounts about common people offered in serialized morsels. (Their first attempt, *The Stolen Husband*, also premiering in 1931, while brief, was a disaster. Yet out of its ruins they gained enough proficiency to establish *Just Plain Bill*, a drama that was a model for scores of series to follow, becoming entrenched in the ether for 23 years.)

The American Album of Familiar Music arrived on the air to the theme of *Dream Serenade*, penned by conductor Gustave Haenschen. (Abe Lyman and his orchestra succeeded Haenschen later in the run.) *Album* was originally introduced as "a program of supremely lovely songs and melodies that capture all hearts." The series' most active vocalists were tenor Frank Munn, billed as "the golden voice of radio" and touted as the program's longtime featured celebrity; coloratura soprano Bernice Claire; tenor Donald Dame; sopranos Margaret Daum, Vivian della Chiesa, Jean Dickenson ("the nightingale of the airwaves"), Lucy Monroe and Virginia Rea; contraltos Elizabeth Lennox and Evelyn MacGregor; and Daniel Lieberfeld. At times there were performances by the piano duo of Arden and Arden; a featured violinist, Bernard Hirsch; a dozen-member Buckingham Choir; and sundry other artists who floated in and out of the lineup. (An astute reporter picked up on the fact that — by the late 1930s — a number of the Hummerts' Fairfield County, Connecticut, neighbors were turning up on *Album*. They included Norwalk's Gustav Haenschen, conductor, and Westport vocalists Jean Dickenson and Elizabeth Lennox.[9])

Although the Hummerts always held firm reins to everything they controlled, James Haupt was the longtime director of the series. A progression of familiar Air Features announcers offered little in the way of monologue, thereby probably substantially increasing the show's delight with music enthusiasts. Notable in that capacity were Andre Baruch, Howard Claney and Roger Krupp.

While the Hummerts often went to great lengths to hide the names of those connected with their serials and crime dramas — including actors, writers, directors, sound technicians and musicians — the individuals performing on their various musicales were usually seen as a "draw," especially those who were talented and instantly recognized by audiences. While there were few "stars," in the true sense, on the aggregate of Hummert programs, an exception was made in music. And the caliber of artists they presented definitely enhanced those series' receptions with listeners.

Because it was "all in the family" — including the same sponsor, announcers, producers and network — the Hummerts would occasionally drop in brief promos for their musical features at the conclusion of their afternoon soap operas. On those occasions the artists performing on the current week's show were individually recounted in an attempt to increase listenership. Nobody realized, of course, that all of those programs were emanating from under the same roof. Dishpan drama addicts probably thought of it as mere chain plugs for a web's future programming.

For their musicals the Hummerts also departed from a longstanding ritual that could be witnessed on all of their dramatic programs — holding rehearsal time to an absolute minimum. With as many individuals as were involved in a performance of the nature of *Album*, the cast was called to begin preparation for a Sunday 9:30 P.M. broadcast at 5 o'clock that afternoon. Practice was intense, and it frequently didn't end until just moments before the program aired live.

On the rare occasions when Frank Munn was absent from his post on *The American Album of Familiar Music*, rising male vocalists, most often Frank Parker ("America's great romantic tenor"— then during his pre–*Arthur Godfrey Time* epoch), filled in, invariably "singing *for* Frank Munn." No one was believed capable of *replacing* Munn, of course. Dubbed "the dean of ballad singers,"[10] Munn was a legendary recording artist and radio entertainer whose career on the ether began even before the mid–1920s. (Parker ultimately replaced Munn upon Munn's retirement, however.)

Munn savored his time away from the microphone. Unlike contemporaries, he routinely turned down concert tours, much pre-

Three *American Album* principals commemorate the show's fifth birthday. Left to right: tenor Frank Munn, soprano Lucy Monroe and musical director Gustav Haenschen. Munn, "the golden voice of radio," was a favorite of audiences and the Hummerts, headlining several of their musicales. His portly frame belied an image of "a dashing amorous troubadour," as his romantic voice urged listeners to swoon. (Photofest)

ferring a quieter subsistence. He cherished his leisure moments, reminiscent of the proclivities of his dual radio producers, Frank and Anne Hummert. In *his* case, however, he may have been persuaded by physical realities: Munn stood five feet, seven inches tall and weighed in excess of 250 pounds. ("Self-conscious of his unromantic roly-poly shape, the short and stocky singer preferred to appeal only to the ear," a pundit allowed.[11])

The Hummerts were genuinely pleased when Munn declined guest spots on other shows. At his request they agreed to shield their fêted pop idol from most studio audiences and public view. Apparently they didn't want "to dispel the illusion of listeners whose image of him as a dashing amorous troubadour had been conceived from his romantic voice."[12] In 1938 the couple banned live theater spectators that— they claimed—were distracting the listeners at home. Despite that, a long-held tradition remained calling for artists to appear in full evening attire, even though only the cast, production crew and sponsor (who might be visiting) could see them.

Frank Munn was in demand as the star of a trio of durable Hummert aural series. In addition to *The American Album of Familiar Music*'s Sunday night broadcasts, he performed concurrently on Tuesday or Wednesday nights as the lead vocalist on *American Melody Hour*. He sustained the same role Friday nights on *Waltz Time*. Munn also starred in a couple of earlier Hummert features: *Lavender and Old Lace* (1934–1936) and *Sweetest Love Songs Ever Sung* (1936–1937).

A determined advocate of time off from such workaholic scheduling, in 1945 at age 51 he suddenly bowed out of all of it. His decision shocked Frank Hummert, while catching his sponsor (Sterling Drugs' Bayer aspirin) and legions of fans off guard. For nearly two decades Munn had been "the golden voice of radio," entrenched as one of the most favored singers of both popular and semi-classical works. Ranking as one of the medium's top male vocalists, he was frequently mentioned alongside Kenny Baker, Bing Crosby, Nelson Eddy and Frank Sinatra. A few years later, in 1953 at age 59, the beloved singer suffered a fatal heart attack.

Munn, vocalists Elizabeth Lennox and Virginia Rea and conductor Gus Haenschen, regulars on *The American Album of Familiar Music*, collaborated on *The Palmolive Hour* (1927–1931) before *Album* premiered. (Munn claimed, "Everything I am in radio I owe to Gus Haen-schen. It is his artistry, musicianship, and advice which have allowed me to achieve whatever success has been mine."[13]) The *Palmolive* show was recognized as NBC's "most esteemed musical presentation" during that period.[14] Its popularity spawned at least seven other features, including *The American Album of Familiar Music, American Melody Hour, The Contented Program, Hammerstein Music Hall, Highways in Melody, The Hour of Charm* and *The Voice of Firestone*. Three of those were Hummert creations (*The American Album of Familiar Music, American Melody Hour, and Hammerstein Music Hall*).

The consumer fanzine *Radio Mirror*, reporting in 1939 on *Album*, perceptively observed: "Not a song is sung or a melody played that hasn't first been selected and okayed by Mr. and Mrs. Hummert. The Hummerts have only one rule for the music they select, but that's a good one — it must be full of melody." On a typical *Album* broadcast, listeners could expect to be treated to such melodic chestnuts as Irving Berlin's "Remember," as well as "The Rose of Tralee" and "Believe Me If All Those Endearing Young Charms."

The second of the most prominent Hummert musical creations was *Manhattan Merry-Go-Round*, which debuted on November 6, 1932, and continued every week through April 17, 1949. For all but its final few weeks on the air the series was sponsored by Sterling's Dr. Lyons tooth powder. During the prewar period the show's featured attraction was the since-forgotten vocalist Rachel Carlay "and her French ditties," providing a Continental affectation. Popular baritone Conrad Thibault and several other vocalists complemented her. The series also dabbled in variety in its early years, with comedy guests like Jimmy Durante, Bert Lahr and Beatrice Lillie making it truly a diverse entertainment forum. Eventually the Hummerts decided to focus everything on melody, however, and the funny business discreetly vanished.

In the show's fading half-dozen years— perhaps its best remembered and most influential epoch — its featured artist was the long established Welsh-born baritone Thomas L. Thomas, "beloved singer of stage and radio." (The "L" stood for "Llyfwny," a common moniker in the singer's native land.) Thomas had bowed at the Metropolitan Opera in 1937 after winning a spot on its radio auditions. He appeared on several other early audio series. Between 1947 and 1954 his voice

Billed as the "beloved singer of stage and radio," baritone Thomas L. Thomas, who came to the forefront after winning a radio audition at the Metropolitan Opera in 1937, starred on the *Manhattan Merry-Go-Round* in its final years. He hosted the Hummerts' *Your Song and Mine,* and became the most frequently featured artist on another popular series, *The Voice of Firestone,* simulcast on radio–TV. (Photofest)

was to become "the most frequently featured on [*The*] *Voice of Firestone* on radio and early television."[15] In 1948 and 1949 he hosted a weekly Hummert musicale, *Your Song and Mine.* It included a singing cast of Mary Martha Briney, Felix Knight and Charles Meynante. Enrico Wahl conducted the orchestra, and Andre Baruch announced.

Incidentally, John Dunning noted that the *Metropolitan Opera Auditions* series was like "no other talent show on the air." Said he: "This was no rich man's Major Bowes, pushing the shaggy dogs of the highbrow set."[16] *Radio Guide,* a popular consumer entertainment publication, defined the program as a "serious attempt to find the most promising singers the country has produced and to make the most of their talents." Dunning allowed: "Many of the Frank and Anne Hummert musical shows ... were staffed by *Auditions* graduates (Evelyn MacGregor, Marian McManus, Thomas L. Thomas, Jean Dickenson, Felix Knight)."[17]

Thomas L. Thomas headlined a *Manhattan* series including vocalists Glenn Cross, Rodney McClennan, Marian McManus, Lucy Monroe, Dick O'Connor, Barry Roberts and Dennis Ryan. The Boys and

Girls of Manhattan, the Jerry Mann Voices and the Men About Town offered choral selections. At other times Victor Arden and multitalented instrumentalist Andy Sannella raised the baton over a house band. (One radio historiographer observed: "Players with Victor Arden's house band on the Sunday night *Manhattan Merry-Go-Round* might be playing in the Campbell Soup orchestra led by Howard Lanin on Monday, Wednesday, and Thursday evenings at 7:15, and on Friday often were turning up with Abe Lyman for *Waltz Time.*"[18]) Paul Dumont directed *Manhattan*, and the Hummert stable supplied Ford Bond and Roger Krupp to announce.

The program leaped onto the airwaves with a bouncy tune that was, in itself, a memorable institution, with lyrics sung by the whole cast:

> *Jump on the Manhattan Merry-Go-Round,*
> We're touring alluring old New York town
> *Broadway or Harlem, a musical show...*
> *The orchids that you rest at your radio.*
> We're serving music, songs and laughter,
> *A happy heart will follow after...*
> *And we'd like to have you all with us*
> *On the Manhattan Merry-Go-Round!*

Manhattan Merry-Go-Round was, as someone aptly pointed out, "the Hummert version of *Your Hit Parade*, but filled with much the same musical sound as the Hummerts' other prime-time musicales."[19] The selection of tunes was driven by current sales of sheet music and recordings. And although the sound may have been similar, its sense of immediacy distinctly contrasted with the traditional melodies that aired back-to-back over the same network (NBC) on *The American Album of Familiar Music*.

Ford Bond introduced the sprightly affair each week, utilizing the idiosyncratic staccato style for which he was infamous: "Here's the *Manhattan Merry-Go-Round* that brings you the bright side of life ... that whirls you in music to all the big nightspots of New York town ... to hear the top songs of the week sung so clearly you can understand every word and sing them yourself." (Clarity was a mandatory Hummert trademark, the reader will recall. Ironically, a couple of the more proficient old time radio historiographers, having listened over and over to the lyrics that launched *Manhattan* each week, wrote: "We found it extremely difficult to decipher the third and fourth lines of the theme."[20] One can visualize Frank and Anne Hummert turning over in their graves.)

The show's format took listeners on an imaginary tour of eight name clubs in the Big Apple where their venues were, by sheer coincidence, presenting the stars of the radio troupe. In truth, of course, those performers never left the NBC studio. That should have been evident from the fact that there was never any applause for anyone and no tinkling glasses nor extraneous murmur from mythical live audiences. No matter. "Listeners were given such full ambiance that they often asked to see cast members when they came to New York and visited the actual clubs," an author noted.[21] The typical fare included such tunes as "Don't Fence Me In," "Together," "Whispering," "The Trolley Song" and "Heartaches."

In an industry dispute fostered by the American Society of Composers, Authors, and Publishers (ASCAP) in the early 1940s, broadcasters found themselves making adjustments in their music playlists. While *The American Album of Familiar Music, The Telephone Hour, The Voice of Firestone* and others of that ilk stressing traditional native tunes and public domain classics were least affected, the popular music series like *The Carnation Contented Program, Manhattan Merry-Go-Round* and *Your Hit Parade* were hard hit.

A cease-and-desist order prohibited radio from airing ASCAP melodies without making costly payments to ASCAP, something the national chains and independent producers like the Hummerts were loathe to do. Therefore, *Manhattan* and its aural peers cranked out substitutions for the hit numbers, consisting of forgotten old songs, disregarded classical pieces and esoteric new tunes. The abrupt moratorium on broadcasting the customary hit parade melodies remained in place until a resolution acceptable to all parties was negotiated.

The third most durable Hummert musicale, *Waltz Time*, premiered on September 27, 1933, and continued (sponsored by Sterling's Phillips Milk of Magnesia brand) for an unbroken 15 years, through July 16, 1948. While it debuted on Wednesday nights, within a few weeks it shifted to Friday nights and became permanently enshrined in that evening's schedule.

The series was headlined by "the golden voice of radio," Frank Munn, previously introduced. In the 1940s contralto Evelyn MacGregor, one of the more popular Hummert artists, was elevated to co-star of the series. In 1945 another Hummert singing trouper, Bob Hannon, joined her upon Munn's retirement. Others in the company were vocalists Lois Bennett, Bernice Claire, Mary Eastman, Lucy Monroe, Vivienne Segal and more. Most of them circulated through additional Hummert musical series. Choral voices included the Amsterdam Chorus.

Abe Lyman's orchestra turned up there just as

The staccato-voiced Ford Bond was one of the premier faithful of the Air Features announcing coterie. He introduced the musical numbers for *Manhattan Merry-Go-Round* and delivered hitchhike commercials on other tune-filled features. Weekdays he narrated the Hummert serial mainstays *Backstage Wife, David Harum, Easy Aces, Lora Lawton, Stella Dallas* and many more. (Photofest)

in the later run of Sunday night's *American Album* show. Actually, some of the musicians were recruited from Victor Arden's house band that played on Sunday night's *Manhattan Merry-Go-Round*. Hummert artists inevitably persisted on several of their series, whatever the breed.

Andre Baruch and — once again — Ford Bond announced this show, while yet another Hummert regular, George Ansbro, delivered the "hitchhike" commercials (those product promos appearing between

Baritone Bob Hannon (left) and contralto Evelyn MacGregor look over a musical arrangement with conductor Victor Arden for the Hummerts' *Waltz Time*. MacGregor co-starred with Frank Munn in the early 1940s. When the latter retired in 1945, Hannon replaced him. Lyman was one of the most prominent musical directors in the Air Features cadre. All three performed on multiple Hummert shows. (Photofest)

the end of the program and the network system cue). Ansbro plugged any one of dozens of Sterling Drug commodities in brief asides: Astring-O-Sol mouthwash, Campho-Phenique canker sore medication, Double Danderine and Mulsified Coconut Oil shampoos, Energine cleaning fluid and Energine Shoe-White polish, ZBT baby powder, ad infinitum.

"Ladies and gentlemen, it's dance time on the air," Andre Baruch informed audiences at the show's beginning. After naming the performers, he'd advise: "*Waltz Time* comes to you from the leading druggists of America who feature genuine Phillips Milk of Magnesia." The mention of the druggists seemed essential in the packaging that the Hummerts delivered for Sterling Drugs—incongruously, they even went so far as to dedicate some of their series to the nation's pharmacists!

Listeners could anticipate songs like "Two Hearts That Pass in the Night," "Time After Time," "Just a Little Bit South of North Carolina" and possibly the most recurring piece heard on all Hummert musicales, "The Rose of Tralee." The latter was the theme song of their popular *Backstage Wife* serial, perhaps not so coincidentally.

The last of their major tune-filled features was a johnny-come-lately NBC Blue — then CBS — insert, *American Melody Hour*, launched on October 22, 1941. It aired for the next seven years, through July 7, 1948 on behalf of Sterling's Bayer aspirin pain reliever. Vivian della Chiesa was singer-hostess for two seasons. Tom DeLong — who, more than any other vintage radio historian, cataloged the musical treats of the medium's golden age — opined: "If there existed a radio music hall of fame to enshrine the airwaves' commanding singers, conductors, and musicians, Vivian della Chiesa and many more would qualify."[22] It was also DeLong who categorized Frank Hummert as "a radio czar who reputedly could 'make or break' performers."[23]

Della Chiesa had won a WBBM Radio battle for unknown singers in Chicago, besting 3,700 competitors, to launch a career on programs originating in the Windy City. When she decided to try her luck in the Big Apple, Hummert asked her to sing for him on an audition recording for a potential new series. In November 1940 della Chiesa simply captivated Hummert, who was observing from the control booth. Effortlessly she handled any piece of music thrust upon her, from "Caro Nome" to "Minnie the Moocher." Hummert promptly signed her for a permanent spot on *The American Album of Familiar Music*.

"Only then did I actually meet Frank Hummert," della Chiesa later recalled. "I was already working with two other Franks — tenor Frank Munn and conductor Frank Black. To avoid confusion, I told Hummert I'd call him Uncle Frank. He was totally disarmed. I became one of his favorites, and he called me Butch."[24]

Nearly a year went by before Hummert created *American Melody Hour*, a midweek spinoff of *Album*, chiefly for Vivian della Chiesa. But after two years she longed to spread her wings by performing serious music in a concert hall. The urge was so great that she finally left the stability and security of the Hummert fold.

"It was an impulsive act," she explained. "I sold Hummert short. He had fallen into a wartime sacred music syndrome, and it seemed every other week I was singing 'The Rosary.' I was so 'bugged' with his choice of inspirational selections that I left all his shows. My family, too, thought I was wasting my talent by not pursuing operatic roles and concert appearances with the likes of [Arturo] Toscanini, who had engaged me for two appearances with the NBC Symphony [in January

Soprano Vivian della Chiesa, star of the *American Melody Hour*, who was brought to fame by Frank Hummert, eventually bit the hand that fed her. She performed regularly on several Air Features musicales and appeared to have an inside track with Hummert, who was enchanted by her voice. Ultimately, her choice to strike out on her own may have diminished her career rather than enhanced it. (Photofest)

and October 1943]. Alas, if I had stayed with Hummert, I would have been heard by many more people, and, in the long run, probably performed more serious music."[25] It would seem that Tom DeLong's assessment of Hummert's czar-like power was in no way misplaced.

In the 1960s della Chiesa was the singing hostess of a five-day-a-week Cincinnati TV talk show. She returned to Long Island in 1970, becoming a vocal instructor.

Paradoxically, when Toscanini signed della Chiesa to perform with the NBC Symphony, Frank Hummert was urged by one of his own staffers to plug the appearance on a Hummert-produced series on which della Chiesa sang. Hummert was aghast: "Does Mr. Toscanini give *me* credit on *his* programs?" he callously inquired.[26] Was Frank Hummert, perhaps, an egomaniac operating under a cunning façade?

Other *American Melody Hour* regulars included soprano Eileen Farrell, baritone Bob Hannon, contralto Evelyn MacGregor, baritones Stanley McClelland and Conrad Thibault, tenor Frank Munn, and Jane Pickens—most of them already familiar to audiences from other aural venues, and many of those Hummert showcases. The Knightsbridge

Chorus and the American Melody Hour orchestra, under the direction of Victor Arden and Frank Black, were also on hand.

From their stable of announcers the Hummerts sent Andre Baruch and Howard Claney to bat for this one, supported by Ford Bond, who delivered hitchhike commercials for Lyons toothpaste and Dr. Lyons tooth powder. One or the other advised that the series was "dedicated to the druggists of America, who supply you with Bayer aspirin," certainly an unconventional epigraph.

The program presented "the songs of the day so you can know them all, sing them all yourself." Typical among the selections were "I Still Get Jealous," "Near You" and "The Whiffenpoof Song."

Perhaps it is also appropriate to include a mention of the theme songs that introduced the many dramatic programs in the vast Hummert repository. Unlike many other producers, they didn't rely on original compositions for most of their narratives. Instead, the twosome selected pieces of standard, easily identified works. Could there be any doubt that their decisions were heavily influenced by cost? Without commissioning someone to pen a tune for a given show, they saved money. They saved even more by choosing scores that, for the most part, were in the public domain. Translation: no copyright fees were paid to anyone for their usage.

By relying on tunes that were already known and loved by listeners, their theme songs bred instant recognition and helped to draw audiences. Thus Hummert melodramas featured listener favorites such as "Juanita" (*The Romance of Helen Trent*), "Red River Valley" (*Our Gal Sunday*), "In the Gloaming" and "Wonderful One" (*Young Widder Brown*), "Finiculi Finicula" (*Lorenzo Jones*), "Darling Nellie Gray" and "Polly Wolly Doodle" (*Just Plain Bill*) and "You and I Know" (*Front Page Farrell*).

The Hummerts possessed an uncanny ability to choose tunes that closely paralleled the themes of some of their individual series. This indicated that considerable care was given to matching the music with a program's premise. A few examples should suffice as illustration.

As the studio organ ground out "How Can I Leave Thee?" weekday afternoons, the saga of *Stella Dallas* unfolded. While the melody played underneath, an interlocutor implored listeners to follow the tale of "mother love and sacrifice in which Stella Dallas saw her beloved daughter, Laurel, marry into wealth and society and — realizing the difference in their tastes and worlds — went out of Laurel's life." Think about it in the context of the song's title.

Immediately preceding that little gem, "the story of Mary Noble and what it means to be the wife of a famous star" wafted onto the airwaves. *Backstage Wife* was ushered in by "The Rose of Tralee," who was a fair maiden from the little Irish burg of Tralee whose name, not surprisingly, was Mary.

Then there was the crime detective thriller *Mr. Keen, Tracer of Lost Persons*. "Someday I'll Find You" seemed utterly apropos, given that drama's title. The familiar tune was unequivocally linked with the mystery in fans' psyches for nearly two decades.

There were many more similar parallels, but you probably have gotten the picture already.

Never let it be said that the Hummerts didn't enjoy a large helping of variety mixed into their entrepreneurial quests. While there can be little question that they clearly favored the dramatic story line as compared to any other form, it's obvious that they didn't limit their thinking to it alone. While they went about it discreetly for a change (e.g., by not having their names read over the airwaves as producers), their musicales were joyous expressions of an age in which popular and classical singing was appreciated by large numbers of American radio enthusiasts.

Frank and Anne Hummert had discovered a niche and — as they so often did — fully capitalized on it. Thousands of rewarding half-hours that millions treated themselves to every week was the satisfying outcome.

4

MYSTERY THEATER

One of the audio forms for which Frank and Anne Hummert derived substantial notoriety was rooted in a handful of dramatic properties commonly classified as crime detective mysteries. As those chilling tales played out over the air, legions of fans sat enthralled by their radios. Fully comprehending where those plot lines would be taking them, the faithful nevertheless remained mesmerized while the Hummert heroes trailed cold-blooded killers to unequivocal conclusions fraught with peril.

The aural sleuth introduced satisfying suspense to American ears daily or weekly through fictionalized drama that — along with the intrigue — offered some of radio's most compelling supermen. These determined detectives of the air, whose inception coincided with a stepped-up war against crime in the real world, brought to the nation's living rooms some of the most popular cultural idols of that epoch. Nowhere in the pages of history can one find greater champions of justice. These artful programs struck a note with vast audiences, holding them virtually spellbound by their radios. In the theater of the mind, after all, possibly no other form could have been as uniquely germane.

What made these shows so stimulating? One pundit proffered a couple of plausible theories: First, there was a self-rating appeal, in which the listeners attempted to solve a mystery or a crime. Second, there was a self-identification factor, which satisfied audiences as they identified themselves with the protagonist-heroes of those dramas.[1]

One should certainly not be duped into thinking for a moment that crime, in its many diverse forms, was ever glamorized in the Hummert narratives. The dastardly deeds of the most conniving miscreants invariably exacted a heavy price. A radio historian observed: "The essence of those [programs'] messages lay in the fact that within each drama the villain never won and the hero never lost. Whether ... a program openly declared that 'crime does not pay,' this was the message expounded in all broadcasts."[2] Any who attempted to gain private property outside the socially accepted channels—whether it was life, currency or possessions—were reformed, imprisoned or executed, "so that the society of the propertied might be secure and enduring."[3]

Some of the Hummert detectives, such as Mr. Keen and Inspector Hearthstone, took particular delight in passing judgment on a culprit's fate in advance of a formal criminal prosecution for murder. With a tinge of euphoria in his voice, Mr. Keen, the kindly old tracer, typically dispensed some foreboding missive to his quarry like, "the state has an electric chair that will provide you with proper recompense for your ill-doing." Air Features investigators seldom deliberated about what a judge and jury would do. They reveled in delivering one's date with destiny.

The Hummerts were strenuously opposed to lawbreaking activity in any form. Anne Hummert once assured an interviewer: "Crime may appear [in the dramas we produce], but either the annihilation or change of heart of the unerring one must follow."[4] The writers stayed true to their superiors' tenet that full punishment must be meted out for heinous transgressions. In Hummert melodrama crime didn't pay, and a day of reckoning was certain and swift for any who violated that basic canon. The fans knew it and embraced it unconditionally.

While the Hummerts were never as prolific in creating crime dramas as they were in bringing musical features to the ether, a quartet from their stable of sleuths resonated with radio audiences over some extended runs. The more familiar names included Chameleon, Keen, Hearthstone and Sabre, four fearless, daunting crimefighters among radio's burgeoning surfeit of private and public gumshoes. The Hummerts preferred that their men of mystery maintain a modicum of anonymity; thus they fielded several detectives who—at least, on the air—were born seemingly without first names (Chameleon, Keen and Hearthstone being among them).

4. Mystery Theater

Chameleon was "the man of many faces" who invariably took on hidden identities to catch a thief or, more likely, a murderer. Keen gained the distinction of lasting longer than any of his broadcast bretheren (18 consecutive years), spending several of them seeking missing persons before applying his efforts to solving whodunits. The other two—inspectors Hearthstone and Mark Sabre—evolved out of *The Molle Mystery Theater* anthology (1943–1948). When the Hummerts acquired that popular series, Hearthstone became the focus under a revamped format and appellation, renamed *Mystery Theater*. A few years later the tales of both Hearthstone and Sabre were spun off into separate, distinctive namesake detective features.

In addition to those four sleuths, at least one other Hummert detective, *Inspector Thorne*, a 1951 summer entry based at the homicide bureau of New Scotland Yard, appeared intriguing. Karl Weber played the lead in all but the final broadcast when Staats Cotsworth supplanted him. Dan Ocko portrayed Thorne's sidekick, Sergeant Muggin. Had that series not arrived just as radio's fortunes were beginning to ebb, the mystery might also have gained standing among a corps of loyal listeners.

No fewer than 10 radio crime detective dramas (eight percent of the Hummerts' total output) were shepherded under the guiding hand of Frank and Anne. Despite such comparatively low numbers in that vein, the couple's many crime-tracking concepts appeared in such characters as *David Harum, Five Star Jones, Front Page Farrell, Jack Armstrong, Just Plain Bill, Kitty Keene, Little Orphan Annie* and *Terry and the Pirates*.

Extending that broad umbrella further, a few of the Hummerts' most beleaguered daytime heroines—who consistently exuded an air of grace and innocence—were on occasion enveloped in sinister plots rivaling those of the traditional nighttime thrillers. Several damsels found themselves in distress as the result of crimes of one type or another, including murder. Some were even accused of it, and they (or their mates) had to defend themselves in terrifying, drawn-out ordeals. Others helped the authorities ferret out the real killers and put them away. *Backstage Wife, Our Gal Sunday, Stella Dallas* and *Young Widder Brown* were routinely perplexed over such indelicacies, particularly after the radio ratings began to slide in the early 1950s. Listeners heard more intense plotting from that time forward, and crime became as prevalent as amnesia in some dramas.

Of the 10 primetime mysteries developed by Air Features (aka Hummert Radio Features), four of them survived for only brief outings. The failed narratives include *Detective Reeder, Inspector Brooks, Inspector Hawkes and Son,* and *Stevens and Son of Scotland Yard.* All except *Hawkes* originated in the 1930s as the Hummerts sought a foothold in the mystery category. (Two other entries in that field were *Inspector Thorne* and *Mystery Theater,* both of which will be considered independently.)

As witnessed elsewhere, the couple appeared to profit from their failures rather than succumb to them. Doggedly they applied newly acquired knowledge to any future attempts, establishing several durable mainstays on the ether only a few years later.

Parenthetically, in a published analysis of 308 American crimefighting dramas carried over network radio between the late 1920s and the early 1960s, 58 series were found with private eyes as their central characters—each one functioning independently of public law enforcement agencies, even though they may have teamed up with those officials at times. Beyond those, 84 additional radio programs featured amateur or part-time sleuths whose livelihoods were derived largely from unrelated professions, if indeed they were gainfully employed at all. The full-time, career-oriented PIs combined with those of the avocational strain to offer radio audiences at least 142 separate opportunities to tune into series with private detectives at their core.[5]

Returning to the quartet of paramount Hummert detective series, each one will be examined briefly in the order of its initial appearance on the air. Noting that the first and most prominent of those protagonists was a private eye, at the outset let us establish how that term is defined. Modern crime fiction buff Al Hubin, who recorded extensive data in a series of published bibliographies, offers a simple definition of the private eye: "[He/she] seeks clients, accepts pay for services, and is not a member of an official law enforcement agency; thus both the likes of Sherlock Holmes and Mike Hammer are included, as are investigators working for private firms—such as insurance companies—and lawyer-sleuths."[6] It is conceivable, Hubin freely admits, that a benevolent, perhaps well-heeled private eye could operate a detective agency, solicit clients, and yet—for whatever reasons—waive all the fees for services rendered.

The latter description certainly pertains to *Mr. Keen, Tracer of Lost Persons*. That PI was affluent and appeared to perform his tasks merely for the benefit of mankind. Many times early in the run he chuckled as he told "clients" not to worry about the debts they incurred for he was "a wealthy old bachelor who enjoys helping people in their time of trouble." The sleuthing series bowed on October 12, 1937, and hung on until September 26, 1955 — 1,693 broadcasts later — before departing forever. Over those 18 years the program broadcast serialized chapters spread over three nights per week. Eventually, these were heard five nights weekly. At other times there were complete 30- or 25-minute episodes.

A third of the way through its long run the show experienced a virtual metamorphosis. For a half-dozen years its protagonist attempted to locate missing persons—individuals who had vanished from sight under mysterious, often baffling circumstances as a result of their own or someone else's choosing. On infrequent occasions the kindly old tracer matched murder victims with perpetrators of their crimes. But more often the sudden disappearances could be explained through less sinister behaviors.

In late 1943, however, the *Keen* plots took on a decided edge, an ominous, foreboding tone that had been heard only fleetingly before. Overnight, a rather jovial Mr. Keen departed and in his place a new personality emerged, one stern and resolute in deportment. The premise of the vanishing acts was gone. In its wake Mr. Keen and a buffoon-prone partner, Mike Clancy (who could be depicted as a brawny-but-sluggish Irishman), began solving murders, dramatized in brief vignettes at the start of each case. (Actually, this became a distinguishing signature trademark near the beginning of nearly *all* Hummert detective programs from that time onward.)

Over the course of his investigations Keen would encounter three or four suspects with apparent motives and opportunities to carry out ghastly crimes. Most assailants were relatives, business associates or acquaintances of their victims. Most had something to hide or to gain through a fatality. In a stunning revelation near the close of each case,

Keen would — one by one — eliminate the suspects and finger the killer. (This procedure, too, was characteristic of the other Hummert detective series.)

Keen then frequently found himself the target of an angry culprit. Only by Clancy's indubitable intervention at a propitious moment was the hero's own life spared. This indisputably proved that "dumber-than-thou" assistants weren't really as dumb as they usually appeared.

Frank and Anne Hummert sustained a predilection for generating the theses for some of their broadcast series from pulp fiction, motion pictures and stage productions. A number of their soap operas, for instance, were derived from such sources. (See chapter 6 for more details.) With several aural matinee successes already adapted from literature, is it any wonder that the creative duo turned to pulp fiction as they pondered a future launch of a private detective series? In June 1906 Robert William Chambers (1865–1933) saw published a manuscript he had ascetically titled *The Tracer of Lost Persons*.[7] How could he possibly have known that some three decades later it would become the basis for the most durable detective drama ever presented in a medium that didn't even exist at the time he conceived his story?

Coincidentally, for several years Chambers maintained a downtown office in New York whose address he kept secret even from his own family, where — for eight hours daily — he created his fictional works.[8] Does this sound like anyone the reader has become acquainted with recently? Among his eccentricities, on more than one occasion Chambers wrote a 30,000-word manuscript, discovered it needed "fixing" and threw it all away, beginning anew to fix it!

In *The Tracer of Lost Persons* his hero ran a New York agency that was limited to romantic matchmaking and not much else. *That* Mr. Keen never stumbled upon the mysterious, life-threatening intrigue that filled the imaginations of millions of radio listeners in the aural drama's heyday. In all probability, the narrative never would have been sustained on the ether for nearly two decades with a mere matchmaking premise.

One of those infamous Hummert dictates was that the audience must know at all times who was speaking to whom. There could never be any hesitancy, no indecisiveness, about that. Thus, on *any* of their programs — daytime *and* nighttime — there was constant — often inane — usage of identifications. To wit:

4. Mystery Theater

A character named Ernest Green might, for instance, state something like this: "Mr. Keen, my brother-in-law Peter Dowling was a very poor businessman. He kept Martha Green, my wife, in the dark about his financial dealings, even though he controlled interests that were of benefit not only to himself but to Martha and his brother, Richard Dowling."

Mr. Keen might respond: "Well, Ernest Green, your observations are most intriguing. I will ask my partner here, Mike Clancy, to look into the public records of your brother-in-law Peter Dowling and determine just how his business was being conducted."

To which the suspect could retort: "Thank you, Mr. Keen. I'm sure Richard Dowling, who is also my brother-in-law, and my wife, Martha, will be grateful to you."

Laughable? Without a doubt. If there was ever a moment's hesitation about who was speaking and who was being spoken to in a Hummert drama, somebody was asleep at the wheel. That was one of the notorious mandated duties assigned to the program directors. If it was missed in the scripting and editing stages, a director could catch hell if repetitious name-calling didn't get on the air.

To this day, there are still those who lambaste the show, claiming it was never on a par with its contemporaries. But beauty is in the eye of the beholder. No sleuth was everybody's cup of tea. *Mr. Keen* brought hours of chilling fables to the ether and mesmerized audiences with them. The fact that people can still poke fun at it probably suggests it must have succeeded at something, even in the face of such awful dialogue.

Lawrence M. Klee may have possessed the most prolific pen among the Hummert coterie of nighttime thriller-writers. He was also one of the most brilliant minds among their band of scribes, as evidenced by a myriad of other singularly successful accomplishments. Internal correspondence suggests that he was highly respected by the Hummerts for his craftsmanship, something not normally accorded most of their wordsmiths. Yet he was relegated to churning out scripts that—from a literary point of view—probably would have satisfied few intellectuals beyond the Hummerts themselves. While working for them, he had few chances to display his true talent.

For years Klee conceived the dialogue and exploits for *Mr. Keen, Tracer of Lost Persons.* Today no fewer than 618 of his *Keen* scripts exist. While penning *Mr. Keen*, at the same time he was writing many of the Hummerts' other enduring dramas, including chapters of *Backstage Wife, Chaplain Jim U.S.A., Front Page Farrell, Hearthstone of the Death Squad, Mr. Chameleon, Real Stories from Real Life, The Romance of Helen Trent, Valiant Lady* and *Young Widder Brown.* Simultaneously, Klee supplied scripts to several other producers for both radio and television. This included TV's early live action mystery series *Man Against Crime,* starring Ralph Bellamy, and a well-received documentary on the life of Franklin Delano Roosevelt.

The Hummerts kept close tabs on the listeners' reactions to their various series, readily witnessed in the audience figures compiled by the C.E. Hooper and A.C. Nielsen national ratings services of that day. When the numbers suddenly spiraled downward, as one actor put it, "All hell broke loose." In 1953 an inter-office memorandum from the Hummerts to Richard Leonard, director of *Mr. Keen, Tracer of Lost Persons,* explicitly addressed an immediate concern:[9]

We are very much alarmed by the drop in rating on MR. KEEN. The last rating shows that it controlled only 18.8% of the audience. Ordinarily MR. KEEN controls well over 30% of the audience.

For that reason, we are returning the script "The Poison Pen Letter Murder Case" which we think requires re-writing in order to hold and build an audience.

This script does not sound like Larry Klee, for it lacks so many of the elements he usually puts into KEEN and which have gone to make it a success.[9]

In a half-dozen paragraphs that followed, specific suggestions were given for improving the script to enhance the "color, movement, switches and surprises usually in KEEN." To say that the Hummerts created shows and forgot about them would be altogether shortsighted. It's obvious that they kept their fingers on every pulse.

Only two actors appeared in the title role over the drama's long run, Bennett Kilpack (1937–1950) and Philip Clarke (1950–1955). Jim Kelly played Mike Clancy for the full stretch. Martha Atwell, Richard

4. Mystery Theater

Leonard and Edward Slattery were the series' only continuing directors.

A plethora of silver-tongued, golden-throated announcers introduced *Mr. Keen, Tracer of Lost Persons* over nearly two decades on the air. While some made only brief appearances, at least seven qualified for enduring status: Ben Grauer (1937–1940), James Fleming (1940–1943), Ken Roberts (1943), Lawrence K. (Larry) Elliott (1943–1951), Jack Costello (1951–1952), Harry Cramer (1952–1955) and Stuart Metz (during a weekday serialized overlap with the weekly half-hour features, 1954–1955). Three more substituted with some frequency — George Ansbro (in the Fleming era), Dick Dunham (for Elliott) and George Bryan (for Metz). Several of them occupied permanent berths in the Hummert camp.

By 1948 Frank and Anne Hummert had gained the expertise that would permit them to introduce a small influx of crime detective figures to the airwaves. While *Keen* may have been their only durable success in the genre until then, experimentation with a few disappointingly short-lived series had led them to the precipice of several enduring entries. The milestone occurred just as a pair of the Hummerts' most imposing musical features (*American Melody Hour* and *Waltz Time*) were leaving the air, while a third (*Manhattan Merry-Go-Round*) was to depart a few months later. With network radio starting to divest itself of long-playing daytime serials, the timing seemed perfect for the Hummerts to jump into the prime time detective fray.

On June 29, 1948, the couple took over an established and admired audio series called the *Molle Mystery Theater*. Its tales of mayhem, murder and the macabre were narrated by an unnerving "crime connoisseur" who was familiar to radio audiences as Geoffrey Barnes (played by actor Bernard Lenrow). When, after five seasons, sponsor Molle shaving cream pulled the plug on its prized NBC marketing vehicle, the Hummerts "adopted" the premise and set about putting their own crime melodrama spin on it. Initially they purchased a CBS half-hour on behalf of longtime partner Sterling Drugs.

(In passing, let us digress for a moment to note that of the trio of major sleuths the Hummerts introduced after 1947, longtime client Sterling Drugs, Inc. underwrote all three. As was Sterling's custom on its afternoon soap operas, the advertising frequently shifted back and

Left to right: Florence Malone (Miss Maisie Ellis, secretary), Bennett Kilpack (Mr. Keen) and Jimmy Kelly (Mike Clancy) played recurring roles in the Hummerts' *Mr. Keen, Tracer of Lost Persons.* The ether's most durable private eye thrilled fans as he sought missing persons. The missing person premise ended in 1943. when Keen began focusing on solving murders. Ellis soon left, and Philip Clarke followed Kilpack in 1950. (Photofest)

forth between a long line of health and personal care wares. Thus there were commercials for Bayer aspirin, Phillips Milk of Magnesia laxative, Double Danderine shampoo, Ironized Yeast supplements, Dr. Lyons tooth powder and many more similar commodities. On the other hand, rival health goods manufacturer American Home Products, another long-time Hummert patron, sponsored *Mr. Keen, Tracer of Lost Persons* over most of its durable run. Anacin pain reliever, Kolynos toothpaste and another glut of family healthcare products were plugged on that show.)

Retaining part of *Molle*'s original moniker, the Hummerts branded their new dramatic venture *Mystery Theater*. Geoffrey Barnes was gone. Instead of offering a variety of thriller narratives from multiple sources, the pair introduced a new continuing character, a highly esteemed mythical Inspector Hearthstone. Operating out of London's metropolitan police department, the "impeccable manhunter" came with a distinctively British brogue.

In addition to his undercover skills, Hearthstone demonstrated an analytical mind that was capable of coping with the fiercest of diabolical menaces. At times Hearthstone could be considered quite ruthless himself. Accusatory in tone as he interrogated bystanders to murders and acquaintances of the victims, he went about his task with a tenacious resolve to place cold-blooded killers where they belonged. On occasion it seemed like his mind was racing so far ahead of the action that he couldn't be held accountable for not waiting for the revelation of more facts.

The inspector had an aide, detective Sam Cook, and the two were joined at the hip. In accepted Air Features style, Cook — like others in the Hummert sidekick cadre — proved his incompetence every time out. Invariably he would ask the ridiculous questions in order for "the great one" to come off smelling like a rose (and thereby achieve the heroic plaudits). There simply couldn't be *two* detectives with superior intellect on *one* show. One was forced to shine by exposing the other as a dim bulb. It went with the turf in all of the Air Features detective thrillers.

One critic lamented the drama's fate after the Hummerts got their hands on it. When it "fell into the clutches of Frank and Anne Hummert" wrote the observer, it "sank into melodrama," replete with "stilted dialogue and cardboard characters."[10] Although the assessment is probably correct, the narrative obviously connected with longtime listeners, who kept it on the air for the next quadrennial. It remained for three years under the *Mystery Theater* banner, resurfaced as a sustained *Hearthstone of the Death Squad* for another year (when Sterling Drugs abandoned it), and departed forever on September 17, 1952. By that time the Hummerts had already spun the original off into yet another augmentation, to be examined presently.

Alfred Shirley portrayed the inspector. While he didn't turn up working for the Hummerts elsewhere, he sustained multiple late–1940s crimesolving roles that required British accents—as Dr. Watson on *The Adventures of Sherlock Holmes* and Sergeant Abernathy on *Scotland Yard.*

None other than Hummert thespian James Meighan portrayed Hearthstone's sidekick, detective Sam Cook. Daytime listeners recognized his voice as that of Larry Noble on *Backstage Wife,* Kerry Donovan on *Just Plain Bill* and from numerous other Hummert serials. *Mystery Theater* directors included Martha Atwell, Henry Howard, Kenneth W. Macgregor, Ernest Ricca, Frank K. Telford and Day Tuttle. Hummert stalwart Harry Cramer narrated.

Mr. Chameleon, "the

Alfred Shirley, displaying a distinct British brogue, played "impeccable manhunter" Inspector Hearthstone twice for the Hummerts — on *Mystery Theater* and *Hearthstone of the Death Squad.* Operating out of London's metro police department, he pursued criminal deviants mercilessly. Shirley also took a turn portraying Dr. Watson on *Sherlock Holmes,* and Sergeant Abernathy on *Scotland Yard* during the same era. (Photofest) man of many faces," a police homicide detective, premiered over CBS that same summer, on July 14, 1948. By 1951 Sterling Drugs withdrew and the series shifted to multiple underwriters, like the General Foods and William J. Wrigley corporations. The crime drama was discontinued on August 7, 1953.

One wag suggested that *Mr. Chameleon* could be the grandson of *Mr. Keen, Tracer of Lost Persons.* Pegging Keen as a "blood brother" of Chameleon, the pundit intimated that Keen was about 60 years of age when Chameleon arrived.[11] "Keen and Chameleon were almost exactly alike," he allowed, "both drawn from the joint well of Frank and Anne Hummert, both working on the same kinds of murder cases, both using simple methods of catching killers and both using dumber-than-thou assistants."[12] Chameleon's albatross was detective Dave Arnold, who precisely fit the mold of clumsy subordinate sleuths. It appeared that most of the time these men had little purpose for being there beyond dialoguing with their partners over an investigation's progress, and applauding the brilliant calculations of their inspired superiors.

Unlike most Hummert mysteries, this one infused its cases with a unique twist to crime-solving. Its principal would appear in camouflage before a crime's chief suspect with the intent of trapping him into giving himself away via a slip of the tongue or some other misstep. Operating out of an ambiguous central police headquarters— whose site was never defined, although probably assumed by most listeners to be New York City—the "famous and dreaded detective" became a scourge to the criminal element as he craftily plied his skills as a quick-change artist. An interlocutor, in the meantime, advised the listeners beforehand that Chameleon's disguise "at all times is recognized by the audience." Some cover-ups were so transparent in practice that on occasion even the killer saw through them!

Several authorities speculated that Frank and Anne Hummert shaped this whodunit especially for one of their most accomplished actors, Karl Swenson, to whom dialects were second nature. The polished thespian could change voices in mid-sentence if need be; he was particularly well suited for the myriad of accents this drama called for.

Swenson distinguished himself every day as the *veddy veddy* British-tongued Lord Henry Brinthrope, the aristocratic spouse of *Our Gal Sunday.* A few hours later he returned to the microphone as the whiny, whimsical inventor with an incessant knack for trouble, *Lorenzo Jones*. He was tapped for roles calling for rare or distant dialects on numerous Hummert series, in fact. Swenson once explained that he didn't consider himself to be that good. But to directors needing someone with an ability to provide unusual inflections with little rehearsal time (a Hummert mandate) on short notice, he was routinely summoned.

Frank Butler, meanwhile, played Detective Arnold, possibly the actor's most celebrated role on radio. Richard Leonard, a Hummert loyalist, was assigned the directing duties. Announcers were mostly members of the elite Air Features coterie — George Bryan, Howard Claney and Roger Krupp.

The last of the Hummert crime detective series was another spinoff from the *Molle Mystery Theater* (shortened to *Mystery Theater* when Air Features acquired it). *Mark Sabre* appeared over ABC on October 3, 1951. The show continued through June 30, 1954.

Sabre was a rather debonair inspector for the homicide bureau of the Los Angeles Police Department. With his arrival one could tell that crime-tracking had moved uptown. He preferred to obtain data from informants by conventional means — usually asking for it in a civilized manner. Yet when an occasion demanded, he wasn't averse to using his left fist to strike a nasty wallop. Obviously no one was aware of police brutality in that era, and lawsuits over aggravated assaults were still far into the future.

While pursuing the down and dirty, the mean and ugly of the L.A. environs, Sabre was routinely shadowed by Sergeant Tim Maloney. A critic pointed to Maloney's "likable awkwardness which meshed harmoniously with the intelligent and coy qualities of Inspector Mark Sabre." Maloney was the last of the great Hummert sidekicks. Even then it appeared that those guys still had incompetence written all over them.

Robert Carroll and Bill Johnstone played the namesake role at different times, while James Westerfield was heard as Tim Maloney. Although Carroll earned few distinguishing radio parts, Johnstone had many (Lieutenant Ben Guthrie on *The Line Up*, the title role on *The Whistler*, and as a support player on *Nick Carter, Master Detective*, *The Shadow* and many more). Westerfield was in the supporting cast of *Have Gun, Will Travel*. Roger Forster narrated *Mark Sabre*.

4. Mystery Theater

While Frank and Anne Hummert produced the longest running private detective in radio history (or television, for that matter), it's obvious (given the numbers) that the field of crime drama was one of their weaker arenas. Aside from Mr. *Keen* they had no other unqualified successes until 1948, just as the bulk of the nation's radio fans were about to turn to another medium for home entertainment. It was really too little, too late.

Had, for instance, inspectors Hearthstone and Sabre and detective Chameleon surfaced in the late 1930s, the Hummert record of fielding criminal investigators might have attained a level of resiliency similar to that of their musical and daytime serial counterparts. Although most of their masters of the macabre arrived late in radio's golden age, those sleuths infused the medium with a set of predictable characters that upheld the traditions, values and expectations of their listeners. With a vengeance they pursued evil in all of its ugly forms until the very last perpetrator was put away. A segment of the aural audience — knowing the outcome well in advance — nevertheless found their exploits captivating.

Such diversionary delights enslaved addicts of the theater of the mind. From that perspective, Frank and Anne Hummert could be labeled successful contributors with their modest attempts in crime.

5

CHILD'S PLAY

One of the more promising programming trends in early radio was that of the juvenile adventure. These typically quarter-hour, late afternoon, serialized yarns featured role models (young and old) who imbued the youngsters they targeted with lofty ideals and ambitions, calling them to become responsible citizens. Mamas and daddies were generally well satisfied with the positive messages contained in their brief, though highly implausible, slices of life. The result was a nation of adolescents focused upon practical concepts that contributed to their own self-esteem and built sterling character to last a lifetime.

The audience was a given. In 1967 radio chronologist Jim Harmon claimed: "You listened to the radio every day at five o'clock. Everybody in the United States of America over twenty-five years of age must have listened intently to the radio at that hour during some period of their lives."[1]

Studies conducted during that epoch confirmed that children began to take an interest in radio as early as three years of age. They showed little selective discrimination between programs, however, until they were four or more. By then certain aired features had begun to captivate their interests. Curiosity increased as they advanced in age, reaching a peak at age 10. The typical youngster was tuning in seven or more programs every week, research suggested. Of a multiplicity of formats offered specifically to adolescents, dramatizations — and, in particular, serialized adventure — inevitably appealed most to both boys and girls.[2]

True to their confirmed sense of timing and what the public (even the "little" public) might find desirable, Frank and Anne Hummert tried producing juvenile adventure dramas from the inception of their radio careers. At least one radio chronologist cites their pubescent series *Skippy*, which aired on the national chains between 1932 and 1935, as the *first* children's serial.[3] But another assigns that coveted honor to their adaptation of Harold Gray's popular comic strip character *Little Orphan Annie*. That one turned into an overnight success in 1930 when it debuted to a Chicago outlet's audience.[4] By 1931 the series, packaged by Blackett-Sample-Hummert, Inc., was picked up by the networks after which it enthralled small fry throughout the land.[5]

The real point worth noting from both a biographical and a historical perspective, however, is just this: *Anne S. Ashenhurst and her future spouse, Frank Hummert, were on the cutting edge of juvenile adventure broadcasting.* They were present at its humble beginnings. Much of what was to follow on the air — on radio and eventually on television — originated in that nascent environment of the early 1930s.

While the Hummerts' offerings in juvenile fiction would be fewer than in any of the other major strains for which they created programming, percentage-wise they were far more triumphant at it than they were in any other genre. Altogether the couple is known to have inspired a mere eight kids' features: *Happy Landing; Jack Armstrong, the All-American Boy; Little Orphan Annie; Penrod and Sam; Popeye the Sailor; Skippy; Terry and Mary;* and *Terry and the Pirates*. But the young ears at whom those features were directed were jubilant. And some of those efforts persevered. *Armstrong, Annie* and *Pirates*, though airing intermittently, hung on for more than a decade, with *Armstrong* continuing for nearly two decades.

Only five of the eight juvenile adventure dramas can be considered prominent.

We are indebted to no less an informed authority than James Thurber for recalling *Terry and Mary*, a children's drama penned by the inimitable Robert Hardy Andrews during what were most likely his early days of Blackett-Sample-Hummert employment. Regretfully, details of that series haven't been preserved, however.

The Hummerts also offered a brief serialized adaptation of Booth

5. Child's Play

Tarkington's comic novel *Penrod and Sam*. The 1934 NBC entry featured actors Billy Halop, Jimmy McCallion and Eddie Wragge. As that program aired at night, it undoubtedly appealed to audiences of widespread ages.

An eighth serial, *Happy Landing*, debuting over Chicago's WBBM in the mid–1930s, may never have aired on a network, although there is unsubstantiated evidence that it did, if only briefly. It could have been a "practice run" for the more popular fare that lay just ahead.

Although the Hummerts didn't remain with some of those programs throughout their extended runs, they strongly influenced them in the critical formative stages. The two set in motion the direction that those programs would take for years into the future. Assessing their most powerful quintet may offer fresh insights into the very nature of juvenile adventure itself. Those five serials will be reviewed in the order of their premiers on the air.

As already noted, *Little Orphan Annie*, which debuted over Chicago's WGN in 1930, moved to a network (NBC Blue) on April 6, 1931. For the next five years it was heard six afternoons a week, then continued for another six years on five weekday afternoons, first over NBC, then MBS. Until 1940 it was sponsored by Chicago-based Wander Company for Ovaltine brand beverage mix aimed at kids. In its last two years the Quaker Oats Company underwrote the series for Quaker Puffed Wheat Sparkies (and, later, Quaker Puffed Wheat) cereal.

Annie focused on a "little chatterbox, the one with the pretty auburn locks" who—with an entourage of tabloid-drawn companions—experienced life as the ward of a rural farm couple, Mr. and Mrs. Silo, in the mythical community of Simmons Corners. One authority labeled the series a tale about youngsters "trying to cope with a strange and complex adult world."[6] Whatever its intent, it launched an array of programming that American audiences, spread across vast territory, had never been exposed to, a forebear of a multiplicity of experiments to follow.

Annie's adventures linked her with pals like Joe Corntassel, who ostensibly was there to draw boys into the listening audience. As in the newspaper scenarios, Sandy, Annie's faithful furry dog, offered an "arf" or two in many episodes. There was Oliver 'Daddy' Warbucks (whom modern audiences recall from the contemporary stage and movie musical *Annie*), a man of great power and wealth. Warbucks routinely challenged the villains that crossed paths with the small waif and her friends. A skeptic lamented: "The major heroine crime fighter in radio was a ten-year-old girl, Little Orphan Annie. This was men's— and teenage boys'—work."[7]

One of the more memorable features of the long-running series was its exploitation of premiums to retain and attract new listeners and thereby increase sales of the sponsor's product. (One wag even hinted that, on *Annie*, "the plots [were] written around the premiums."[8]) The Hummerts gained firsthand knowledge of the value of supplying decoding badges, rings, milk shakers and mugs to young fans that mailed in a dime and a label from a jar of the sponsor's product. Greater loyalty to the program and the product resulted. Employing the premium (or giveaway) was a practice those producers would repeat on scores of occasions in the years ahead on behalf of several sponsors. They habitually applied the concept to all of their juvenile features, for instance.

When by 1940 the Wander Company believed it had milked the *Annie* series for all it was worth (no pun intended), it decided to invest its advertising dollars elsewhere. Wander selected yet another kids' radio venture, *Captain Midnight*, then just completing an engaging 24-week tryout on WGN. "Her producers, faced with the choice of canceling the program or selling Annie's soul, chose the sellout," an informant admitted.[9] The Quaker Oats Company rescued *Annie* and kept it on the air, but at the price of robbing it of its childhood innocence.

Joe Corntassel was put out to pasture. Little Annie became little more than a combat pilot's elbow tagging along with newly-added aviator Captain Sparks in a sky-spy thriller that folded a couple of years down the runway. It was outwitted by competing aerial shows that were doing it all better. "At the last she had little to do but gasp 'Leapin' lizards!' [a recurring catchphrase from tabloid days] when Captain Sparks pulled his plane out of a power dive," wryly noted a commentator.[10]

The part of Annie was played by Shirley Bell and (temporarily) Bobbe Deane during the show's first decade, and by Janice Gilbert from

1940 to 1942. Until 1933, when NBC connected its West Coast stations with the rest of the country, a separate cast, featuring lead actress Floy Margaret Hughes, performed the same scripts for Western audiences from San Francisco studios. Jerry O'Mera and Henrietta Tedro played Byron and Mary Silo. Allan Baruck and later Mel Torme were Joe Corntassel, with animal imitator Brad Barker as Sandy. A trio of thespians was heard as Daddy Warbucks—Stanley Andrews, Boris Aplon and Henry Saxe. Alan Wallace directed much of the run. Pierre Andre announced.

At its inception *Annie* had "hit" stamped all over it. And none of its early promise was lost on Anne Ashenhurst and Frank Hummert; they set about to duplicate its instant acceptance. *Skippy* was their next adolescent sensation. It, too, was based on a highly popular 1920s newspaper strip, drawn by cartoonist Percy Crosby. There was also a 1931 Paramount film by that title starring Jackie Cooper. General Mills, Inc., the maker of Wheaties cereal, brought it to the ether (first on NBC, later CBS) on January 11, 1932. The program aired through March 29, 1935, about half of that six afternoons weekly until it was reduced to five weekdays.

Initially penned by Robert Hardy Andrews (and later by Roland Martini)—one of the Hummerts' most prolific serial scribes—*Skippy* was a Tom Sawyer character perceived as "a less neurotic Charlie Brown."[11] Andrews depicted him as "a rascal, ever testing his parents' patience by figuring out honorable ways of fooling them without actually lying."[12] (A *Radio Digest* review applauded the "child acting" but was less charitable concerning the wordsmiths, dubbing the scripting "weak" and intimating that the cartoon's creator might also write the radio show.[13] That was not the case, however.) Promotional plugs, meanwhile, assured the parents of radio fans that the program was "a great character-building force free from objectionable situations."[14] Despite that claim, not all listeners were as enchanted as the children and General Mills:

> A Scarsdale woman told a meeting of her Parent-Teacher Association that "Skippy" was a dangerous and degrading form of entertainment, and newspapers everywhere printed her charges. A panel of psychologists hired by Hummert pooh-poohed the Scarsdale lady's fears and said that the loud and rambunctious

adventure serial was a good thing for America's over-cloistered young. A kidnapping sequence in the story aroused criticism. Although it was written long after the Lindbergh case, indignant ministers and editorial writers denounced it as an attempt to profit by exploiting a tragedy. A new story line was instantly devised, and Andrews wrote twenty-five scripts in five days to catch up. Percy Crosby, who had been moaning and wringing his hands over his mild little character's lost innocence, breathed easier. But "Skippy" was not to last much longer. General Mills were disturbed when they heard that Andrews was not only a newspaperman but a writer of books; the chances were they had a drinking fellow and a bohemian on their hands, and this might get to the listening women and distress them. To forestall old wives' tales and young mothers' fears, Andrews had himself photographed eating Wheaties and sliced bananas with the child actors of "Skippy."[15]

Skippy Skinner stood out among "his fellow small boys." His body and ethical character were strong, a combination that positively enhanced the wisdom and courage he so aptly demonstrated beyond his years. His cohorts included Sooky Wayne, Jim Lovering and Carol (who, oddly enough, had no known surname). The kids' specialty was in engaging trouble, although the series took a humorous twist rather than a serious one most of the time. Needless to say, the fearless foursome probably appealed to more boys than girls in Radioland.

Rejected for the narrative's lead, actor Charles Flynn was to turn up in an even more important Hummert fixture a while later. The title role of Skippy was instead awarded to Franklin Adams, Jr., Francis Smith appeared as Sooky, St. John Terrell as Jim and Patricia Ryan as Carol. David Owen directed.

Their very next entry into the field of juvenile adventure narratives was to be Frank and Anne's most enduring and celebrated of all time. Some purists might debate the degree of influence that this pair exhibited over *Jack Armstrong, the All-American Boy* and its 18-year run (including a spinoff). But the fact that the Hummerts held the reins during the serial's important formative stages signifies that they contributed significantly to guiding it to its ultimate destination. It also seems noteworthy that — of the handful of Hummert juvenile adventure entries— their most successful, *Armstrong*, was created from scratch. Indeed, it was *the only one not adapted from comic strips or the fictional works of other authors.* There was quite possibly a lesson worth learning there.

Somewhere down the line Blackett-Sample-Hummert (BSH) bowed out as *Armstrong*'s packager. By then one of the most important and popular juvenile adventures on the air, the serial was relinquished at that point to Knox-Reeves advertising agency, who accepted both the writing and production of it.[16]

But before this shift transpired, the BSH agency was about to make what some consider its single greatest practical contribution to the annals of advertising. Recall that Frank Hummert possessed an intrinsic, absolutely phenomenal ability to turn just the right word or phrase into powerful marketing messages. Those missives resonated with millions of recipients, and motivated them to respond with affirmative behaviors.

For instance, Hummert created memorable mottoes like *Bonds or Bondage* and *For the Skin You Love to Touch.* But he saved his crowning achievement, his ultimate masterpiece and easily his most brilliant line of all time for a mere bowl of cereal: the immortal *Breakfast of Champions.*[17] Still in use today, through the years that marvelous emblem has appeared on billions of boxes of General Mills' Wheaties, picturing scores of athletes in many diverse sports. (The mythical Jack Armstrong was the first to be shown, in 1934.) That three-word slogan has been broadcast on the airwaves thousands, possibly millions, of times.

Synonymous with the product name for more than seven decades, it's emblazoned in the minds of billions of the globe's inhabitants. It appears on merchandise and apparel distributed in nations around the earth. Today the phrase even claims its own web site. *Breakfast of Champions* may be unequivocally the single most enduring icon of the talented and fertile Hummert mind. Indubitably, it holds a distinct spot among the most memorable advertising axioms ever created.

Despite the colorful and influential history, it's unclear when that advertising banner floated onto the airwaves for the first time. Wheaties sponsored *Skippy* as well as *Jack Armstrong, the All-American Boy.* Regrettably, no transcriptions of the former series have ever surfaced, therefore leaving the precise debut of the advertising catchphrase open to speculation.

One fable has it that Hummert wordsmith Robert Hardy Andrews was inspired by a box of Arm-and-Hammer baking soda when he concocted the name Jack Armstrong. The strong-armed symbol on the package helped him focus on the youth as an all–American hero, as that story goes. Another legend indicates that Andrews adapted the hero's name from an actual General Mills staffer who bore the appellation. Whatever the case, the resulting show was among the foremost juvenile fiction narratives ever to ride across the ether.

In its heyday it was well written, its characters were believable, lines were enunciated clearly, the story was directional but simple, and the series drew heavily upon the masterful effects of a talented sound technician. One reviewer confirmed: "*Jack Armstrong* was the adventure for boys who spent hours with Lionel trains or Gilbert chemistry sets, an aperitif for future engineers and scientists who built crystal sets and loved gadgetry."[18] After only a brief while it was obvious that the Hummerts and their successors were producing a spellbinding tale. *Armstrong* enraptured millions of imaginative youngsters who sat mesmerized by radios across the land during its twilight quarter-hour installments.

Armstrong premiered in a six-afternoon-a-week serialized format on CBS on July 31, 1933. By the time it left the air on June 1, 1950 — coupled with an extended run known as *Armstrong of the SBI* (Scientific Bureau of Investigation) that departed June 18, 1951, all of it for Wheaties — the series had eventually broadcast in 15- or 30-minute chapters one, two, three, five or six days a week over all four national chains.

One authority credited it as the symbolic start of the globetrotting characteristic of juvenile adventure serials. From *Armstrong*'s inception, "It was nothing for a hero to range all over the world in search of something or someone."[19] Jack and his pals trekked across Africa and sailed the Sulu Sea in pursuit of valuable data or objects or conspirators as they tried to keep the planet from falling into the hands of ruthless despots.

Jack was, himself, an athletic hero of Hudson High, whose familiar fight song performed *a cappella* by a male quintet brought the show on the air:

5. Child's Play

Wave the flag for Hudson High, boys!
Show them how we stand!
Ever shall our team be champions,
Known throughout the land!

The transition to a *Breakfast of Champions* plug was an easy one from there.

Jack's companions, siblings Billy and Betty Fairfield and their uncle Jim Fairfield, accompanied him on those far-away jaunts.

In 1950 a makeover, perhaps as dreadful as the one that brutalized *Little Orphan Annie* a decade earlier, overwhelmed *Armstrong*. Uncle Jim had vanished by 1946, replaced by a younger Vic Hardy, director of the SBI. Agents Jack, Billy and Betty assisted him. But the show had lost the charm that mesmerized legions of American youngsters in the 1930s and 1940s. As an after-dinner half-hour twice weekly it was no match for the spirited adventure of an earlier epoch. It folded in less than a year.

Jack Armstrong was successively played by Jim Ameche, St. John Terrell, Stanley (Stacy) Harris, Frank Behrens, Charles Flynn and Michael Rye (Billsbury). Flynn, who was in the part from 1939 to 1943 and 1944 to 1951, was un-

Actor Charles Flynn, shown with his pedigreed English bulldog, failed to gain the title role in the Hummerts' *Skippy* juvenile adventure. But he was soon tapped for an even more prestigious lead, as *Jack Armstrong, the All-American Boy* and the subsequent *Armstrong of the SBI*. Except for a brief period while away in Army service, he carried that important role from 1939 to 1951. (Photofest)

doubtedly the actor most closely identified with the part. Playing Billy were, consecutively, John Gannon, Roland Butterfield, Milton Guion, Murray McLean and Dick York. Portraying Betty, in order, were Shaindel Kalish, Sarajane Wells, Loretta Poynton, Naomi May and Patricia Dunlap. Jim Goss was Uncle Jim Fairfield and Ken Griffin was Vic Hardy. Directors included Jim Jewell, Ted MacMurray, Ed Morse, Pat Murphy and David Owen. Among the show's interlocutors were Truman Bradley, Paul Douglas, Norman Kraft, Franklyn MacCormack, Bob McKee, Ken Nordine, David Owen, Ed Prentiss and Tom Shirley. When Hummert writer Robert Hardy Andrews left, Irving Crump, Lee Knopf, Talbot Mundy, Colonel Paschal Strong and Jim Jewell (who had initially directed *The Lone Ranger*) followed him.

A fourth Hummert series aimed at adolescents, *Popeye the Sailor*, didn't repeat the triumph of the All-American Boy. Debuting over NBC on September 10, 1935, the thrice-weekly quarter-hour shifted to CBS a year later. Plagued by interruptions— off the air for five months, back on, then off 14 months more before resuming— it was gone for good by July 29, 1938, surely a disappointment to producers and cast alike.

The show was based on Elzie Crisler Segar's animated strip. It featured the gravelly-voiced character fondly recalled by movie theater patrons (and, subsequently, from televised cartoons). On radio Popeye supplanted spinach with the sponsor's Wheatena cereal to give him steel biceps so he could move mountains or whatever required his super-strength at the moment. (In the show's final three months Popsicle sponsored, however.)

Aimed at little tikes, the narrative often dramatized familiar fairy tales (*Jack and the Beanstalk, Robin Hood*, etc.). Invariably Popeye gained power from a bowl of Wheatena for his last-minute rescues from giants and other menaces. It was one of broadcasting's earliest instances of working the client's message into the story line, a precedent that others shamelessly copied.

Popeye was surrounded by traditional figures from the illustrated strip, among them love interest Olive Oyl, an orphaned newsboy whom Popeye adopted named Matey, and their good friend J. Wellington Wimpy. Victor Irwin's Cartoonland Band, which accompanied the theater animation, also backed the radio series.

Floyd Buckley, Jack Mercer and Det Poppen took turns in the cast as Popeye. Olive LaMoy and Mae Questel portrayed Olive Oyl. Jimmy Donnelly was Matey, while Charles Lawrence played Wimpy. Kelvin Keech announced.

Following that less-than-stunning-success, the Hummerts returned to the sound stage with one more children's adventure, *Terry and the Pirates*. Based on yet another comic strip — this one by Milton Caniff — a drawing that was introduced to newspaper readers in October-ber 1934, the drama pre-miered over NBC on November 1, 1937, airing three days weekly for Dari-Rich. It moved to the Blue network the following season. At the time, the nation was simply too isolationist for adventure stories set in the Far East (Terry's locale) to catch on. The show left the air on March 22, 1938.

It was off for two-and-a-half years before being picked up for eight months by Libby, McNeill and Libby (for its tomato juice and other diverse lines of foodstuffs) over Chicago's WGN. At that point it aired five afternoons weekly. The show was off for another seven months before returning to the Blue/ABC chain on February 1, 1943, for the cereal-manufacturing Quaker Oats Company.

Bill Fein was one of several actors who played the namesake role in *Terry and the Pirates*, a cartoon-inspired Hummert fantasy of the Far East. Before the war that area held little appeal to young ears and the show departed within months. But when things heated up there, it quickly returned, captivating young minds unable to get their fill of the Dragon Lady's exploits against Col. Terry Lee and pals. (Photofest)

By then World War II gripped the nation and listeners were interested in whatever transpired in the Far East. Ironically, according to a web site dedicated to the program, Japan was never mentioned throughout the run. With minor interruption, the serial continued until permanent cancellation on June 30, 1948.

Terry and the Pirates focused on the Orient, where an evil Eurasian, Lai Choi San (aka the Dragon Lady), was the archenemy of U.S. Air Corps Colonel Terry Lee and his buddies. Those pals included adult companion Patrick Ryan, Hotshot Charlie, Flip Corkin, Connie the Coolie, Burma and Eleta.

They fought Axis powers during World War II, and other global villains and crime cartels before and after that period. During the war, working for the Chinese government, the Dragon Lady joined forces with Lee and his team to vent their collective wrath against the Japanese. Given Dragon Lady's penchant for making life miserable for the Americans during the prewar era, the fans were never quite certain just how far she could be trusted. When the war ended, she showed her true colors again, resuming her diabolical tirade against Lee and his compatriots.

Cliff Carpenter, Bill Fein, Owen Jordan and Jackie Kelk played the title role. Adelaide Klein, Agnes Moorehead and Marion Sweet portrayed the nemesis Dragon Lady. Wylie Adams, Marty Andrews and Cyril Armbrister directed. The program's announcer was Douglas Browning. Once again the Hummerts tapped their prolific writer Robert Hardy Andrews to pen the early episodes, setting the direction for all that was to follow.

In summary, the influence that Frank and Anne Hummert had on the juvenile adventure radio serial was enormous. It was they and a few others who set in motion how melodrama would play out to the nation's youngsters in the decades just ahead. While it may be true that the couple brought only a handful of creations to the air, during that genre's embryonic stages they made a lasting impression. Ultimately they determined what would appeal to little ears. And most of their instincts were right.

The permanent legacy that the Hummerts left on the genre loomed much larger than any transitory glance might indicate. Their enormous output in other programming categories usually places their identities within those other confines. But for a few years, at least, without youngsters in their own home, they defined kids' shows and influenced the content and focus of serialized tales for adolescents as much or more than anyone else.

6

MATINEE MELODRAMA

In 1940 Katherine Best told her *Saturday Review of Literature* readers that the "daily dilemma-dramas" concocted by a host of soap opera producers were designed to "ease drudgery at the drainboard."[1] She also correctly observed that the true agenda of those narratives on the installment plan was to "sell soap at the counter." At the time, soap was their primary sponsor and the origin of the breed's "soap opera" epithet.[2] U.S. soapmakers were then spending $30 million to advertise their cleansers every year on radio serials, accounting for a third of that medium's annual revenues.

"The industry justifies itself by claiming that it gives the public what it wants," electronic media critic Charles A. Siepmann observed of the audience's preoccupation with serialized melodrama.[3] Writing in 1947, he cited at least three reasons why "our two greatest networks continue to fill daytime listening hours with programs which investigation proves to be unpopular with, or disregarded by, the majority of available listeners."[4]

First, soap operas were relatively cheap programs to produce.

Second, they were especially convenient vehicles for advertising plugs.

Third, the suspense and excitement of the serial, as it unfolded, created a peculiar attentiveness.

Siepmann delineated: "These fictional characters are very far from fictitious—to this morbid coterie of listeners. Soap operas, for many of them, are more real than life itself. Many of these listeners *escape*

95

from life into the world of fantasy and daydreams that many soap operas deliberately offer.... The intense interest of the addicts, their morbid frame of mind, their pitiable credulity, make them a pushover for the advertiser.... Soap operas sell goods. That is why they continue."[5]

In the meantime, the chief of Columbia University's radio research unit, Dr. Paul S. Lazarsfeld, determined that women were appreciative of some of seemingly contradictory dynamics they found in soap opera: the utter escapism that Siepmann also cited, which "removed the listener from the drudgery of daily life"; and moral guidance, which "helped the housewife solve her own personal problems." Network studies suggested "there was little difference in social and cultural activities between listeners and nonlisteners."[6]

Finally, another scholar hypothesized:

> Radio serials attract the listener by offering her a portrait of her own shortcomings, which lead to constant trouble, and of her inability to help herself. In spite of the unpleasantness of this picture, resonance can be enjoyed because identification is drawn away from it and transferred to an ideal type of the perfect, efficient woman who possesses power and prestige and who has to suffer not by her own fault but by the fault of others.[7]

Meanwhile, cultural critics postulated that agony on the airwaves impeded the moral fiber of American femininity. In the wartime era, New York psychiatrist, physician and author Dr. Louis I. Berg complained that those recurring anguishing predicaments faced by the beleaguered daytime heroines could be likened to Adolph Hitler's party line communications. Both corrupted the human nervous system, Berg allowed.[8]

Katherine Best admitted that a nationwide "I'm Not Listening" campaign seeking to "stem the tide of daylight radio drivel" had little effect. Siepmann inferred that listeners who did refuse to tune in to such programming gave as their chief reason "that they want to be cheered and not depressed, soothed and not whipped up daily to a tense pitch of excitement and anxiety."[9] Promoted by the National Federation of Women's Clubs and other feminine groups representing an estimated one million individuals, the national effort to curtail serialized melodrama publicly upbraided sponsors for willfully "underestimating the nation's taste and intelligence, ... stupidity, ... [and] not knowing women."[10]

At that juncture (1940) there were 81 dramatic serials broadcast every weekday, the highest number in the history of radio. And Frank and Anne Hummert were plainly the champions of the form, the couple cited as the "most prolific" producers, with 55 (68 percent) of the total number aired. Those drainboard dramas appealed to a weekly audience of 500 million listeners. The Hummerts were simultaneously generating another 25 programs in other formats every week.[11] "Nothing," surmised Katherine Best, "succeeds like excess."[12]

As this tome previously delineated, Frank Hummert's presupposition that American homemakers—who were chiefly women during the golden age of radio—might revel in some serialized fiction as they labored over their daily chores was little short of genius. Modestly, he referred to it as "a shot in the dark."[13] His conjecture bordered on brilliant deduction nonetheless.

About 1930 Hummert's intuition told him that the chief cooks and bottle-washers of millions of U.S. households might be predisposed to some stimulating audio matinee fare. Programming of that nature hadn't been tried, at least not on a national platform. Until then daytime schedules were replete with cooking tips, beauty secrets and other personal advice. It wasn't very imaginative; much of it was delivered by employing lecture techniques. (Even the Hummerts would be guilty of perpetuating the agenda, as they soon proffered shows like *Beatrice Mabie* and *Blanche Sweet*, two women headlining separate features offering hints for good looks, plus the aural features *How to Be Charming* and *The Mystery Chef*.)

Until then marketers were only dimly aware that those stay-at-homes who, on weekdays, rarely left their domiciles were also the nation's principal purchasing agents. These women figured prominently in making a family's brand-name buying decisions. Yet nearly all of Hummert's contemporaries had already assumed that the ladies were too busy to pay more than cursory attention to the radio. The homemakers, they felt, joined with other family members returning home in the evening to give their full attention to the fledgling entertainment medium following dinner. Thus, in radio's formative years, one scholar may have quite perceptively allowed that the medium was limited almost exclusively to "evening, family, and father-controlled entertainment."[14]

But Frank Hummert had other ideas. He intended to seize the housewives' attention and alter the pattern of their daily existence. One source credits him and his future bride with "the actual invention of soap opera."[15] While he didn't get on the air with the first daytime drama, he and Anne, without question, became the most prolific exponents of the form.[16]

The itinerant wordsmith Robert Hardy Andrews possessed the most facile Hummert pen. He must have seen what Frank Hummert envisioned when he contemplated the stay-at-home housewife of that era and composed a few lines that he entitled "A Voice in the Room":

> The average woman lives by a schedule in which no element changes from one day to the next....
>
> The accomplishments of such days may be great in their value to humanity, but the hours are — or were, in the past — long, empty, and deadly dull. But now a new thing has happened.
>
> There is, or can be, a voice in the room. A friendly, unhurried, likable, listenable, neighborly voice that is created by the turning of a dial....
>
> The housewife turns on her radio. She goes here and there, into her living room, upstairs to make the beds and clean the bathroom, out in the yard to hang up the washing, back to the kitchen to prepare lunch for the children....
>
> She knows, without thinking much about it, that the voice in her room tells her what is being heard by other women like herself. Therefore, she is a member of a great group....
>
> She is grateful, because in the world at last she has at least one neighbor, who is many voices in one, who talks to her all day long every day. And it is talking, the sound of a voice, not music or a joke that must be thought about or drama so artistic that she must sit down to listen to it, that the woman wants to hear. That is what she is grateful for: the voice in her room.[17]

Andrews surely grasped the diversionary release from the monotonous routines and demanding drudgery of millions of American women that daytime radio drama could provide.

6. Matinee Melodrama

The first of the breed was *Painted Dreams*, an Irna Phillips creation. Phillips would soon become the Hummerts' foremost competitor as a soap opera creator-producer, although she would be greatly
outdistanced by them in yield. (Her contributions are scrutinized more
extensively in the next chapter.) *Painted Dreams* debuted as a local feature on Chicago's station WGN on October 20, 1930. A few informants
stipulate that Frank Hummert actually produced the series.[18] While
that revelation is unsubstantiated by other authorities, it certainly *could*
have transpired. Because of Hummert's proximity to Phillips, plus his
rapidly developing interest in bringing drama-by-installment to the
airwaves, it's possible he might have collaborated with her. Hummert
also might have served in a consulting or advisory capacity, if not outright as producer. His influence is unclear. For now it's sufficient to
honor Phillips as the initiator of the line, without specific ties to anyone else.[19]

"Those voices over the air … seemed real," recalled one account
of the Hummert discovery. "Radio drama could be closer to gossip or
to the family stories women tell each other in traditional cultures,
which don't always have beginnings, middles and closed and conclu-
sive ends: the narrative flow is all."[20]

Ironically, the Hummerts made the happy discovery that there
was also a nighttime audience for their daytime fare — notably comprised of working people who were unable to hear narratives by installment when they were broadcast originally. By the late 1930s they
purchased a weeknight block for two hours on New York's WMCA
Radio to air eight of their quarter-hour dramas back-to-back in that
one gargantuan metropolitan market.

In the 1920s narratives by installment had become popular in magazines and newspapers. To implement his new initiative, Frank Hummert employed a practicing journalist, Charles Robert Douglas Hardy
Andrews (*one* man, although his accomplishments would seem like
many!). While one source would downplay him as little more than "a
hired gun writing for someone else's creations,"[21] a colleague labeled
Andrews a writing "syndicate." Meanwhile, James Thurber acknowledged that Andrews was eminently equipped with "an indestructible
typewriter, strong wrists, a story sense, and the knack of stringing out
words."[22] He was "beyond their [the Hummerts'] dreams of stamina

and fluency," asserted Thurber. Andrews, "who was eventually to become one of radio's legendary figures,"[23] presents a fascinating case study in his own right.

Born in Kansas in 1903, Andrews produced a 100,000-word serialized story for a newspaper contest at age 16. At 20 he was the city editor of *The Minneapolis Journal.* Until he moved to New York in 1932 he maintained his day job with *The Chicago Daily News* while hammering out five radio scripts per night, astounding skeptics with an amazing fluency and stamina. This was only a warm-up for the main attraction, however.

For a decade, until he acknowledged that he "got tired," Andrews kept anywhere from four to seven daily radio shows going, most of them soap operas. Working in a penthouse apartment on New York's Central Park West, he consumed 40 cups of coffee and chain-smoked 100 cigarettes between the hours of noon and midnight seven days a week while typing his scripts. His weekly production rate typically surpassed 100,000 words. And as a diversion he wrote numerous novels and dozens of movies, either alone or jointly with other writers. Of course, the Hummerts never replaced him, and when he died on November 11, 1976 it was surely the passing of an era among electronic media scribes.

But we have gotten ahead of ourselves. Andrews had achieved regional status as the author of serialized features for *The Chicago Daily News* at the time Frank Hummert employed him. His first assignment for Blackett-Sample-Hummert was to pen a radio serial called *The Stolen Husband.* Its plot was to be about (a) a handsome young businessman, (b) a voluptuous secretary, eager to advance her boss's career and (c) a dense but attractive wife who would learn too late that a man spending nights at the office with a gorgeous assistant could become preoccupied beyond his occupation.

The Stolen Husband, with a single actor reading all the parts, couldn't be declared a phenomenal success in any sense. But it gave Hummert, Anne Ashenhurst and Andrews invaluable insights. And in a short while it led to three extremely successful serials, against which almost all others could be measured for more than two decades: *Just Plain Bill* (1932–1955), *The Romance of Helen Trent* and *Ma Perkins* (both 1933–1960).

6. Matinee Melodrama

There could be no doubt that *Just Plain Bill* set the tone for more than 200 melodramatic serials that followed. A critic correctly identified the narrative as "the first smash hit network soap,"[24] while an aural thespian dubbed it the Hummerts' "first hardy perennial."[25] It was "the first daytime serial with lasting power," one scribe correctly assessed.[26] Another proclaimed it "a fifteen-minute giant of the air."[27] Yet another thought it a "cultural juggernaut."[27] One more dubbed it "the template for soaps."[29]

Bill Davidson, the philosophizing tonsorial artist of Hartville, was the guardian of his community. He boasted a demeanor that was attractive to the local citizenry — calm, quiet, gentle, sympathetic, tolerant, understanding, kind, firm, strong, wise — qualities he displayed throughout the long run. Here was a man folks could go to in time of need, assured that — without pretension — he would give them sound advice and offer the personal assistance within his power. The part was always played by distinguished thespian Arthur Hughes, dubbed "an actor's actor" by his counterparts; he memorized his lines before going on the air. *Bill*'s tale was the first with "staying power," and it established a genre that maintained permanent appeal for millions of radio listeners.[30]

In developing the series, writer Robert Hardy Andrews recalled a rather gregarious barber from his younger days — friendly, bordering on nosy, yet a reassuring presence to customers. Andrews, who had already tried his hand at *The Stolen Husband, Betty and Bob, Judy and Jane,* and *Easy Aces,* created situations that were set in a small town around this character, allowing him to become the conscience of the community. The writer labeled his drama *Bill the Barber.* But Anne Ashenhurst, claiming to understand precisely what women wanted, corrected him: "*Just Plain Bill,*" she injected.

Incidentally, a family member recalls that John Ashenhurst used to tag Andrews as simply "one of Anne's hacks."[31] A *hack*, by the way, shouldn't be interpreted as a pejorative term. A seasoned author explained: "A hack writer was a person who could hack it out day after day after day…. You don't demean a person like that."[32]

"Once this astute couple had taken hold of radio's daytime serial (as their careful planning allowed them to do almost overnight)," historiographer Raymond William Stedman recalled in 1971, "its course

was fixed with little wavering by the guiding star they seemed to see shining so brightly. With a full complement of enraptured passengers, the newly launched dramatic craft would sail to Oblivion, by way of Scorn and Derision, with few side trips to the Isle of Quality and no real chance to remain there."[33]

In a 1939 newspaper interview the Hummerts claimed they followed four steps in creating and producing their daytime serials.[34]

Dubbed "an actor's actor" by peers, Arthur Hughes became a fan favorite as the Hummerts' long-playing *Just Plain Bill* (Davidson), barber of Hartville. Actually, he had little time for cutting hair; he was swept up into the crises of the townsfolk, who routinely turned to him in their time of trouble for counsel and crimesolving. Hughes persevered for the duration of the drama's 23-year run. (Photofest)

First, they established a theme while insisting that their programs could be certified as "successful stories about unsuccessful people." Secluding themselves in their Greenwich mansion, Frank and Anne Hummert emerged with a title and a rough draft of a projected serial's motif. Returning to the office, they whipped it into a four- or five-page typewritten outline.

Second, they created a "story line," sketching out perhaps a half-dozen episodes of the proposed drama. It usually consisted of a quartet of double-spaced typewritten pages.

Third, a staff writer was engaged to take the material that the pair had generated in the first two steps and flesh out the dialogue for the narrative. Their scribes were thus often referred to as "dialoguers" as opposed to "authors" or "writers."

Fourth, that wordsmith (or another) penned a finished script that was to be broadcast over the air.

The Hummerts often adapted generating the theses for their soap opera series from pulp fiction, motion picture and stage productions. Early in their audio careers, for instance, they adapted *David Harum* from a best-selling novel by that name that was released in 1898. Before they carried it forward, the tale also had been turned into a 1934 box office smash featuring renowned homespun entertainer Will Rogers.

After their experiment was successful in turning *David Harum* into a radio serial, the Hummerts soon offered listeners *Our Gal Sunday*. That narrative was taken directly from a turn-of-the-century Broadway production simply titled *Sunday* that had starred Ethel Barrymore.

Another of their durable melodramas, *Stella Dallas*, was based on Olive Higgins Prouty's turn-of-the-century novel of the same name. In a pair of celluloid versions, Belle Bennett (1925) and Barbara Stanwyck (1937) portrayed the heroine before the Hummerts recalled that indomitable figure before aural audiences.

At about the same time they adapted *Mr. Keen, Tracer of Lost Persons* from pulp fiction. (See chapter 4 for further details.)

The dramas' schemes included revealing disclosures or unexpected developments, called cliffhangers, on Fridays that were specifically designed to compel audiences to tune into Monday's broadcasts. Ratings-takers found that the bigger the shock, the higher the return. A reviewer suggested, "The serials ... [routinely] followed a formula of histrionic dialogue, larger-than-life characters, sudden plot twists, and improbable resolutions."[35]

The Hummerts were credited with introducing the capsule thesis into soap opera that invariably followed the titles to their washboard weepers, a ritual which soon appeared on other daytime producers' wares. These epigraphs helped acquaint new listeners with a dishpan drama's premise.

Thus there evolved "the story of Mary Noble, a little Iowa girl who married one of America's most handsome actors, Larry Noble, matinee idol of a million other women — the story of what it means to be the wife of a famous star." There were also "couples like lovable, impractical Lorenzo Jones and his devoted wife, Belle. Lorenzo's inventions have made him a character to the town — but not to Belle, who loves him. Their struggle for security is anybody's story. But somehow with Lorenzo, it has more smiles than tears." And then there was "a continuation on the air of the true-to-life story of mother love and sacrifice in which Stella Dallas saw her beloved daughter Laurel marry into wealth and society and, realizing the difference in their tastes and worlds, went out of Laurel's life." In such brief daily morsels, listeners were reminded just what their stories were about.

In a story that brought more smiles than tears, Karl Swenson — one of the Hummerts' most versatile thespians — portrayed lovable *Lorenzo Jones* from 1937 to 1955. Shown with support player Colleen Ward, Swenson (who turned up as the police detective *Mr. Chameleon,* and as Lord Henry Brinthrope, *Our Gal Sunday's* long-suffering spouse), played a man whose inventions made him a character to the locals. (Photofest)

6. Matinee Melodrama

Actress Mary Jane Higby mischievously recalled in her memoir that, of all the dramatic capsule theses aired, her favorite was easily the one repeated every day on *Amanda of Honeymoon Hill*.[36] George Ansbro elaborated on this state of affairs in his book *I Have a Lady in the Balcony*[37]:

> Frank Gallop was the regular announcer, and his occasional tendency to almost break up but still manage to hang on for dear life while on the air was the giggly gossip of New York radio. The reason was the opening announcement which, as on all the Hummert soaps, was written by Anne Hummert. This particular lead-in indicated how truly naïve Mrs. Hummert must really have been: "We bring you now the story of Amanda of Honeymoon Hill, laid in a world few Americans know. The story of love and marriage in America's romantic South, etc., etc." The attention-getting word remained for the entire run of the program because, evidently, none of Anne Hummert's subordinates at Air Features had the temerity to approach her about deleting the double entendre and replacing it with a word or phrase less suggestive. Rather than chance it, they skipped it. But by substituting for Gallop myself once in a while, I found out what it must have been like for poor Frank to not break up. And for five years yet.

Incidentally, the Hummerts routinely plucked announcers from their vast stable of interlocutors at will and transferred them between serials like they were property rather than people. Several who turned up here and there on their daytime dramas included Pierre Andre, George Ansbro, Andre Baruch, Ford Bond, Howard Claney, Harry Clark, Jack Costello, Frank Gallop, Roger Krupp, Larry Elliott, Fielden Farrington and Ed Fleming. The reader will rapidly recognize that many of those same individuals appeared at night on their various musical and crimefighting features.

One of the most formidable concerns the prolific pair of producers encountered while developing their serials, admitted Frank Hummert, was in selecting proper names for the hundreds of new characters who peopled the many Air Features dramas. He solved the dilemma, he said, by randomly copying the names from signs that he saw at various retail establishments.[38]

Hummert further explained that — to diminish the voice-change shock to listeners when an actor departed from a series— the part in question would be temporarily written out for a short period of time. To allow for that incidence, the figure in the story line might, for instance, become ill or perhaps take an extended trip for a time. Returning to the daily lineup with a new actor then portraying the role, the character's new voice would result in a "less jarred" audience, according to Hummert.[39]

In the genre of soap opera there were two clearly defined types of melodrama: the sluggish story line that almost never reached an explicit conclusion; and the sequence-driven formula that did.

In the former, wholeheartedly embraced by prolific soap opera author Elaine Sterne Carrington (*Pepper Young's Family, Rosemary, When a Girl Marries*), the action extended continuously without noticeable pause. This has been termed the "meanwhile, back at the ranch" approach. The plot evolved simultaneously in a multiplicity of segments, never really drawing its breath. (Carrington's philosophy as applied to soap opera is examined in greater detail in the next chapter.)

In the second technique, a small cluster of permanent figures interacted with a group of individuals who were introduced into the story line for a given period of time — usually a few weeks to a few months. The Air Features assembly line showed a strong preference for this approach. In its dramas, the temporary troupe was nearly always predominated by wily women, sly men and universal troublemakers. Once those rapscallions were exposed, routed and banished, they were superseded by yet another group of malefactors.

"Before the main crisis was resolved," noted media reviewer Erik Barnouw, "the next one was stirred in as a subplot, which was brought up to a full boil as the old story was resolved and dropped."[40] To which author John Dunning added: "It was the simplest kind of radio, ripe for satire; comics Bob Elliott and Ray Goulding had little to exaggerate in their *Mary Backstayge, Noble Wife* skits [parodies of *Backstage Wife* that the two popularized]."[41]

The task of maintaining acceptable ratings rested heavily on the predicaments in which the dialoguers engaged the principals. While most Hummert serials might include two or three such drawn-out story lines in a year's time, there were some entanglements that ran considerably longer — particularly if there was strong listener interest. *Ma Perkins* sparred with some deceptive, distant kinfolk for a full calendar year in 1950, while *Perry Mason* (which was *not* an Air Features property) pursued a single murder case over an 18-month time frame.

In most Air Features serials there was a rather lengthy "lead-in," during which the announcer set the scene, often harping back to what had previously transpired. He droned on and on to be certain that listeners who had missed an episode or two of their favorite soap opera were brought up to speed. To be sure of it, many of those dramas featured just two scenes following the "lead-in." In the first, called a "recap," previous actions and/or conversations were repeated or told to someone else (all with the intent of keeping audiences up to date). In the final scene, new action occurred which, of course, would be repeated on succeeding days.

If any housewives caught on to this repetitious formula, they could carry out the trash, hang the clothes on the line, run the carpet sweeper or chat on the telephone during the first six to eight minutes of most Hummert serials and never miss *any* action! Surely some listeners must have became conscious of that practice after a while.

In spite of all honorable intent to the contrary, one radio historiographer's research revealed a plethora of deficiencies in Soapland: "While the use of dialoguers did increase greatly the output of the Hummerts, ... it did not lead to a high literary quality in the programs so manufactured. The dialoguers had little control over their writing and were bound by the outline whether they thought it right or not."[42] This often led to some of the most banal conversations on the air, several critics attested. One lamented that the Hummert shows "were so heavy-handed that they were parodies of themselves."[43]

The story lines themselves were far-fetched, frequently outrageous and certainly repetitious. Gerald Nachman expounded: "The astonishingly prolific but remote Hummerts rang an amazing number of changes on the reliable theme of female unfulfillment, male unreliability, and general domestic knavery; their original guiding inspiration was *The Perils of Pauline*."[44] He elaborated further: "The serials' major faith was an unswerving, fundamental belief in marital harmony. Eternal misery awaited every soap opera spinster, whereas any bachelor was considered eligible and desirable, and any woman who failed to convert his heathen ways to home life must be some kind of hag."[45] Though perhaps a bit exaggerated, these comments possess a ring of truth.

"Evil sirens were forever luring Larry [Noble] to the brink of infidelity, and Mary herself was pursued through her twenty-three-year air run by the usual Hummert host of maniacs," proclaimed John Dunning, describing *Backstage Wife*, a typical Hummert daytime property. "The villains were so deliciously evil that murder, blackmail, and double-dealing were Mary's constant companions."[46] Let's also recognize that not only was this normal for Mary, it was commonplace for a whole lot of other Hummert heroines as well.

The earliest antecedents of the assembly-line approach to writing can be traced as far back as the nineteenth century.[47] They include the Victorian-era novels of Beadle & Adams; juvenile thriller fiction that spotlighted the Bobbsey Twins, the Hardy Boys, the Rover Boys, Nancy Drew, Tom Swift and several other characters manufactured by the Stratemeyer Syndicate; and the fantastic applications of Alexandre Dumas. With 60 anonymous apprentices in tow, Dumas turned out 277 volumes—a practice stifling originality and creativity that was embraced and perfected by Frank and Anne Hummert in the twentieth century.[48] Underpaid hacks were given little leeway to depart from set parameters. They seldom reached personal fulfillment as they ground out reams of stilted, predictable word patterns that rarely rose above mediocrity.[49]

When a wordsmith's efforts began wearing thin on a given drama, the scribe was transferred to another, hopefully netting both inspired scripts and writers. "To lighten the burden further, there was the hack's best friend, the narrator," the historian recalled. "While skillful writers were able to keep narration within reasonable bounds, letting it enhance the drama, the less talented often allowed the narrator to give the listener more information than the characters themselves provided."[50] Little of it was of sterling quality. To paraphrase a hack who had invested his career in the Hummert system, he freely admitted some years later, "I had only slight interest in what I wrote."[51] What a telling declaration!

In her engrossing memoirs, actress Mary Jane Higby, a major pres-

ence in a multitude of Hummert dramas, offered an aside concerning
the actual physical documents from which she and her contemporary
thespians read their on-air lines:

> To the eye, most soap opera scripts were alike. Mimeographed
> in clear black lettering, they all had a cover page that included
> only the title, the author's name, and the cast list. A radio actor
> could spot an Air Features script from across the room. Pale
> lavender ink covered the title page. In addition to the usual
> information, we were reminded that this was a "Hummert Radio
> Feature," that the "authors of title and original story line" were
> Frank and Anne Hummert, and that "this unpublished drama
> or radio adaptation is the property of Frank and Anne Hum-
> mert and is being used under special license to Air Features,
> Inc.... [As far as I could see, Air Features was Frank and Anne
> Hummert, too].... It is fully protected under common law copy-
> right law. Damages will be demanded for unauthorized perfor-
> mances thereof or for the making of unauthorized copies thereof
> either for publication, radio, or motion pictures. It may not be
> broadcast, published, or made into motion pictures without
> specific individual authorization in each performance thereof."
> The Hummerts took soap opera seriously.[52]

The scripts for other Hummert shows—beyond soap opera—
were also printed in lavender and carried identical information, credits, stipulations and warnings. One of the Hummerts' eccentricities,
incidentally, specified that everyone who worked on their programs
must turn in their scripts to the directors at the end of every broadcast to prevent other producers and writers from studying them.[53]
Given what we have learned about their story lines, what competitor
can the reader think of who would be hankering to emulate most of
those Air Features scripts? Were the overprotective Hummerts simply
flattering their own egos in that respect?

The fact that so many serials were brought to the air in rapid succession, and that only the hardiest perennials survived, need not be
disturbing. Raymond W. Stedman explained that such quick disappearances were a result of "overplanting." Said he: "Most well-rooted
shows managed to hold on, and often thrive, showing that the fault
was not in the serial form itself. New plantings, however, were as likely

to wither as they were to grow. And when one failed, there were many others waiting to take its place."[54] Thus, with such a vast number of Hummert creations concurrently on the air, no one should expect that all would thrive.

Frank and Anne Hummert adopted similar values to those they believed most mainstream Americans revered. Certain tenets became sacrosanct in their organization and were virtually inscribed in stone. The pages of Air Features scripts were awash with them. "Ours is a religious country, so we try to embody the idea of right," Anne Hummert told a reporter. "Crime may appear, but either the annihilation or change of heart of the erring one must follow. Divorce is not unknown among our characters, but it is deplored and does nothing to make the participants happier."[55] The latter comment is insightful, if not instructive, considering it fell from the lips of one who had been there — at a time in which it definitely was an anomaly.

The pair provided directives to those who penned their story lines, delineating the type of figures about whom they would write. *Ma Perkins*, for instance, whose heroine was labeled by a pundit "the mother of the airwaves," was painted as "a woman with a heart of gold and a world of common sense ... a philosophy of the Golden Rule ... unselfish in her interest in individuals ... doing unto others rather than doing others." (Actress Virginia Payne portrayed Ma as a warm, tolerant character at odds with only the small-minded residents of mythical Rushville Center. She carried off her part as a woman possessing a compassionate heart who believed in everybody's dreams. In playing a role that was considered by many scholars to be soap opera's most beloved protagonist, Payne never missed an episode across 27 years on the air.)

One reviewer prudently assessed: "Misery and the Golden Rule are intertwined to oil the lady listener into the satisfying confirmation of her own virtue and the hardness of her lot. The majority of Hummert listeners being mothers, no mother on a Hummert show can be bad. And certainly not domineering."[56]

The Hummerts' personal excesses and idiosyncrasies turned up in the story lines of their many narratives. They maintained an exalted deference for sexual purity at all times, never giving the network censors or advertisers any occasion to question an impropriety. There simply was none. But their modesty went to unbelievable extremes, even in a day in which chastity was highly regarded. Helen Trent, for example — a goddess of goodness who never had an immoral thought in her life — exhibited an unapproachable virtue that gave her a superiority not enjoyed by any other serial heroine. (Coincidentally, Helen was "one of the best known non-existent people in the United States," according to one of Anne's collegiate classmates who wrote about her in an alumnae journal in 1957.)

Frank and Anne Hummerts' interpretation of sex was patently naïve. When on one occasion a fiancé (Helen had several) asked to hold her hand, she snapped at him, letting him know that a mere engagement ring didn't buy such privileges. Helen and her kind had a way of making a peck on the cheek appear to be sexual excess.

As late as 1957, when villain Kurt Bonine had Helen right where he wanted her — snared in an abandoned house — he advanced lustfully toward her. "Kurt, you're mad!" she screamed. Her life, and her reputation, was spared for another 60 seconds as a commercial interrupted him. But he would have his way with her as he pursued his revenge immediately following the ad. As the day's episode drew to a close, Kurt informed his quarry: "When I'm through with you...."

And Helen, her back to the wall, cut him off with the injunction that Hummert heroines always relied upon when cornered by a menacing villain: "Kurt, Kurt, you wouldn't!" (What sounded like attempted rape in those programs sometimes resulted in something less heinous by Hummert standards, such as attempted murder, maybe.)

All this simply galled a media analyst, particularly when Frank Hummert explained to an interviewer that their programs' central figures were "high principled" as a result of being "so close to the audience and so much a part of their daily lives." The observer charged:

> That was an understatement of the serial formula, at least as compounded by the Hummerts. High-principled women did not have to be given the impossibly pure character of Helen Trent. Consistency did not demand that heroines always should be stronger and nobler than their husbands in almost any situation. The canvas of American life was not filled with so many crimes, trials, strange diseases, lost mates, and causes for

extended suffering as was the canvas of the daytime serial, especially as painted by Frank and Anne Hummert.[57]

When Anne Hummert was 80 years of age, a reporter asked her if she watched soap operas on television. She claimed she didn't. "Too much sex in them," she allowed, then added: "My husband always said, 'For God's sake, leave something to the imagination!'"[58]

Helen Trent seldom showed any temper; she never smoked and never drank alcohol. For 27 years on the air she remained utterly chaste. Yet housewives who themselves smoked three packs a day were probably convinced that any woman who smoked or drank on *The*

The cast of *The Romance of Helen Trent*, the Hummerts' virtuous "goddess of goodness," prepares for a reading of the script during its one-hour rehearsal. Director Ernie Riker wears glasses. In the foreground are Don McLaughlin and Susan Douglas. At back (left to right) are David Gothard (Helen's most durable swain, Gil Whitney), Julie Stevens (Helen), Riker, Mary Jane Higby, and Bess McCammon. (Photofest)

Romance of Helen Trent had low ethics and loose morals. That was a Hummert tradition and it could never be compromised.

Helen wasn't alone when it came to upholding the virtues espoused by Frank and Anne Hummert. Popular Air Features actor Ned Wever loved to recount how he fell into a 17-year run as Dr. Anthony Loring, the heroine's principal suitor on *Young Widder Brown.* (Long-time series announcer George Ansbro branded that melodrama as "eighteen years of the most excruciating radio torture ever devised by Frank and Anne Hummert."[59]) Another swain also pursuing Ellen Brown, Dr. Peter Turner, played by versatile actor Clayton (Bud) Collyer, preceded Wever on the air. Unfortunately for Collyer, when the Hummerts took an extended vacation to Europe in 1939— leaving *Young Widder Brown* in the hands of a new writer—the aforementioned scribe somehow failed to comprehend that anything even hinting at intimacy in a Hummert script was an absolute faux pas.

Ned Wever used to smile when recalling how he became Dr. Anthony Loring, male lead in *Young Widder Brown.* One of the Hummert scribes, a neophyte for sure, broke a cardinal rule, which carried Ellen Brown's previous beau to the brink of disaster. The Hummert resolution was to push him over the edge and replace the character (and the actor playing him). No word on what became of the miscreant who caused it. (Courtesy of Patti Wever Knoll)

These events must have occurred at a time when the producers were lax about plotting out everything in an episode or making sure that the rules were clearly understood. Before long the hero and heroine were sipping coffee while attired in their bathrobes at Ellen Brown's home. It didn't go any further than that, but when the Hummerts returned, according to Wever, "All hell broke loose, and Bud Collyer was out of a job." They simply had to rid the drama of any perception of tainted vice. Replacing the hero was their "fix." Wever didn't say what became of the offending wordsmith, but his eminence and perhaps his career in that organization was presumed doomed.

There was also a darker side to some of the Hummerts' dealings, or so it was perceived. Some might classify their demeanor as meanspirited, although that might be too strong a label. The bottom line always was that the dynamic duo—invariably shrewd businesspersons who maintained a take-charge stance—constantly tinkered with the product they delivered to advertisers and audiences, ostensibly under the guise of improving it.

One of the methods they routinely relied upon was to surreptitiously hold auditions for replacements of their lead actors—both for their short and long-running series. Anne Hummert, in particular, seemed to relish such secret auditions. On those occasions, seasoned talent, as well as aspiring thespians, might be brought into a studio and tested at a time when whoever was then playing the lead role wasn't present (and often was not informed of it).

Vivian Smolen, one of their most durable leading ladies, related to this author just such an incident, which left her totally "devastated." Having played the namesake role of *Our Gal Sunday* for several years, on one occasion she was tipped off by the show's director that he had been ordered to conduct auditions for the heroine's part behind her back.

"Nothing ever came of it," she allowed, "but I was nervous for awhile." Ultimately, the director let her know that the storm had passed; Anne Hummert hadn't found a voice that satisfied her more, and she finally let it go. Smolen said she never heard directly from the Hummerts about it at any time. She remained in the part about 13 years, until the network finally canceled the durable series.

Florence Freeman, on the other hand, who played *Young Widder Brown* from that series' debut in 1938, was forced out in 1954 when Anne Hummert evidently tired of her voice. "She wanted a fresh, younger-sounding Ellen Brown," long-running announcer George

Ansbro told this writer. When the producer held auditions behind Freeman's back, Hummert picked a virtual neophyte, Millicent Brower, as the new lead. "Her voice didn't possess the range and empathy nor quality of Florence's," Ansbro allowed. The striking difference in the younger woman's voice contrasted negatively, in his opinion, with that of the more seasoned leading man (Ned Wever). After all, Dr. Anthony Loring had been Ellen Brown's intended for ages and hardly sounded like a man who would suddenly date a much younger-sounding woman. Within a few months Brower was also put out, replaced by a more mature-sounding Wendy Drew, who carried the part to the end of the run. "Wendy was no Florence Freeman, but she was a big improvement over her immediate predecessor," Ansbro confirmed.[60]

Vivian Smolen played major roles on two Hummert serials. At 12:45 P.M. over CBS she was the orphan girl from the little mining town who married England's richest, most handsome lord, *Our Gal Sunday*. At 4:15 P.M. she appeared on NBC as beloved daughter Laurel (Lolly-Baby), who married into wealth and society. In theory, her mom, *Stella Dallas*, went out of her life. But only in the epigraph! (Photofest)

Ansbro himself was subjected to such a trial by fire when *Young Widder Brown*'s ratings failed to improve. After hearing scuttlebutt that his job was on the line, he learned from director Richard Leonard that Leonard was—at the Hummerts' bidding—to conduct an audition to replace him. Leonard, a longtime friend, suggested that

Ansbro show up for it despite the fact that the Hummerts hadn't told him of his impending release. Ansbro did so and recalls the tryout encounter like this:

> I remember Mrs. Hummert smiling courteously at me from the control room. What it boiled down to was that I was auditioning for something I had been doing successfully five days every week for the previous fifteen years. On the day of the competition, I faced many of the top announcers of the day, including such impressive names as David Ross, Frank Gallop, Ed Herlihy, Jack Costello, Nelson Case, and Ken Roberts. The fascinating conclusion to this little saga is that I continued doing the show. For the next week or so, I kept expecting to hear from the Hummert office that I was through and would be replaced by announcer so-and-so. But such a message never arrived. Whatever made the Hummerts decide to keep me I never learned. Needless to say, it was a good thing for me that I had found out about the audition.[61]

Such tactics were common practice in doing business in the Hummert regime. The fact that an individual in a given role was familiar to audiences for many years was no guarantee that he or she would continue until a show departed the airwaves. For some it was a persistent struggle. And while the examples presented are drawn from Air Features' soap operas, similar conditions prevailed on Hummert programs in other genres. In fact, except for those name personalities who headlined a handful of Hummert music and variety features, nearly everyone connected with their narratives—including daytime and nighttime fare—could be subject to replacement at any time, seemingly on sheer whim.

We have presented a disturbing picture that characterized the Hummerts as shrewd operators who looked out mostly for themselves, with little regard for others. But in all fairness it must be acknowledged that working for them often offered some very attractive aspects as well.

Julie Stevens, the heroine of one of the Hummerts' most popular women's serials, *The Romance of Helen Trent*, was unprepared for the menial salary figure that appeared on her contract when she initially signed for the part of Helen. The Hummerts' legal representative (quite possibly Mickey Scopp on that particular occasion) assured her that she would work on *all* their serials nonetheless. That would translate into a banner income, she was advised. She — and others—found this to be entirely true. In one evenhanded assessment, a critic allowed that when the Hummerts liked an actor, "there were no more loyal employers." Said he: "The couple slid their favorite actors from serial to serial like floating bars of Ivory soap."[62]

There was also considerable crossover for those working Air Features daytime and nighttime programs. Long-standing heroes and heroines on such serials as *Backstage Wife, Our Gal Sunday, Stella Dallas* and *Young Widder Brown* who were in particular good graces with the Hummerts and their program directors often found themselves enjoying bit parts in nighttime thrillers like *Hearthstone of the Death*

Florence Freeman was the heroine of not one but *two* serials that ran more than a decade, one Hummert-produced. At high noon over CBS she reported "news of the women's world" on straight-talking broadcast journalism's *Wendy Warren and the News*. At 4:45 P.M. she returned as tearoom proprietor Ellen Brown, otherwise known as the Hummerts' *Young Widder Brown*, with nary a chance to arrive at the altar. (Photofest)

Squad, Mr. Chameleon and *Mr. Keen, Tracer of Lost Persons*. By the same token, the principals of those mysteries frequently turned up in support roles and occasionally in the leads of Hummert washboard weepers that were aired in the daytime.

Another point in Frank and Anne Hummerts' favor concerned the Communist scare that swept the land during the late 1940s and early 1950s. Ad agencies, sponsors and networks panicked as a result. Any writer, actor or other industry professional suspected of ties to leftist causes was suddenly blacklisted — and out of work. Since overt accusations were seldom made, a defense was often impossible. But the Hummerts, seemingly alone in the industry, defied all of it. Going about their business as usual, they ignored the call to ferret out subversives and continued employing actors, announcers, directors and writers as if nothing was happening. If for no other reason than that, they were revered above most other producers. Their open-mindedness on that singular issue earned unswerving allegiance from many in the profession, both among Hummert employees and those who worked for other producers as well.

Brownlee Corrin was communication program chairman at Goucher College, Anne Schumacher Ashenhurst Hummert's alma mater. Corrin claimed that the Hummert serials "contributed to, as well as reflected, the lives of many microcosms and subsets of our society. They gave people a way to model themselves in anger, in joy, in passion. You couldn't write scripts for that without the richest kind of education and breadth of experience. Anne Hummert set the model.... It's hard to improve."[63]

One of their most durable radio actresses, Mary Jane Higby, acknowledged the Hummert contributions: "Unquestionably, they had a profound influence on the whole literature of soap opera. They, more than anyone else, determined the shape it took."[64]

The same leading lady recalled an illuminating perspective that she and her peers gained of the infamous recluses after many years of viewing the couple in a somewhat curious, possibly judgmental manner. Perhaps the pair had mellowed by then; perhaps, also, some hearts had thawed. Either way it appears that, on this occasion at least, these hirelings weren't kept at arm's length:

> In the late forties, the Hummerts put on two new evening shows and held the auditions each week themselves. [In all likelihood the actress is referring to *Mystery Theater* and *Mr. Chameleon*, both of which were summer 1948 acquisition-creations and drew heavily upon their matinee players.] For the first time we got to know these hitherto remote, but, as it developed, pleasant people. Their programs had led us to think of them as a somewhat

naïve pair from the Midwest. Now we learned that he had been one of the top copywriters in the nation, and that she had been a reporter on *The Paris Herald*. Hardly an unsophisticated background. We began to wonder if the naivete [*sic*] had not been on our side of the control-booth window.[65]

Anne Hummert was convinced that her task was to offer something to the listeners that they would not have had otherwise. "Worry, for women, is entertainment," she proclaimed. "The silence throbs ... the empty hours are endless ... then a friend in need is brought into the room by the turning of a dial. Misery loves company."[66] She countered: "Nobody can understand the phenomenal success of the soaps without knowing when they were born. It was during the Depression. The housewife was at home worrying about everything. Would her husband lose his job? Where was the family's next meal coming from? They found escape in the lives of the people on the soaps."[67]

An astute analyst decreed that — precisely *because* the Hummerts *did* comprehend the desires of the economically strapped housewife in the 1930s — they had little interest in characterization (as their major counterparts in producing radio serials did). "What they aimed for, always, was the spectacle and glamor [*sic*] beneath the plain words their writers wrote, bringing dreams to life for adult women much as comic-book heroes did for children."[68]

Another point can be made — one whose extent cannot be accurately measured, yet which left an indelible impression upon the industry: Frank and Anne Hummert infused their programs with common sense, basic efficiency, advertising expertise and production competence. *From them the radio serial gathered its purest and most durable traditions*, which often spilled over to their auxiliary forms of aural amusement. Without them, much of the success that those series enjoyed might never have been realized. In volume alone they were in a unique position to fashion discerning trends that could enhance the feasibility of broadcast programming. Their legacy includes a number of innovations that their peers often simply copied.

One of the traits both Hummerts displayed throughout their working careers was a fervent devotion to country a devotion reflected in their many radio features. Patriotism was a prominent theme exhibited unashamedly in a great host of their musical and juvenile adventure series. The concept also turned up, especially during the war years, in their matinee melodramas. As noted in chapter 2, during the Second World War Anne Hummert, in particular, devoted herself to a consulting mission on radio production for both the U.S. War and Treasury departments. Luther Sies expounded on their collective efforts:

> The Army found daytime serials useful for civilian morale purposes, because so many women had seen husbands, brothers and other male relatives and friends go off to war. Many women were left with little or no information about how their men were clothed and fed, or how they coped with the everyday routine activities in service. In order to remedy this lack of information, the War Department appointed daytime serial experts Frank and Anne Hummert to act as consultants, who would share their expertise with the government's Radio Branch.
>
> First, the Hummerts had informative morale messages inserted in many regular daytime serials in the speeches of the program's main characters. Second, they assisted in the development of new daytime serials with the express purpose of maintaining and improving civilian morale. One of the most successful daytime serials developed was *Chaplain Jim, USA*. This program in dramatic form answered letters from relatives seeking servicemen with whom they had lost contact. At other times the listeners' letters asked moral questions.[69]

A mythical religious chaplain played the central figure in *Chaplain Jim, U.S.A.* He was a compassionate young man assigned to both European and Pacific theaters during the Second World War. The Hummerts viewed their drama as appealing to a particular audience. According to Howard Blue, "They directed it at the little-educated, anxious ones who could not quite understand why 'Uncle Sam' had taken their loved ones and sent them to faraway places. Most of the young soldiers whose families were the show's target audience had never been outside the limits of their home towns or counties before being drafted. *Chaplain Jim* was designed to put their loved ones at ease. The notion that there was someone else to whom a troubled soldier could turn besides an often-unsympathetic sergeant was a source of comfort to mothers and wives."[70]

The Hummerts supplied a whole lot more to stimulate patriotism at home, however. Not only did they alter many of their soap opera plot lines to insert wartime themes, many of their leading characters were suddenly involved in the national effort in some direct way. Only one daytime radio serial figure actually died on the battlefield, Ma Perkins' only son, John. That unexpected incident prompted strong negative reaction from her devoted fans. It also allowed the widow who had comforted so many townsfolk in mythical Rushville Center to receive an outpouring of love and empathy from her people — including the nation — and to properly reflect on the challenge she faced, just as millions of wives, mothers, sisters and sweethearts were then doing.

In addition, a number of the Hummert protagonists made specific contributions to the war's homefront effort that served as a role model to other Americans. Stella Dallas, for one, did her part by laboring in a factory that made products for the defense lines. In so doing she may have implanted an idea in the hearts and minds of women in the listening audience who had time to spare for volunteer efforts while their men were away.

The kindly old New England bachelor banker, David Harum, who devoted time away from the office to a love of animals, relinquished his horse-trading and ledger sheets for a while to serve his country as the manager of a plant manufacturing secret weapons for the government. A cast member in a supporting role of *Front Page Farrell* also devoted skills to a wartime job. The fabled actor Larry Noble, infamous husband of Mary and matinee idol to millions of star-crossed women, answered the nation's call when asked to wear the uniform of a service branch. This temporarily altered the title of *Backstage Wife* to *Mary Noble, War Wife*.

Thus the Hummerts, in particular among the creators of daytime soap opera (because their volume of shows was so great), served their nation unselfishly during World War II. The assistance they rendered by inspiring thousands, if not millions, to sacrifice time, jobs, family and personal interests on the altar of homeland service is incalculable but enormously credible. Little public acclaim has been awarded their laudable efforts. Yet such factors demonstrate that — while operating under a perceived façade of grabbing everything for themselves — Frank and Anne Hummert possessed hearts of gold that beat unfalteringly for worthy causes in which they strongly believed. They were patently noble American patriots. Such actions seem important when assessing and appreciating the legacy and contributions of the pair.

Frank and Anne Hummerts' programs and characters, frequently held up to public scrutiny and ridicule of the day, were favorite subjects of many of that era's impressionists. Perhaps the best of the lot were the legendary comics Bob (Elliott) and Ray (Goulding). Radio comfortably suited Bob and Ray's style, and they had a field day poking fun at numerous archetypal entertainers. Their hilarious takeoffs have been preserved via the magic of tape recording so that successive generations may continue to laugh at their antics, including parodies of some well-recognized Hummert figures, several of them from Soapland.

Among their better impressions are those of *Mr. Treat, Chaser of Lost Persons*; *Mr. Trace, Keener Than Most Persons*; *Mary Backstayge, Noble Wife*; *Jack Armstrong, the All-American American*; and *Our Fella Thursday*. In occasional baseball matches pitting a couple of non–Hummert shows against one another, Bob and Ray called the play-by-play for games featuring *One Fella's Family* vs. *Pepper Young's* "group." The two humorists completed their lineups by borrowing players from the Hummert camp. Stella Dallas might be at first base for Pepper's team, while Lolly-Baby was out in left field (literally) with One Fella's clan. Helen Trent was pinch-hitting for Mary Noble because she was a fast runner. And (Just Plain) Bill Davidson could be called up from the bullpen to close out the game after Dr. Anthony Loring's successful starting pitches.

Bob and Ray had a ball (no pun intended), and so did their audiences. The Hummert guys and gals surfaced spasmodically in their satire, and those familiar with the Air Features shows undoubtedly caught it all and loved it. It was fun to make sport of what was— to still another segment of the population — hilarious of its own accord.

A dozen Hummert-inspired daytime dramas surpassed a decade on the air, a fairly good barometer of success as few serials achieved such longevity. With their number of broadcast years in parentheses, they were: *Backstage Wife* (23), *David Harum* (15), *Easy Aces* (13), *Front Page Farrell* (13), *Just Plain Bill* (23), *The Light of the World* (10), *Lorenzo*

Jones (18), *Ma Perkins* (27), *Our Gal Sunday* (22), *The Romance of Helen Trent* (27), *Stella Dallas* (18) and *Young Widder Brown* (18).[71] The 12 programs collectively aired an aggregate of 227 years, an average of 19 years per narrative, yet another impressive record in that genre.

Another eight Hummert-influenced serials aired at least five years each, indicating strong staying power in a breed accustomed to quick cancellations: *Amanda of Honeymoon Hill* (6), *Arnold Grimm's Daughter* (5), *Betty and Bob* (8), *John's Other Wife* (6), *Lone Journey* (6), *Lora Lawton* (7), *The Strange Romance of Evelyn Winters* (5) and *Valiant Lady* (9).

Ultimately, no matter what type of show they presented, Frank and Anne Hummert attempted to provide the sponsors with simple, inexpensive, unobjectionable programming concepts. Across the years, the bulk of their air time was sold to just two major underwriters, (surprisingly, neither of them a soapmaker): American Home Products (for such popular consumer brand names as Anacin pain reliever, Kolynos toothpaste, Bi-So-Dol analgesic, Freezone corn remover, Black Flag insect repellent, Aerowax and Olde English floor cleaners, Wizard room deodorizer, and many more healthcare and household commodities) and Sterling Drugs, Inc. (for many similar wares, including Bayer aspirin, Astring-O-Sol mouthwash, Double Danderine and Mulsified Coconut Oil shampoos, Energine cleaning fluid, Dr. Lyons' tooth powder, Phillips' Milk of Magnesia, Haley's M-O mineral oil laxatives and numerous comparable goods). Those sponsors often advertised their products interchangeably on the programs they purchased, shifting their healthcare aids from program to program every day.

American Home Products' arsenal across many years offered such favorites as *Mr. Keen, Tracer of Lost Persons*, *The Romance of Helen Trent*, *Our Gal Sunday*, *Just Plain Bill* and *Front Page Farrell*. Meanwhile, Sterling Drugs purchased an hour's block of time every afternoon over NBC that included *Backstage Wife*, *Stella Dallas*, *Lorenzo Jones* and *Young Widder Brown*. The firm also underwrote several Hummert-produced crime dramas (*Hearthstone of the Death Squad*, *Mark Sabre*, *Mr. Chameleon*, *Mystery Theater*) and all of their major musical features (*American Album of Familiar Music*, *American Melody Hour*, *Manhattan Merry-Go-Round*, *Waltz Time* and more).

As the 1950s arrived, television began to erode audiences for the nation's original medium that millions had relied upon for instant entertainment and information for decades. Looking for new horizons to conquer, advertisers began to shift their long-supportive budgets from an aural-only channel to the newer challenges of a visual medium. Radio networks, also simultaneously losing audience share, were faced with yet another dilemma: some of their most prestigious local affiliates threatened to end long-established contracts and associations if the big chains didn't reduce their programming schedules, permitting them to sell time more profitably to local advertisers in their respective markets.

Consequently, entire blocks of programs were cut from both the daytime and nighttime agendas, including many of those durable bastions of melodrama created by the Hummerts that had been staples in American households for many years. "What's to become of all my actors?" Anne Hummert plaintively inquired in a missive to Frankie Thomas (*Tom Corbett, Space Cadet*) as the pillars of an empire began to crumble.[72]

The Hummerts weren't interested in the tube; indeed, they could never replicate the simple dishpan dramas there that had enjoyed such loyal followings in the theater of the mind. By the mid–1950s virtually all of their series were gone. Only three in which they still maintained controlling interest —*Backstage Wife, Our Gal Sunday* and *The Romance of Helen Trent*— survived. The first two of those checked out on January 2, 1959, the last, on June 24, 1960, five months shy of "the day radio drama died," November 25, 1960, when all of the network serials were permanently banished from the ether.

Ahhh! But while it lasted, through their matinee melodramas the Hummerts offered satisfying amusement to millions of individuals who tuned in across three decades, while also simultaneously providing steady employment opportunities to thousands of gifted artists. In all, the pair developed, supervised or influenced no less than 61 separate soap operas that were primarily targeted at the American housewife — representing 49 percent of their total production output. No one has equaled their harvest. And it's doubtful that anyone ever shall.

124

7

THE TROIKA

It's an undisputed fact that Frank and Anne Hummert were the foremost architects of daytime serialized melodrama that appeared on U.S. radio in the 1930s, 1940s and 1950s. No one has come close to reaching their dynamic output. They produced wares in such a volume that will probably never be equaled. The pair infused the continued story with a visibility that gave it instant recognition, markedly distinguishing it from other fictionalized genres.

Like it or not, drama by installment caught hold of the contemporary American homemaker, who heretofore was accustomed to performing the grunge chores with little or no chance for distraction and amusement. Rapidly finding a receptive audience in her, ongoing narratives became a fixture in the housewife's home. And more than anybody else, the Hummerts assumed the credit for that development.

They were not alone, however, in creating the daytime serial. Scores of other individuals contributed to the surfeit of more than 200 separate quarter-hour stories that were carried on the ether by the national chains during the medium's golden age. Many of those dramas strongly resembled one another, as they bore comparable themes, characters, locations, titles and writing styles. In addition, a handful of firms underwrote the bulk of those fabricated tales; in many cases they were soapmakers, giving rise to the "soap opera" label that was applied to the surplus of shows they sponsored.

Sometimes the creators, writers and producers worked on more than one show. Occasionally they were responsible for several. In a very few cases they were able to raise the literary content and production values of the genre. Yet, more often than not, the serials were permitted to wallow in matinee goo, unable to rise above a basic level of mediocrity. It appeared, in fact, that the serials that were universally acclaimed for reaching the highest levels of quality often stood alone, frequently distinguished by the fact that their originators focused upon just one, or only a limited number of, creations.

Sandra Michael, for instance, penned the only daytime drama (*Against the Storm*) to earn the distinguished Peabody Award for literary excellence. With her concentration there, she is known to have contributed to the writing of but two other serials during her career. Those who produced fewer dramas seemed to have better chances to get it right than those whose quivers were full of arrows.

If one accepts that hypothesis, then the natural assumption is that producers like Frank and Anne Hummert routinely offered inferior merchandise. The profusion of their wares alone suggests that they couldn't possibly have given the tender loving care required by three score or more serial dramas— dozens of them airing concurrently — that authors like, for example, Addy Richton and Lynn Stone could. Richton and Stone who sometimes combined their names under the pseudonym Adelaide Marston, were responsible for writing *Hilltop House* and contributing to only a couple of other serials. Industry insiders regarded their work on *Hilltop House* as of superior literary quality.

When that level of achievement was challenged and about to be diminished following an internal transition that shifted the series to another advertising agency (the agency just coming aboard expressed an immediate commitment to lower production costs over and against literary quality), producer Edwin Wolfe responded by pulling the drama off the air. He said he would rather do that than to dilute the high standards the program had achieved. Not many serials reached comparable lofty plateaus, and fewer still sustained such unqualified support. Of course, it was easier to react in that manner when the focus was on just one or two dramatic programs than it would have been with a warehouse full of them.

In one sense, Frank and Anne Hummert had no serious competitors in generating daytime dramatic programming. Anne

7. The Troika

Hummert, riding herd over the empire's plethora of serialized fiction, was indisputably the Queen Bee of the genre. Under her, scores of worker bees dutifully performed their tasks. And from that hive a brand of narrative programming emanated that was repeated many times on their myriad classic daytime features.

But their formula contrasted sharply with the dramatic creations of two other high profile, inexhaustible daytime programming designers: Irna Phillips and Elaine Carrington. If the Hummerts had any potential rivals in the business of radio soap opera they were clearly Phillips and Carrington. (One wag called the three camps "the daytime-tragedy troika."[1]) Both of those women developed multiple serialized sagas and indelibly put their own labels on the strain. Each crafted independent methods of churning out reams of scripts in unbelievably brief periods of time. Their inspired dialogue contributed heavily to the substance of soap opera and encouraged some of their peers to adapt or copy their literary techniques.

Soap opera was clearly the domain of Frank and Anne Hummert, more so than any other field. But in truth they didn't own that dominion exclusively. As this chapter progresses, the influences of Phillips and Carrington on the daytime drama will be explored. Their individual styles will be compared and contrasted with those of the Hummerts. The trio of suppliers will be examined for their differences, strengths, weaknesses and impact on the genre. In the end, the reasons why the Hummerts proliferated to a far greater extent than the others will become evident.

Before continuing, a brief introduction of these two important figures that also made indelible marks upon radio soap opera is in order.

In the summer of 1930, Irna Phillips, still in her twenties (and for several years a teacher in a Dayton, Ohio, normal school) returned to her native Chicago seeking seasonal work between academic terms. One of the doors she knocked on was that of radio station WGN, a Midwest powerhouse whose regional scope extended far beyond the confines of the Windy City. Harboring a longtime interest in performing, it became her good fortune to be accepted by the station as an actress. She initially appeared by herself, then with Ireene [sic] Wicker, another schoolmarm-turned-thespian, in various dialoguing exchanges.

As previously noted in chapter 6, Phillips created the very first daytime serial, *Painted Dreams*, which debuted over WGN on October 20, 1930.[2] Phillips would soon become embroiled in a legal quagmire over ownership rights to that drama, a controversy that would drag on in the courts for nearly a decade. While she lost the ultimate battle, her indomitable spirit marched resolutely onward, displaying little evidence that she had been sidetracked for even a moment. The experience turned her into an astute businesswoman just like Anne Hummert. From that day forward she established her rights to the material she created, and persisted in that vein throughout the remainder of her career.[3] And, like her counterparts, it made her into a very affluent woman.

In time, Phillips, a spinster, would create no less than nine radio serials (*Painted Dreams, Today's Children, The Guiding Light, Road of Life, Woman in White, The Right to Happiness, Lonely Women, Masquerade, The Brighter Day*) while influencing yet another (*Young Doctor Malone*). Of the three major suppliers of radio soap opera, only Phillips would succeed in television — and do so in a powerful way. She is credited with authoring or co-authoring eight TV incarnations (*These Are My Children, The Guiding Light, The Brighter Day, As the World Turns, Another World, Days of Our Lives, Our Private World, Love Is a Many Splendored Thing*). One astute authority fondly referred to *The Guiding Light*—currently in its seventh decade on the air at this writing — as "the longest story ever told."[4]

In addition, through protégés her ideas appeared in no less than five other television serials (*One Life to Live, All My Children, Loving, The Young and the Restless, The Bold and the Beautiful*). When she died on December 23, 1973, Phillips left a legacy that influenced serialized melodrama in two mediums. Some of the precepts practiced in the modern era stem directly from ideas concocted by this creative genius.

In light of the Hummert production factory that issued 10,000 or more new scripts during its peak years— relying on scores of individuals to turn out that exalted quantity — Irna Phillips pursued a much less complicated method of scriptwriting: she wrote them all herself — for a while, at least. *Every* word. Impossible? Actually, no. In the beginning, when she had only a few shows on the air, she typed those scripts

herself, using a manual typewriter and carbon paper
to make enough copies for
every cast member in a single typing.

Numerous stories have
circulated over the years,
and are believed to be true,
that when changes were
made in her scripts during
rehearsals—just before air
time — Phillips raced to the
typewriter to hammer out
corrected pages for everybody. Sometimes she fed
new dialogue to actors while
a show was *on the air*, just
moments before those lines
would be spoken live!

Later, when Phillips
expanded her repertoire of
daytime serials, it became
impossible for her to type
enough scripts to provide for
every show. This was no
problem for the spirited Irna
Phillips, however. She merely
acquired a dictating machine
and *said* those important
lines of dialogue.[5] Clerical

Shown in this 1935 portrait, Irna Phillips is
credited with airing the very first soap
opera with the inception of her *Painted
Dreams* over a Chicago station on October
20, 1930. While her creations would never
begin to approach the volume of Frank and
Anne Hummert, Phillips left a mark on the
genre with a style that focused on character development and the professional as
central figures in her dramas. (Photofest)

workers turned her dictation into completed scripts. In the early radio
years she dictated as many as six scripts daily, amounting to 60,000
words weekly and three million words annually. Phillips was depicted
as a good storyteller but not an especially effective dialoguer. As a
result, her performers often attempted to rewrite many of her lines.

Still later, when even dictating the lines became too burdensome,
Phillips acquiesced. Admitting her personal limitations to herself,

though never defeat, she hired a group of nameless scribes to derive some of the verbiage that she previously had been accustomed to writing.

Does that sound familiar? Yet there are at least two consequentially distinguishing factors that separated her practice from that of the infamous Air Features assembly line.

For one, and in spite of some reviewers' criticisms (which may have been directed at soap opera universally), the dialogue was still a decisive cut above that of most of the Hummert shows. This was true when Irna Phillips wrote it and when she hired a few wordsmiths to do it for her. The triteness found on Air Features programs was seldom demonstrated to any appreciable extent on Phillips' series.

Secondly (and the first point may be logically linked to this one), Irna Phillips compensated her scribes much better than Air Features ever did. Typically, a Phillips writer could anticipate $100 per quarter-hour script ($500 weekly), a far cry from the well-documented $25 per show ($125 weekly) that Hummert writers received for similar efforts. That alone makes it appear that working for Phillips could be far more attractive to scriptwriters seeking employment than toiling for the Hummerts. That includes the later years when Air Features increased its top wages to $35 and even $50 an episode, primarily the result of improved American Federation of Television and Radio Artists union contracts.

Meanwhile, Phillips herself wasn't going to the poorhouse. After paying all of the production costs associated with her dramas, as an independent producer she reportedly netted at least $260,000 annually from her radio ventures.[6] By the time she got into TV that increased many fold. There were certainly no paupers among creators who reached her level of success.

Recall that, from his earliest inspiration about dramas by installment, Frank Hummert wondered if women might be amenable to audio serialized melodrama that had provided a captivating diversion to many through the popularity of pulp fiction in the 1920s. It turns out that Elaine Sterne Carrington was one of those scribes who published a lot of the literature upon which Hummert's notion was based.

A native New Yorker, Carrington, like her contemporaries, was well educated. She married an attorney and was the mother of two. She earned a noteworthy reputation as a short story writer, seeing her material appear in numerous widely circulated slick magazines, including *Collier's, Good Housekeeping, Harper's, Ladies' Home Journal, Pictorial Review, Redbook, The Saturday Evening Post* and *Woman's Home Companion.* Furthermore, she wrote a successful Broadway play, *Nightstick,* which enjoyed a fair run. The production was twice turned into screenplays, each time under the title *Alibi.*

Her foray into serial writing at age 40 was something of a fluke, however. While waiting one day under the marquis of the NBC building for a rainstorm to let up, she struck up a conversation with the chain's head of program continuity. He encouraged her to try writing a radio play. The year was 1932. Her effort turned into a subsequent request that she write a serialized drama, to be aired in primetime. The result was *Red Adams,* forerunner (after several recurring name changes) of one of serialdom's most popular daytime features, *Pepper Young's Family.* That soap opera enjoyed an aggregate air life of 27 years.

Carrington was not done by any means, however. The success of that feature awakened other dreams in her. In time she would bring to the ether an additional quartet of daytime dramas: *Marriage for Two, Rosemary, Trouble House* and *When*

Elaine Sterne Carrington imbued the daytime serial with strong characterization that majored on common people. She broke into radio after success in writing fictional tales for women's magazines. Carrington touted a somewhat irreverent attitude and — unlike her creative rivals — literally dictated every word of her scripts. (Courtesy of Library of American Broadcasting, University of Maryland)

a Girl Marries. She experienced a failed attempt with a single TV serial, *Follow Your Heart,* in the early 1950s. That show's story line closely paralleled the early scripts of her very successful *When a Girl Marries.* When Carrington died on May 4, 1958, the writing of her surviving drama, *Pepper Young's Family,* passed to her son and daughter, who continued churning out scripts until the narrative finally departed the airwaves eight months later.

Carrington's methodology was never that of the Hummerts, nor that of Irna Phillips, at least not beyond Phillips' earliest years. Carrington dictated *every word* of *every character* of *every show* until she died. And she acted out every role as she spoke her figures' lines into dictating equipment. After clerical help transcribed it, she personally made the cuts and revisions rather than relying on an editor to do it.

Of the three leading suppliers of radio soap opera, most critics agree that the serials of Elaine Carrington achieved a level of enhanced writing quality that was seldom witnessed in the dramas of her two nearest rivals. One observer termed her "the most literate of all soap writers."[7] Another noted that when Carrington expanded the number of shows for which she was writing, the additions "did not appear to dilute the quality of her product."[8] Yet another classified her *Pepper Young's Family* as "one of the best scripted soaps"[9] The distinction that separated Carrington from the others clearly arose because she lavished tender loving care on every word of dialogue she uttered. With her, there were no intermediaries to be concerned about. She wrote — *said* — it all. And for years it showed in the performances the listeners heard.

At about 10 o'clock every Monday morning Carrington would stretch out on a large davenport at her home near the waters of Long Island Sound and begin dictating. Her weekly volume exceeded 38,000 words — more than two billion words annually! Working around the clock, at times she talked past midnight. Unless unusual circumstances prevailed, she finished a week's work by Thursday night and recuperated for three days, normally relaxing with her family. She seldom listened to playbacks of her dictation.

Only rarely did she hear one of her own shows. Yet she loved to drop in on rehearsals unannounced. Radio serial heroine Mary Jane Higby recalled that it wasn't unusual for the notorious author to

7. The Troika

unhesitatingly brush past studio warning signs flashing the cautionary "On the Air" message. To no one in particular she would bellow: "Are you all on the air?" Higby observed, "She just didn't give a damn!" On those occasions, Carrington went to the mat for her dialogue, defending it against any alterations a cast member or director might request.

Carrington possessed a mischievous, gregarious personality, industry insiders allowed. She dotted her writing with humor. She slipped double entendres into her scripts to see if she could get away with them. At one and the same time she could confound, mesmerize and incense her associates. Occasionally she showed up at public events wearing lace and old tennis shoes. She chain-smoked cigarettes, enjoyed risqué stories and appeared oblivious to what anybody thought. In that regard, she could have been a protégé of the Hummerts.

This one-of-a-kind author was no dummy, however. Perhaps as a result of Irna Phillips widely publicized, precedent-setting legal battle over rights to material Phillips created, Carrington retained ownership of *all* her serials. Like her counterparts, she too became fabulously wealthy. By the late 1940s her annual earnings were reportedly nearly a quarter of a million dollars. (Because Carrington was strictly a writer and did not *produce* her own shows, as did the Hummerts and Phillips, she was the highest paid *writer* of soap operas.[10]) Her achievements allowed her to maintain three domiciles: a New York penthouse apartment, a waterfront estate on Long Island and another residence in Florida. The high income, much of it from her efforts for Procter & Gamble shows (including *Pepper Young's Family* and *Rosemary*), entitled her to dub her Bridgehampton riverside retreat "the house that Camay built." For most of the years that *Pepper Young's Family* was on the air, in fact, its commercials exclusively featured Camay, "the soap of beautiful women."

Now for a comparison of the differences in writing styles employed by soap opera's three major suppliers.

The Hummert mode has been carefully delineated at various points throughout this book. One pundit conceded, "The Hummerts had a formula that was surefire: appeal to the lowest common denominator, make it clear, grab the heartstrings, and reap the rewards."[11]

133

To carry it out, Frank and Anne Hummert fashioned an assembly-line approach to producing drama that would, by sheer volume, readily surpass anybody else's attempts to match their output. From their ivory tower they handed down basic plotlines to scores of minions who fleshed out their instructions into finished scripts, and did so speedily and for minimal compensation. According to many pundits, the dialogue they created was some of the most hackneyed ever to reach the air. One of the most respected researchers of vintage radio, John Dunning, gamely disparaged their efforts, summarizing it as little more than "jerky, obvious, and corny melodramas."[12]

In the previous chapter we learned that the Hummerts possessed a proclivity for a sequence-driven narrative. That method consisted of integrating a handful of ongoing figures with a few new characters who were introduced to the story line for a specified period of time. When the situations involving the latter group were resolved, those temporary personalities were banished and a new group of malefactors were ushered in. The formula was clearly evident on nearly every Hummert washboard weeper. Over the years hundreds of such interactive exchanges were broadcast for a period of a few weeks or, more likely, a few months. Ratings often determined how much blood could be squeezed from a particular turnip. If the audience numbers sagged, a sequence could be brought to an abrupt end within a few days; but if the show prospered, the action would be extended and milked for all it was worth.

There were other traits that trademarked Hummert serials. Some were eventually borrowed by other producers and resurfaced elsewhere. Frank and Anne Hummert are duly credited with originating the "lead-in" to serialized drama, for instance. An interlocutor set the scene at the start of each new chapter by offering lengthy details of previous action. A "recap" dramatization usually followed in which one or more figures recalled developments, dialogue or personal reflections of what had transpired on another day. This allowed the homebodies to go about their household pursuits without missing a beat. It virtually made certain that they were on board for the scene or scenes to follow.

The Hummert theory was that everything should be repeated often to assist any fan having missed part or all of an episode to be able to plug right back into the drama upon returning to it. This, of course, had the additional effect of slowing down the action in their story lines to a bare crawl, thereby giving the skeptics a slow-moving target to shoot at.

There was also that inviolable Hummert dictate that clarity of speech was the essential ingredient of every program. "Their preoccupation with clarity gave rise to soul-searching throughout the field," related actress Mary Jane Higby.[13] During each scene no overlapping conversations could occur, nor could music or previously unapproved sounds be inserted under the dialogue. Not ever. And characters had to identify themselves and those to whom they were speaking frequently to avoid even the mere possibility that listeners—presumably distracted by matters requiring their full attention at home—could momentarily forget who was speaking to whom. As seen in several examples, there was just no way that such confusion could ever occur on a Hummert serial.

Realism was in short supply in their soap operas. Many of the things that happened there simply didn't occur to anyone in normal life. Raymond W. Stedman, an astute observer of the form, commented

> Radio writers learned quickly that random sounds, unless explained, usually confused or annoyed listeners. Thus, the isolation from life's sights and sounds, seldom noticed in stage plays because of their short duration, merely appeared to be greater in serials, which continued for years and years. There may be reason to wonder why Helen Trent never met the milkman. Yet serial creators well knew that adding a touch of realism by having the deliveryman stick his head in the door or having a chair squeak in the background also meant hiring an additional actor or paying a sound-effects man. For financial as well as artistic reasons they put their characters on milk-free diets and kept them out of rickety furniture.
>
> In over-all analysis, *it was not the absence of the ordinary that interfered most noticeably with the illusion of reality in the daytime serial drama. Rather it was the presence of the extraordinary* [italics mine]. Serials were filled with court trials, amnesia victims, lost mates, and scheming criminals far in excess of the number a normal person might expect to encounter in a similar period of years—or in a lifetime. Serial characters had

unusual susceptibilities to strange diseases and afflictions, none of which the ordinary person had reason to fear.[14]

All of the above was certainly true of the Hummert dishpan dramas. If misery beyond any semblance of veracity failed to afflict a Hummert hero or heroines, the show probably was not one of their humorless melodrama; more likely, it was one drawn from a comic persuasion.

Meanwhile, the Hummerts' competition held other ideas, some of which differed significantly from the Hummert formula.

For one, Phillips placed strong emphasis on characterization in all of her serials. (It was a stance that was also firmly espoused by Elaine Carrington, as shall be presently confirmed.) Claimed Phillips: "The important factor ... is that the story grow out of characters rather than story superimposed upon characters. [The Hummerts were guilty of weighing down their central figures with heavy plotting.] This I have found to be most successful, realistic and believable. We do what we do because we are what we are."[15] An informed pundit, familiar with Phillips' obsessive bent toward realism, conjectured: "The success of Irna Phillips' serials came from her devotion to reality and from her careful understanding of the women who comprised her audience."[16]

Over time, little by little, Phillips revealed innate details about the people in her stories, allowing her audiences to identify with those individuals. A couple of her subjects might spend an entire quarter-hour on radio dialoguing with one another. That is something that ostensibly never happened on a Hummert serial, despite those producers' intense efforts to hold down costs by reducing the number of players appearing in each installment.

It's reliably reported that Phillips—certainly as shrewd a businesswoman as Anne Hummert—soon realized that not only could the characterization be advanced by such lengthy chats but also her bottom line would be significantly enhanced in doing so. The technique became a staple in her modus operandi. Whereas the Hummerts limited their dialoguers to inserting a maximum of 25 speaking roles in their serials over any five-day period, Phillips usually got by with a substantially smaller number, perhaps no more than 15. Applying her simple blueprint, consider how much Frank and Anne could have saved!

Furthermore, Phillips was the first serial writer to focus on the career professional as a protagonist. Such figures as clergymen, physicians, nurses, attorneys and others of like persuasions dotted the landscape of her drainboard dramas. (She maintained, for instance, "The pathway of a physician is the road of life," the premise and title of one of her most durable features.[17])

Unlike the Hummerts, who wanted their narratives to primarily reflect the ordinary citizens that the middle class could readily identify with, Phillips insisted that the professional crowd made far more *interesting* subjects for her stories. In pursuing that route she capitalized on an area that many other radio producers simply missed, intentionally or otherwise. It probably can be safely stated now that a preponderance of such skilled artisans in today's daytime television serials emanated from her astute perception of seven decades ago.

Parenthetically, Phillips may be also credited with another concept that was to profoundly influence the soap operas currently aired. When she became convinced that televised serials were the wave of the future, she relentlessly lobbied the networks and sponsors to increase the traditional quarter-hour drama to a half-hour show. It took two years before both CBS and Procter & Gamble finally either grew weary of her persistence or were won over and finally gave in. On April 2, 1956, they instituted not one but two 30-minute serials on the same day—*As the World Turns* and *The Edge of Night*. The new practice eventually led to the hour-long daytime drama, which Phillips championed. In time she would be acclaimed "the single most important influence on television soaps."[18] Years later there is still little reason to doubt it.

Phillips' strong accent on character development opposed story fantasy or "common heroes"—concepts that the Hummerts embraced in their serials. (Think *Stella Dallas, Lorenzo Jones, Just Pain Bill, David Harum, Ma Perkins* and a myriad of other Air Features weepers that fit those dynamics.) Phillips' stories had unique qualities in which strong personalities were placed within credible situations. The essential distinctions (and strengths) of her plots were in how those mortals acted—and reacted—in their environments. More often than not, the plausibility factor in her serials was high, and was rooted in Phillips' realistic dialogue and her subjects' literal common sense. Their conduct and speech were often a cut above that of characters in many Hummert serials. This, together with strong acting, offered a winning combination.

As mentioned previously, Phillips also possessed a good grasp of who comprised her audience and what was important to them. The primary craving of women, she maintained, was to create a warm and protected family—"to build securely for herself a haven, which means a husband, a family, friends, and a mode of living all wrapped up neatly and compactly into a tight little ball with the woman as the busy center of the complete, secure little world."[19] It was out of that context that her plots were developed. Very real evil and other unsteadying forces railed against a woman's tight, secure universe, attempting to penetrate it. It was up to her to defend it against all threats that might destroy it.

Robert LaGuardia, a prominent student of the genre, claims that the amnesia attacks eventually adopted by almost all serial writers originated, ironically, with Irna Phillips. In those silly diversions protagonists could wander for days, weeks or longer (Lorenzo Jones did so for three years), asking, "Who am I? Where am I?"—in most cases simply to juice up the show's ratings. There were times when several serials simultaneously featured an amnesiac, a bit much to ask loyal audiences to swallow. Air Features segued into this memory morass with some regularity in its multiple dramas. LaGuardia lamented: "Even Irna was not above Hummert tricks when they suited her purposes."[20] If indeed she was responsible for this madness, it seemed somewhat out of character for the doyenne of the daytime serial.

Another critic, assessing Phillips' work, declared: "The writing, direction and playing are in the most intense terms. The tone is lugubrious and the pace is torpid. There is never the slightest suggestion of lightness or enjoyment, but the emphasis is constantly on emotional contortion, and mental anguish."[21]

In 1943 yet another pundit testified: "Over the last few years, Miss Phillips' stories have contained a variety of brutal physical situations, divorces, illegitimate births, suggestions of incest and even murders."[22] While her tone and pace might have remained "lugubrious and torpid," it was obvious Phillips was challenging reality head-on, demonstrably running well ahead of her peers via some major human issues of conflict and debate.

Finally, still another source characterized her serials as both "vehicles of evil" and "documents sincerely devoted to public welfare."[23] With Irna Phillips it appeared that every fan could find something in which she could take refuge.

Meanwhile, radio historiographer Raymond W. Stedman observed that one of Phillips' contemporaries, Elaine Sterne Carrington, gained an understanding of soap opera out of her experiences with slick magazines. This placed her "one step away from the domestic novels that provided the frame of reference for some of her associates," he said, in what could be considered to be a veiled swipe at the Hummerts.[24] He noted that the tribulations experienced by characters in Carrington serials "were troubles which might come to a family living on this planet and that characters resembling real people were facing them."[25] Another media author opined: "Carrington's unique ability to make listeners feel as if they were hearing actual conversations instead of radio plays made her shows immensely popular."[26]

Characterization was as important to Carrington as it was to Phillips. The former mocked the Hummerts' preoccupation with story lines and cliffhangers (big climaxes at the ends of episodes—particularly those aired on Fridays—to prompt the fans to return for Monday's chapter). "The establishment of character is far more important than plot," assured Carrington. "The story must be written about people you come to know and like and believe in. What happens to them is of secondary importance. Once characters are firmly established and entrenched in the hearts of listeners, the latter will have to tune in to find out what becomes of the characters because of what they feel for them."[27]

She also took a poke at Phillips' penchant for favoring the upper crust (e.g., the professionals) in her washboard weepers, whom Phillips considered "more interesting" as subjects than mere common folk. Carrington theorized: "Stories about middle class families have the widest appeal. People can identify the characters with their own friends and relatives. Simple, homely little episodes are those which happen in the listeners' homes, too, and they understand them and love them."[28]

Recall that Frank Hummert insisted that their serials were "successful stories about unsuccessful people." He explained that by "unsuccessful" they meant only that their characters weren't wealthy people. "In other than a material sense, they were by no means failures," said he. "They may be very successful in their family life or in the way they manage to help their neighbors and their friends. [Think *Ma Perkins, David Harum* and *Just Plain Bill.*] Our stories are about the everyday doings of plain, everyday people — stories that can be understood and appreciated on Park Avenue and on the prairie," Hummert attested.[29] (A pair of pundits couldn't resist a jab at his assessment: "The Hummerts' own story did not deal with unsuccessful people. Indeed, it was the archetypical [*sic*] American success story. Within a few years of their meeting, they were running a large and enormously profitable mass-production manufacturing operation.")[30]

Although historian Stedman acknowledged Carrington's efforts weren't literary masterworks" ("no drama heard five days a week every week could be"[31]), he postulated that had there not been such a proliferation of daytime serials in the late 1930s, "and if one serial factory had not been in such a dominant position" (a pretty clear reference to Air Features), the quality of soap opera would have been greatly improved.[32]

The point is just this: Carrington inculcated her serials with big helpings of realism, including live-action situations and relevant banter. Many others didn't. Frank Hummert's protestations to the contrary, his and Anne's serials invariably found a resting place in the latter camp and put down permanent roots.

Unlike her contemporaries, Carrington also populated her serials with younger personalities. She based her initial drama, *Red Adams*, on this thesis: "It ... is, the story of an average American family doing their darndest to give every advantage to a son and daughter, to understand them and encourage them and correct their faults. It seemed to me that in this time of flux, the only thing stable was American family life itself. And that is what I built the story around — the best family life I could possibly offer my public."[33]

The fact that she was personally in the throes of rearing a son and daughter was anything but coincidental. "All I knew about was an American family, such as I was trying to raise myself," she allowed.[34] Thus, an overabundance of younger figures turned up in her dramas. She liked them and obviously identified with them. That may be one of the reasons why she could get away with sprinkling big helpings of colloquialisms into her dramas' conversations.

There were occasions of genuine laughter (or at least an occasional chuckle) in her dialogue, too, something noticeably lacking on most Air Features shows. "Programs created in serial factories seldom contained much humor," an observant scholar attested. "Humor is hard to write and requires a reasonable degree of freedom. For dialoguers it was almost beyond reach. Their efforts to supply occasional moments of comedy relief on order were painfully apparent."[35] Carrington, however, seemed to handle it with grace, making it a natural part of her subjects' conversations.

She further prided herself on the romantic scenes that appeared with some frequency in her story lines. Staunchly she defended them, refusing to allow any alteration. Often she would dot them with such demonstrative lines as, "I'd like to give you the whole world as a bauble to swing at your wrist." At least two of her three most popular narratives, *Rosemary* and *When a Girl Marries*, were launched as love stories, a theme obviously close to Carrington's heart. While the shows dipped into all sorts of diversionary substances later in their runs, both maintained affection and matrimony as their centerpiece. The "effusive romantic quality" found in her serials was "one of the most striking aspects" they established, a reviewer declared.[36]

Simply stated, Carrington's serials dealt with "the frustrations, heartbreaks, kindliness, nastiness, cruelties and tragedies of the middle class," insisted one pundit.[37]

Carrington demonstrated her feisty and rebellious nature when she borrowed an oft-repeated Hummert theme — that of the girl from the sticks who marries an unstable man of prosperity, culture, education, influence and social status — and turned it 180 degrees. In *When a Girl Marries* it was the lawyer's daughter, the town's leading practitioner in his profession, who married the boy from the wrong side of the tracks. Not surprisingly, completing the makeover of a well-used theme, he was about as unstable as any man she could find. Carrington was obviously enchanted by the thought of being considered a maverick, and looked for opportunities to continually prove it.

She flaunted her ability to appall any agency or network brass that might try to muzzle her. Once Benton and Bowles, the advertising agency that produced *When a Girl Marries*, constructed an elaborate, expensive papier-mâché model of Stanwood, the fictitious hamlet in which the show's action took place. They invited Carrington in to view it. Agency officials pointed out that the model would help them instantly realize if any positional errors occurred in her scripts. Carrington gave tacit approval of the concept and moved on. That wasn't the end of it, however. Soon the male lead purchased a farm in nearby Beechwood (notably, a town *without* a papier-mâché layout). He abruptly moved his family to Beechwood, and Carrington persevered without being encumbered by a model town!

Turning to more practical concerns, one authority pinpointed the real reason for the success of daytime melodrama. Formula and style were related only indirectly: "Despite the obvious and important contributions to the soap opera form made by Irna Phillips, Frank and Anne Hummert, and, in the television era, Agnes Nixon [a Phillips protégé], it is clear that the idea of presenting continuing stories focusing upon domestic concerns on daytime radio was the result of the conjunction of corporate desire to reach a particular audience (women eighteen to forty-nine) and broadcasters' need to fill the daytime hours with revenue-generating programming. The soap opera represents a form of cultural production that has been fully penetrated by capital since the moment of its conception, a form driven and sustained by corporate imperatives."[38] That observation puts the genre's success in a perspective that can be quickly grasped. The methods of achieving an inflated bottom line would appear to have been immaterial to the industry's economists. All that truly mattered to them was getting there.

The disparities between the writing styles of the three most prolific suppliers of radio soap opera — Elaine Carrington, Frank and Anne Hummert, Irna Phillips — have offered a fascinating investigation in contrasts. On occasion, two of the three were aligned in thought and practice. Together, allowing for the fact that the Hummerts and Phillips collaborated on at least two serials, the troika was responsible for influencing no less than 75 radio soap operas — about a third of all the dramas known to air in the daylight hours.

Each member of this triumvirate developed an independent method of churning out large volumes of scripted melodramas quickly, while placing his or her own stamp upon the genre. Serious scholars of the form habitually observe their marked differences in style.

A modern media communications instructor, John Leasure, recently said, "Each had a distinctive style and yet, in his or her own way, defined the medium of soap opera even today. I think shows like *General Hospital* and *Days of Our Lives* and even *Passions* follow the Hummert style of plot-heavy story; while the Agnes Nixon-William Bell shows [major TV soap opera producers] follow Irna's family-based formula, with Carrington's influences seen in individual story lines as opposed to whole show concepts."[39] The guiding hands of all of the breed's originators, it seems, still can be viewed today.

Regarding the contributions of Frank and Anne Hummert (particularly as it relates to radio melodrama), it certainly is clear that their work was often held up to public scrutiny and ridicule.[40] That includes reactions not only by professional reviewers, historiographers, academicians and literary critics, but by their own peers as well.

There are some obvious reasons why: with so many voicing disdain over their trite plots, implausible situations and hackneyed dialogue, the Hummert dramas were sitting ducks. If anyone supplied the pundits— most of whom routinely scoffed at serialized melodrama as an inferior form of amusement anyway — with the ammunition that Air Features' assembly line did, the guilty party had best run for cover or be prepared for the ensuing barrage. With its almost universal emphasis on quantity as opposed to quality, the Hummert machine had a huge bullseye drawn on it.

A second reason for its vulnerability is tied directly to that enormous production volume: with so much territory to defend, Air Features dramas were mercilessly exposed to the crossfire.

That the Hummerts' most formidable challengers in manufacturing soap opera attempted to separate their own dramas from those of the masters of the craft speaks volumes. Carrington and Phillips both infused huge doses of reality into their daytime serials. One centered her stories on the same commoners that attracted the Hummerts; the other often idolized a more cultured, erudite class of subjects. Characterization was all-important to both women, something of little consequence to the Hummert dialoguers.

Despite those major differences, each camp offered several long-running serials that widely appealed to the masses tuning in to their radios every day. The ratings invariably were the ultimate test. They indicated that there wasn't a right or a wrong way to produce melodrama. Instead, there were different strokes for different folks. And between Carrington, the Hummerts and Phillips, just about every soap opera–lovers' tastes could be satisfied.

8

THE MOGULS OF
MELODRAMA

It should come as no surprise whatsoever that Frank and Anne Hummert — the legendary, celebrated, inexhaustible architects of serialized daytime melodrama — plunged headlong into nurturing still more thriving programming developments in the music, crime drama and juvenile adventure categories. As has been repeatedly observed, they were two highly motivated workaholics who utterly focused their entire beings upon a single spectacular mission: *to produce radio entertainment for a variety of listener tastes with the intention of satisfying a broad spectrum of the potential audience, and to do so at the least possible capital outlay, thereby appreciably enhancing their own bottom lines.* If there was any rationale for their combined efforts that radically departed from that, this author admits to having missed it.

Coupled with their passionate drive for achievement, the Hummerts were extremely fortunate to be endowed with indispensable business proficiencies that complemented the innate creative abilities they both possessed. Furthermore, they had the connections *and* the resources that could turn their dreams into realities. Only very rarely have two individuals been as extraordinarily blessed with as much practical raw material as that held by the Hummerts when launching a mission of such enormous magnitude. In addition to what they had been given already, they were also abundantly endowed with the gift of perfect timing. That permitted them to combine those critical circumstances to their ultimate advantage. With all those factors working in their favor, they were in a strategic position to pursue their aims expeditiously.

The result of their maximized efforts brought immense pleasure to millions of fans that never actually heard their voices nor saw their faces but merely recognized their names. And among *their* rewards, the Hummerts became millionaires many times over. It was the classic win-win situation for both audiences and producers. In the time frame in which they persevered, there were simply few broadcasting executives with greater opportunities or more striking achievements.

To date, no less than 125 separate programs have been identified which Frank and Anne Hummert either wholly or partially controlled. That figure exceeds by almost 100 the number of features that their closest competitors provided. The couple originated or adapted nearly all of those entries while simultaneously serving in the strategic capacity of owners-producers of the vast majority of them.

There were also instances in which they influenced a program's content or direction while supplying expertise as an advisor to other show operatives. There were still other times when they supervised or packaged a series for yet other radio executives who sought to capitalize on the Hummerts' competencies in advertising.

Sometimes a client, aware of the Hummerts' sterling reputation in that domain, requested that they inaugurate marketing schemes for a given series. The Hummerts furnished a program's commercial content, created mailhook premiums (typically trinkets offered for a dime and a label from the sponsor's product), developed strategies that integrated those premiums into the story lines while making them available for widespread public distribution, devised series promotions, and served in a myriad of other consultative and advisory capacities.

Returning momentarily to the 125 Hummert broadcast features, 61 may be classified as soap operas, 37 as music or variety shows, 10 as crime detective mysteries and eight as juvenile adventure serials—a total of 116 programs in a quartet of Air Features' most fruitful breeds. The reader will note that a balance of nine displaced series is still unaccounted for. Those are to be found in a diverse lot of strains, including advice-self help, games, current events, sports-fitness and situation comedy.

8. The Moguls of Melodrama

Among these remaining nine features, four may be classified as advice–self help series: *Beatrice Mabie*, who offered glamour and grooming hints; *Blanche Sweet*, an actress who conducted interviews, gave reviews and provided beauty secrets; *How to Be Charming*, a self-explanatory title, with hostess Beatrice de Sylvara; and *The Mystery Chef*, featuring cooking tips from John MacPherson.

Scramby Amby, starring Perry Ward as master of ceremonies, appears to be the lone Hummert entry in the game show category.

A single current events feature was *Who's Who in the News*, a series purporting to introduce youngsters to the day's (late 1930s) major public figures.

Dual sports-fitness shows were headlined by a couple of well-recognized athletes of the day: *Jack Dempsey's Gymnasium* and *Russ Lamb's Sportscast*.

Finally, situation comedy. Although to this author's knowledge no published documentation exists linking Frank and Anne Hummert directly to *any* television series, there are some pretty convincing indications that they *did* work in that medium at least once. A register of Hummert features housed among the couple's personal papers is an initial clue. It references an early video domestic farce, *Mary Kay and Johnny*. A pair of newlyweds, Mary Kay and Johnny Stearns, real names of real people who were married to each other in real life, starred on the live TV series. Eventually it aired over three different television networks—Dumont, NBC and CBS—between November 18, 1947, and March 11, 1950.[1]

Several signs point towards a Hummert connection. For one, the live program initially was a quarter-hour feature, a format with which the creative pair had long been well acquainted. Not long after the series premiered it became a serialized five-night-a-week program, another Hummert hallmark.

But the most convincing piece of evidence is the fact that American Home Products Corporation (AHP) underwrote the show for its Whitehall Pharmacal Company subsidiary. Whitehall manufactured many drug products, including a popular brand of pain reliever, Anacin, which was advertised on the show. (In those days, commercials on the screen weren't too advanced: While an announcer extolled the virtues of Anacin, viewers were treated to a simple outline sketch depicting a human form. Flashing lights indicated the path of Anacin as it traveled throughout the body, bringing fast, effective relief. For that day, it was high tech for sure.)

At that same juncture Anacin was sponsoring several Hummert radio features under the guiding hand of Frank and Anne Hummert. Included were *Mr. Keen, Tracer of Lost Persons* and *Our Gal Sunday* on a permanent basis, with occasional plugs for the commodity on *Front Page Farrell* and *Just Plain Bill*. As AHP had been a satisfied user of Hummert services for perhaps 15 years, it stands to reason that the firm might entrust its brand advertising for the fledgling enterprise — or consultation on the series, at least — to its established, proven advertising operatives, Air Features.

There's still an even more telling piece of evidence linking the Hummerts to the show. Early in the series' run — in an attempt to define audience size — AHP asked the show's viewers to send in their written opinions of the show. To the first 200 who replied, AHP would send a free compact mirror. Frank and Anne Hummert, of course, had spent their broadcast careers devising such simple mailhook premium schemes, satisfying millions who tuned in to their plethora of programs in the process. This would certainly have been familiar territory to them.

To avoid disappointing any viewer, AHP took pains to have 400 compact mirrors manufactured, relying solely on guesswork up to then to tell them how many were watching. They found out all right: when the results were tallied, 8,960 letter writers had responded.[2]

It is improbable that Frank and Anne Hummert produced *Mary Kay and Johnny,* or even had anything to do with the story line. There were others who were already skilled in those areas by that early date in TV's ascendancy. But it is plausible, even reasonable, to assume that the couple's long association with AHP could have resulted in a trial experiment packaging the commercials.

The fact that there is no verification that Frank and Anne Hummert pursued other TV ventures hints at either a lack of opportunity or of success. Whatever the case, it's understandable how media historiographers might have overlooked what appears to have been a brief foray by the Hummerts into the new world extended by the tube. If they tried it and merely didn't adjust well to it, they would have joined a large band of people with extensive radio credentials who reportedly never felt comfortable with a visual medium, and therefore bypassed it.

Leaving that subject, it's possible — even probable — that there were still further attempts made by the Hummerts to launch even more radio series beyond those that have been documented. There are, for instance, several programs that appear well suited to the Hummert fold by type, time and sponsorship, although to date there are no conclusively proven ties that connect them.

The musical reverie *Acordiona*, as a prime example, is one that bears a strong resemblance to Hummert wares. The 1934 musicale, launched during the era in which so many of their tune-filled features were premiering, included vocals by soprano Vivienne Segal (who regularly appeared on their *Waltz Time* during that same epoch) and tenor Oliver Smith. The vocalists were backed by the orchestra of Abe Lyman, one of the Hummerts' most dependable bandleaders, who for many years raised the baton on multiple Air Features musicales. Sterling Drugs, which brought virtually all of the most popular Hummert variety programs to the air, underwrote the show. Yet, nothing to date confirms that the Hummerts were the program's creators and producers.

Another unsubstantiated example is that of a 1939 dramatic series headlined by actress Helen Menken. Sterling Drugs sponsored it, too.

Then there was a juvenile educational program begun in 1937, *Paul Wing's Spelling Bee*, which was also backed by Sterling Drugs.

Once again, nothing conclusively ties the Hummerts to any of these; but, as they were so well identified with Sterling, it seems unnatural that the firm would divert its trust to the hands of other producers that had not yet reached the Hummerts' exalted levels of prestige and achievement.

Beyond these, there were several other Sterling shows for which no direct links have been found to a particular production house. This adds to the speculation that the Hummerts may have been responsible for considerably more than the 125 shows for which they are credited in this tome. In truth the list could be far longer. The table of shows (delineated in some detail in appendix B) is limited to those programs for which records exist that prove they were influenced by Frank and Anne Hummert.

Frank and Anne Hummert's Radio Factory

The Hummerts' closest competitors in developing broadcast programming would most likely be Mark Goodson and Bill Todman. Almost all of that pair's 29 innovations were created exclusively for television, however. The two men are included in the present comparison because a portion of their work was performed in radio.

No fewer than a half-dozen Hummert rivals, in fact, were responsible for bringing at least 10 series to the air (some of those in television). Following the Hummerts, the most prolific innovators in an admittedly unscientific survey of this imposing clan (with the numbers of their series appearing in parentheses) are: Mark Goodson and Bill Todman (29), Himan Brown (18), Irna Phillips (16), William N. Robson (14), Louis G. Cowan (13) and Charles Vanda (11). (For a more intensive comparison of individual broadcast wares, turn to appendix A, which includes the programs of several prominent radio programming creator-producers.)

Even with such lofty figures as these, however, their collective output pales when measured by the volume of Frank and Anne Hummert. Taken together, the top six producers—several of whom worked in *two* mediums instead of one—churned out just 101 combined features, no less than 24 *fewer* than those of Frank and Anne Hummert, who operated virtually in radio alone!

Despite the enormity of the Hummerts' accomplishments, few people actually knew them or comprehended what they did in the epoch in which they lived. Unmistakably, a large part of that can be attributed to their preferred reclusive lifestyle. Yet today they are hardly recalled by anybody. Even their names have been forgotten by all but broadcasting scholars and those who casually hear their monikers repeated on recordings and transcriptions of vintage radio shows.

No matter.

Frank and Anne Hummerts' achievements still rank them among their industry's foremost personalities, whether they are so credited or not. They were, without parallel, *the moguls of melodrama*. In that province, there simply was no one else who ever came close.

Appendix A

PROLIFIC
PRODUCERS

In the golden age of radio— between the late 1920s and early 1960s—
a coterie of program developers, commonly referred to as producers,
emerged. While many individuals were so branded, a handful acquired
reputations that approached legendary status. Their superlative achievements netted audiences who often became quite familiar with their
names. The notoriety could be attributed to a number of factors, including the entertainment they provided, the standards they upheld, the span
of projects under their control and possibly a combination of dynamics.

A concerted effort has been made to offer what is believed to be a
never-before-published list of the most active players among radio producers from the golden age. Because Frank and Anne Hummert so totally
dominated this aspect of broadcasting by sheer volume (extending to
the present day), the register contains names of individuals who were
responsible for introducing at least three series (as opposed to only one
or two). While not purporting to be unconditionally exhaustive, a sin-
cere effort has been made to include the names of every salient producer
meeting the criteria. In no way does this diminish the contributions of
those who focused their careers on only one or two programs. At the
same time, it substantiates the diverse complexity and contributions of
the considerable Hummert influence.

The primary works for which each producer is best remembered are listed. At times, radio historiographers disagree on the proper classifications of some figures, one assigning duties as producer while another designates tasks as director. The list was derived from a preponderance of sources favoring one or the other when such conflicts arose. There are also instances when a producer and director are the same individual. For our purposes, they are recognized as producers.

Producers sometimes owned a portion of their series, and in some cases owned them outright. In other situations they merely managed a show for somebody else. Whatever the circumstance, a great deal was riding on their shoulders, for their decisions often contributed markedly to a production's ultimate success or failure.

Listed alphabetically, in addition to the Hummerts, here are the individuals who appear to be the most prolific at that task.

Don Becker
As the Twig Is Bent
Life Can Be Beautiful
The Light of the World
The Parker Family
We Love and Learn

Roger Bower
The Adventures of Leonidas
Witherall
Can You Top This?
Crime Club
Famous Jury Trials
It Pays to Be Ignorant
The Paul Winchell-Jerry
Mahoney Show
The Rookies
Take a Note

Himan Brown
The Adventures of Nero Wolfe
The Adventures of the Thin
Man

The Affairs of Peter Salem
Bulldog Drummond
The CBS Radio Mystery
Theater
Flash Gordon
The General Mills Radio
Adventure Theater (aka
The CBS Adventure Theater)
Grand Central Station
Green Valley, U.S.A.
The Gumps
Inner Sanctum Mysteries
Joyce Jordan, M.D.
Little Italy
Marie, the Little French
Princess
The NBC Radio Theater
The Private Files of Matthew
Bell
The Private Files of Rex
Saunders
Spy Secrets

Elaine Sterne Carrington
(including radio and TV series)
Follow Your Heart
Marriage for Two
Pepper Young's Family (pre-
ceded by the monikers *Red
Adams, Red Davis* and *For-
ever Young*)
Rosemary
Trouble House
When a Girl Marries

Norman Corwin
An American in England
An American in Russia
Columbia Presents Corwin
One World Flight
Passport for Adams
Twenty-Six by Corwin

Louis G. Cowan
(including radio and TV series)
Cloak and Dagger
Down You Go
Hollywood Jackpot
Murder at Midnight
Musico
The $100,000 Big Surprise
Play Broadcast
The Quiz Kids
RFD America
The $64,000 Challenge
The $64,000 Question
Stop the Music!
Who Said It?

Jaime del Valle
The Line Up

*Richard Diamond, Private
Detective*
Yours Truly, Johnny Dollar

Ralph Edwards
(including radio and TV series)
Crosswits
It Could Be You
The People's Court
Place the Face
This Is Your Life
Truth or Consequences

Dan Golenpaul
*The Heinz Magazine of the
Air*
Information Please
Raising Your Parents

Mark Goodson and **Bill Todman**
(including radio and TV series)
Beat the Clock
Call My Bluff
Card Sharks
Family Feud
Get the Message
Hit the Jackpot
It's News to Me
I've Got a Secret
Judge for Yourself
Match Game
Missing Links
The Name's the Same
Now You See It
Number Please
Password
Play Your Hunch
The Price Is Right

Rate Your Mate
Show-offs
Snap Judgment
Spin to Win
Split Personality
Tattletales
Time's a-Wastin'
To Tell the Truth
Treasure Salute
What's Going On?
What's My Line?
Winner Take All

John Guedel
Art Linkletter's House Party
People Are Funny
You Bet Your Life

Elliott Lewis
Broadway Is My Beat
Crime Classics
The Line Up
Mr. Aladdin
On Stage (aka *Cathy and
    Elliott Lewis On Stage*)
Pursuit
The Sears Radio Theater
Suspense
The Zero Hour

Phillips H. Lord
By Kathleen Norris
Counterspy (aka *David
    Harding, Counterspy*)
Gangbusters (aka *G-Men*)
Mr. District Attorney
Policewoman
Seth Parker
Sky Blazers

Treasury Agent
We, the People

Norman Macdonnell
*The Adventures of Philip
    Marlowe*
Escape
Fort Laramie
The Green Lama
Gunsmoke
Have Gun, Will Travel
Rogers of the Gazette
Romance
Suspense

Tom McDermott
Perry Mason
Portia Faces Life
Rosemary

Carlton E. Morse
Adventures by Morse
Family Skeleton
His Honor, the Barber
I Love a Mystery
I Love Adventure
One Man's Family
The Woman in My House

Arch Oboler
Arch Oboler's Plays (aka *Arch
    Oboler Presents*)
Everyman's Theater
Everything for the Boys
Four for the Fifth
Lights Out
Plays for Americans
The Sears Radio Theater

Irna Phillips
(including radio and TV series)
Another World
As the World Turns
The Brighter Day
Days of Our Lives
The Guiding Light
Lonely Women
*Love Is a Many Splendored
  Thing*
Masquerade
Our Private World
Painted Dreams
The Right to Happiness
Road of Life
These Are My Children
Today's Children
Woman in White
Young Doctor Malone

William N. Robson
*The Adventures of Christopher
  London*
Calling All Cars
Doorway to Life
Escape
Four for the Fifth
Hawk Larabee
Life with Luigi
*Luke Slaughter of Tomb-
  stone*
The Man Behind the Gun
Pursuit
Request Performance
The Saint
Shorty Bell
T-Man

William Spier
The Adventures of Sam Spade
The Philip Morris Playhouse
Suspense

George W. Trendle
American Agent
The Challenge of the Yukon
  (aka *Sergeant Preston of the
  Yukon*)
The Green Hornet
The Lone Ranger
Ned Jordan, Secret Agent

Charles Vanda
The Free Company
G. I. Laffs
Hollywood Premiere
Hollywood Showcase
Intrigue
Jubilee
Millions for Defense (aka *The
  Treasury Hour*)
Nature of the Enemy
Rogue's Gallery (aka *Band-
  wagon Mysteries*)
Suspense
Theater of Romance

Orson Welles
The Campbell Playhouse
Les Miserables
*The Mercury Summer Theater
  of the Air*
The Mercury Theater on the Air
The Orson Welles Theater
  (aka *The Orson Welles
  Almanac*)
This Is My Best

Carl Wester

The Guiding Light
Masquerade
The Right to Happiness
Road of Life
The Story of Holly Sloan
Today's Children
Woman in White

Bruno Zirato Jr.

The Right to Happiness
Suspense
The Woolworth Hour
Yours Truly, Johnny Dollar

Appendix B

HUMMERT
BROADCAST SERIES

The following is an alphabetical listing of all broadcast series that were created, adapted, supervised, augmented or directly influenced by Frank and Anne Hummert. While their involvement was limited to a portion of the air lives of some of these, for the majority the couple oversaw production from the inception of the program to its cancellation. Where substantiated, genres, premises, air years and networks are included. Sometimes the only information that could be found on features they produced came from the permanent Hummert archival collection.

Abe Lyman and Movieland's Favorite Band — (*Musical*). One of a series of orchestra features under the baton of one of radio's most prominent and popular 1930s conductors. *1932–1934, CBS.*

Album of Familiar Canadian Music — (*Musical*). A series featuring standard compositions traditionally associated with our nation's northern neighbors. *c1933–1935.*

Alias Jimmy Valentine — (*Soap Opera*). An ex-con and reformed safecracker uses his talents and enormous underworld contacts to aid the forces of law and order — while going straight as a bank clerk and falling for the banker's daughter. *1938–1939, NBC Blue.*

Along the Boulevard — (*Musical*). No details preserved. *c1940.*

Appendix B

Amanda of Honeymoon Hill — (*Soap Opera*). The theme is similar to that of many Hummert washboard weepers, revolving around a young maiden who married above her station in life. Amanda Dyke, a "beauty with flaming hair," was the offspring of a working class family. She wed Edward Leighton, the son of a wealthy aristocratic Southern family. Domestic tensions and rivalries kept them at odds at their Honeymoon Hill estate in Virginia. Actress Mary Jane Higby called this serial's epigraph her favorite for its intriguing premise: "Amanda of Honeymoon Hill — the story of a young girl — laid against a tapestry of the deep South." *1940–1942, NBC Blue; 1942–1946, CBS.*

America the Free — (*Musical*). No details preserved. *c1941–1942.*

American Album of Familiar Music — (*Musical*). Introduced as "a program of supremely lovely songs and melodies that capture all hearts." Tenor Frank Munn, "the golden voice of radio," was featured originally; succeeded by Frank Parker, "America's great romantic tenor," in the mid–1940s. Classical vocalists and instrumentalists included Arden and Arden, Bernice Claire, Donald Dame, Margaret Daum, Vivian della Chiesa, Jean Dickenson, Bernard Hirsch, Elizabeth Lennox, Daniel Lieberfeld, Evelyn MacGregor, Lucy Monroe and Virginia Rea. Orchestras of Gustave Haenschen and Abe Lyman performed. *1931–1950, NBC; 1950–1951, ABC.*

American Melody Hour — (*Musical*). Introduced as "the songs of the day so you can know them all, sing them all yourself." A showcase spotlighting soprano Vivian della Chiesa until she grew tired of it within a couple of years. Other artists included Eileen Farrell, Bob Hannon, Evelyn MacGregor, Stanley McClelland, Frank Munn, Jane Pickens, Conrad Thibault. Victor Arden and Frank Black conducted the American Melody Hour orchestra. *1941–1942, NBC Blue; 1942–1948, CBS.*

Arnold Grimm's Daughter — (*Soap Opera*). All the makings of a family feud on the boil: a father who dispossessed his child upon her marriage, a moody groom who fretted over dire conditions that he perceived the couple's fathers could alter, a mother-in-law who despised her son's wife, a father-in-law who initiated tension when the girl melted his heart. Add determined suitors for her hand who never quit and the

158

accidental death of the young groom, and the beleaguered heroine was mired in constant emotional upheaval. Principal characters included Connie Grimm, who married Dal Tremaine, and her father, Arnold Grimm. *1937–1938, CBS; 1938–1942, NBC.*

Aunt Jemima — (*Musical*). Part of a variety series that extended from 1929 to 1953 highlighting the traditional Southern Negro minstrel. Three white women (Tess Gardella, Hariette Widner, Vera Lane) hosted as the stereotypical "blackface mammy" depicted on the sponsor's pancake mix box, before African-American actress Amanda Randolph acquired the role late in the run. Exaggerated black dialect, plus vocalists Mary Ann Mercer, Bill Miller, William Mueller, the Mixed Chorus, the Old Plantation Sextet and Harry Walsh's Dixieland band, were featured. *1931–1933, CBS.*

Backstage Wife — (*Soap Opera*). Marrying above one's station is once again the thesis as a stenographer from Podunk weds an attractive Broadway thespian that scores of wily women would kill for. Several try. The wife is innocence personified, while the husband's suspicious nature and jealousy rages out of control. The epigraph sets the stage: "Now, we present once again, *Backstage Wife*, the story of Mary Noble, a little Iowa girl who married one of America's most handsome actors, Larry Noble, matinee idol of a million other women — the story of what it means to be the wife of a famous star." *1935–1936, MBS; 1936–1938, NBC Blue; 1938–1955, NBC; 1955–1959, CBS.*

Barry Cameron — (*Soap Opera*). Initially titled *The Soldier Who Came Home*, the show revolves around the difficulties of a returning war veteran (Cameron) and his young bride Anna as the pair face the throes of adjustment. *1945–1946, NBC.*

Beatrice Mabie — (*Advice*). Beauty secrets and tips offered to milady. *1932, NBC Blue.*

Betty and Bob (*Soap Opera*). Purportedly *"romantic melodrama that turned into a turbid exercise in distrust and deceit — but not before it had caught millions of women in its spell,"* according to one reviewer. A girl from the sticks marries her heir-to-a-fortune boss, Bob Drake, who's disinherited for it. Man-hungry mamas salivate over him as jealousy and mistrust have a field day, the progenitor of themes to come.

159

Appendix B

When a son is born, the audience departs as the disparaging partners bicker, headed for divorce. In an attempt to regain listeners, the show's scripters have the infant die. But more intriguing tales on newer serials ultimately keep fans away. One wag suggests the program offered radio its "first and greatest" matinee idol in Don Ameche. *1932–1936, NBC Blue; 1936–1938, CBS; 1938–1940, NBC.*

Beyond These Valleys—(*Soap Opera*). The tale of Rebecca and John Lane, penned by one of radio's most talented authors and composers, Don Becker. He collaborated with Carl Bixby on *Life Can Be Beautiful* and wrote several other serials by himself or with Bixby. He created the theme song for this show and several more. *1939–1940, CBS.*

Blanche Sweet—(*Advice*). A motion picture veteran, star of both silent and talking films, conducts interviews, comments on the theater and cinema scene and offers beauty hints for women. *1935, CBS.*

Broadway Merry-Go-Round—(*Musical*). Here's a spin-off of the eminently popular *Manhattan Merry-Go-Round* (separate entry) sporting a distinct French flair (also appearing under the monikers *Folies Bergere of the Air, Folies de Paree* and *Revue de Paree*). Fanny Brice followed by Beatrice Lillie as major attractions. *1936–1937, NBC Blue.*

Broadway Varieties—(*Musical*). The orchestra of Jerry Freeman and then Victor Arden back vocalists Fifi D'orsay, Eugene and Willie Howard, Elizabeth Lennox, Helen Morgan, Carmela Ponselle, Guy Robertson and Oscar Shaw on a program beginning as *Broadway Melodies*. Light, popular and semi-classical chestnuts featured. *1933–1937, CBS.*

California Theatre of the Air—(*Musical*). No details preserved. *c1939.*

Caroline's Golden Store—(*Soap Opera*). Small town locals are subjects of humorous exchanges in a rib-tickling comedy and country-western music sketch. Activity focuses on the hamlet's general store, owned by fun-loving Caroline Ellis. Think *Lum and Abner* for the ladies. *1939, NBC; 1939–1940, CBS.*

The Carters of Elm Street—(*Soap Opera*). In the little burg of Galesville, Mara Carter rails against the odds as the new spouse of husband Jeff in "the story of a second wife and her fight for happiness."

The Carters include a trio of offspring, two at home and a married daughter and her husband living a few doors away on Elm. Virginia Payne, the admired actress portraying *Ma Perkins*, is the heroine. *1939–1940, NBC; 1940, MBS.*

Central City—(*Soap Opera*). A blue collar manufacturing hub of 50,000 citizens, Central City witnesses the tribulations of an allegedly classic American family. Presaging *Peyton Place* on TV, it is a *Grand Hotel*-style tale of entanglement. *1938, NBC Blue; 1939–1941, NBC.*

Chaplain Jim, U.S.A.—(*Soap Opera*). Serialized narratives of a young enlisted clergyman's encounters with boys on the battlefields of World War II and crises back at home. Sponsored by the U.S. War Department, these stories are based on true incidents. The intent is to boost patriotism as the hero asks the audience to write to servicemen overseas. He frequently concludes with prayer. *1942–1945, NBC Blue/ABC; 1945, 1946, MBS.*

The Couple Next Door—(*Soap Opera*). Never referred to by name, a dialoging married couple witness life from opposite perspectives as they incessantly quarrel (though never with the intensity and malice of *The Bickersons*). She's a persistent nag and he's a classic henpecked hubby. In between runs under this title the series continues as *Ethel and Albert* (1944–1950 over the NBC Blue/ABC chain). *1937, MBS; 1957–1960, CBS.*

David Harum—(*Soap Opera*). A New England hamlet's banker, Harum, a confirmed bachelor, impresses the townsfolk as a friend. Confirming it, he fights plenty of sinister rogues with personal gain on their minds at the expense of local citizens. Epigraph: "Once again we present *David Harum*, one of the most beloved stories in American fiction, for David Harum is America. It's the story of every one of us—of our search for love ... for happiness ... and the good way of life." *1936, NBC Blue; 1936–1947, NBC; 1947–1950, CBS; 1950–1951, NBC. Concurrent runs: 1937–1938, MBS; 1942–1943, CBS.*

Detective Reeder—(*Mystery*). No details preserved. *c1939.*

Doc Barclay's Daughters—(*Soap Opera*). Focus on the discord faced by a widowed dad, a small-town druggist who clashes with a trio of

161

grown daughters. Socialite Connie, the eldest, leaves a millionaire play-boy spouse to return to her hometown. Middle daughter Mimi, flirta-tious and egocentric, resents Connie's affluence; she's married to Tom Clark, a lowly hardware clerk, vulnerable to her impetuous decisions. The youngest, Marge, attractive, single and showing more stability than the others, is housekeeper for her dad. The blueprint is riddled with potential for conflict, and doesn't disappoint in that quest. *1939–1940, CBS.*

Don Donnie's Orchestra — (*Musical*). One of numerous lesser-known bands on the airwaves during its epoch; guest vocalists featured. *c1935.*

The Dreft Star Playhouse — (*Soap Opera*). Originated as *The Holly-wood Theater of the Air*, it is an ambitious project. It features major cinema luminaries (like Mary Astor, Maureen O'Sullivan, Jane Wyman) typically in one- to five-week serialized adaptations of pop-ular movies on weekday mornings. Think *Lux Radio Theater* in quar-ter-hour installments without the trappings of a live audience. *1943–1945, NBC.*

Easy Aces — (*Soap Opera*). Goodman and Jane Ace are spotlighted, a married couple portrayed in a gentle tone of light humor with con-tinuing plot lines. A *New York Times* reviewer pegged the two as "a couple of ordinary people set against an average background, except that something screwy is always happening to them." They are fre-quently dubbed "radio's distinctive laugh novelty." *1931–1935, CBS; 1935–1942, NBC; 1942–1945, CBS; 1945–1947, transcribed syndicated repeats; 1948, CBS.*

Evening Melodies — (*Musical*). This is one of numerous nondescript and seldom-recalled purveyors of tunes on the ether. *c1939.*

Five Star Jones — (*Soap Opera*). An ace reporter for *The Register* finds himself entangled in challenges at home with wife Sally and in jour-nalistic exploits for his city newspaper. Not to be confused with *Front Page Farrell*, in which David and *his* Sally probably do it all better. *1935–1936, CBS; 1936–1937, NBC Blue.*

For America We Sing — (*Musical*). This show arrived shortly before America's involvement in World War II, promoting sales of defense and savings bonds for the U.S. Treasury Department. Frank Black conducts a 44-piece orchestra and chorus. Donating time and talent are guest vocalists Rose Bampton, Helen Jepson, Elizabeth Lennox, Dorothy Maynor, Frank Munn, Frank Parker, Lanny Ross, Gladys Swarthout and Robert Weede. *1941–1942, NBC Blue.*

French Mignon Trio — (*Musical*). This is one of the less memorable ensembles that performed in this era. *c1937.*

Front Page Farrell — (*Soap Opera*). The program is introduced with this epigraphical synopsis: "We now present the exciting, unforgettable radio drama *Front Page Farrell*, the story of a crack newspaperman and his wife — the story of David and Sally Farrell." In its formative years the show fixates on domestic issues. But by the 1950s it undergoes a subtle transformation, turning into a hard-hitting mystery investigation saga as Farrell tracks and exposes a murderer every week. It's a Hummert primetime crime drama with a daytime twist. *1941–1942, MBS; 1942–1954, NBC.*

La Gaiete Parisienne — (*Musical*). One of numerous Hummert musicals with French themes; no specific data appears to have survived. *c1937–1938.*

Gems of Melody — (*Musical*). Featured artists on this early song series (running for several months on two chains, differentiated by times, days and stars) include John Herrick, Fred Hufsmith, Muriel Wilson and Harold Sanford's orchestra. *1933–1934, NBC; 1933–1935, NBC Blue.*

The Girl Who Lives Next Door — (*Soap Opera*). A brief romantic drama three afternoons weekly that floats onto the airwaves with the theme "Alice Blue Gown." It's not to be confused with a couple of other serials of the same period with similar monikers but distinctly different premises, *Girl Alone* and *The Girl Next Door*. *1932–1933, NBC.*

Hamburger Katie — (*Soap Opera*). Its fleeting existence is documented by multiple authoritative sources (including actress heroine Mary Jane Higby). Specific details beyond that fact apparently do not survive.

Hammerstein Music Hall — (*Musical*). Ted Hammerstein and Lucy Laughlin are featured personalities on a half-hour music-variety series. *1934–1935, CBS; 1935–1936, NBC; 1936–1938, CBS.*

Happy Landing — (*Juvenile Adventure*). Mitzi Green starred. No details are available on the plotline of this serialized feature. Not to be confused with a 1950 ABC game show under the same title hosted by quizmaster Clayton (Bud) Collyer. *WBBM, Chicago, mid–1930s, with some sign of a network extension.*

Hearthstone of the Death Squad — (*Mystery*). In acquiring the *Molle Mystery Theater* in 1948, the Hummerts christen it *Mystery Theater* and introduce a tenacious murder investigator, Inspector Hearthstone, operating out of London's metropolitan police department. Detective Sam Cook, a bobble-headed primate who works hard to make the boss appear grand, follows on his missions. This series is an extension of the earlier one, merely spun off under the "impeccable manhunter" appellation. *1951–1952, CBS.*

Helpmate — (*Soap Opera*). The interconnected lives of a trio of neighboring couples — Holly and George Emerson, Linda and Steve Harper, Grace and Clyde Marshall — form the basis for this narrative. *1941–1944, NBC.*

Hollywood Nights — (*Musical*). Singer Frank Luther stars in one of numerous revues bearing the film capital's name in the title. *1931–1932, NBC Blue.*

Houseboat Hannah — (*Soap Opera*). After Dan O'Leary loses an arm in a cannery accident, his financially strapped family moves to a Shanty Fish Row houseboat on San Francisco Bay. Wife Hannah, a woman of resolute strength, persists with integrity, determined not to allow their dilemmas to totally beset them. *1936–1938, transcribed primarily on MBS stations; 1938–1941, NBC Blue.*

How to Be Charming — (*Advice*). Beatrice de Sylvara offers milady tips on improving her looks and alure in a Monday–Wednesday–Friday quarter hour. *1936, NBC Blue; 1936–1938, NBC.*

The Imperial Hollywood Band — (*Musical*). This is one of many instrumental groups headlining their own shows during this period. *c1935–1936.*

Inspector Brooks — (*Mystery*). No details preserved. c1939.

Inspector Hawkes and Son — (*Mystery*). No details preserved. *c1943–1949*.

Inspector Thorne — (*Mystery*). Thorne of the Homicide Bureau of New Scotland Yard is purportedly "an investigator smart enough to claim he is dumb, and modest enough to believe it." A narrator assures listeners that his quests "rank with many of the most celebrated cases in the annals of crime fiction." Sergeant Muggins, the inspector's faithful subordinate, accompanies him to the crime scenes. Even at this late date in radio's life victims are still spouting immortal lines like "You killed me" as they fall to the floor. Though the landscape has changed, some things never do. *1951, NBC*.

Jack Armstrong, the All-American Boy — (*Juvenile Adventure*). A flag-waving high school hero who, accompanied by several companions, traipses the globe, putting criminals in their places while exposing young ears to lofty ideals. It is one of the most popular adolescent series ever aired. In 1950 *Armstrong of the SBI* becomes a faltering single-season successor. *1933–1936, CBS; 1936–1941, NBC; 1941–1942, MBS; 1942–1950, NBC Blue/ABC*.

Jack Dempsey's Gymnasium — (*Sports-Fitness*). No details preserved. *c1933*.

John's Other Wife — (*Soap Opera*). An insecure wife whose suspicions of her spouse's clerical helper (perhaps with good reason), plus his gorgeous assistant, keep the pot boiling in a seething romantic triangle-quartet. John Perry owns Perry's Department Store. Married to Elizabeth, he's accused of carrying a torch for secretary Annette Rogers and dallying on the side with Martha Curtis. He's so besieged by domestic problems he can barely prevail against a nearby sumptuous retail competitor. *1936–1940, NBC; 1940–1942, NBC Blue*.

Judy and Jane — (*Soap Opera*). Heavy into comedy, with much of its laughter generated by two fun-loving friends, *Judy and Jane* is limited to listeners in the Midwest, where the sponsor's product (Folger's coffee) is a staple on supermarket shelves. *1932, CBS; 1932–1935, NBC; by transcription in local markets until 1947*.

Just Plain Bill — (*Soap Opera*). The good-natured tonsorial artist is everybody's friend, quick to champion principal over deception, and willing to get involved in improving anybody's lot. He'll take action, if required, and offer some grandfatherly advice otherwise. His own little clan includes Bill Davidson, daughter Nancy Donovan, grandson Wiki Donovan and son-in-law Kerry Donovan. The epigraph summarizes his theme: "Now, to the many friends who wait for him ... we present *Just Plain Bill*, barber of Hartville, the story of a man who might be living right next door to you — the real-life story of people just like people we all know." *1932–1936, CBS; 1936–1940, NBC; 1940–1942, NBC Blue; 1942–1955, NBC.*

Katie's Daughter — (*Soap Opera*). The protagonist is primed to open in a Broadway show. At that juncture she quarrels with her boyfriend. Can she overcome her personal conflicts to become a successful thespian? *Variety* contends that she departed the airwaves before the question could be satisfied. *1947, NBC.*

Kitty Keene, Incorporated — (*Soap Opera*). A feminine private eye discovers that her professional pursuits tend to take a back seat to domestic crises at home. She's married to Bob Jones and has a daughter, Jill. *1937, CBS; 1938–1941, MBS.*

Lavender and Old Lace — (*Musical*). "Songs of other days" featuring tenor Frank Munn, Fritzi Scheff and soprano Muriel Wilson (later replaced by soprano Lucy Monroe), the Gus Haenschen and Abe Lyman orchestras, a male trio, and organist William Meeder. Ballads and waltzes are featured prominently. *CBS, 1934–1936; NBC Blue, 1936.*

Lazy Dan, the Minstrel Man — (*Musical*). Versatile comic and tenor Irving Kaufman takes all the speaking and singing roles. It's blackface humor with light music set in a hardware store, with the proprietor playing a straight man. When it's time for a tune, the radio is turned on. *1933–1936, CBS.*

The Life of Mary Sothern — (*Soap Opera*). It's "the fast-paced story of a young mother who finds it difficult to keep her well-meaning husband's two feet on the ground." Another husband goes awry. Two men had fought for Mary and we're left to wonder if the victor was her most common-sense choice. This is the Mutual network's first daytime soap opera. *1934–1935, WLW, Cincinnati; 1935–1937, MBS; 1937–1938, CBS; 1939–1943, aired by individual stations transcribed.*

The Light of the World — (*Soap Opera*). Action based on narratives of the Old Testament, most of them recounted in multi-part dramatizations. Attesting to the drama's quality and commitment to faithfully interpret the scriptural context is the fact that this program is solely underwritten by a single sponsor (General Mills, Inc.). *1940–1944, NBC; 1944–1946, CBS; 1946–1950, NBC.*

Little Orphan Annie — (*Juvenile Adventure*). Based on a popular comic strip, this program cuts the pattern for future kids' fare as young Annie — ward of a simple farm couple — and her dog Sandy follow thrilling exploits throughout the world. The premise turns sour in 1940 when Annie becomes little more than an aide to Captain Sparks, a fly-boy in pursuit of bad guys, and who plugs a new sponsor's product with his name (Quaker Puffed Wheat Sparkies). *1931–1936, NBC Blue; 1936–1940, NBC; concurrent run, 1937–1938, MBS; 1940–1942, MBS.*

London Merry-Go-Round — (*Musical*). Aired in Great Britain, this is an English version of the Hummerts' well-liked *Manhattan Merry-Go-Round. c1939.*

Lone Journey — (*Soap Opera*). Unhappy with life in Chicago, architect Wolfe Bennett and his wife Nita retreat to Judith Mountain in Montana, buying the Spear-T Ranch. The narrative trails their attempts to start a new existence. Peabody Award winner Sandra Michael and her brother Peter penned the serial — she lived in Montana and knew the environment. They increased daytime dramas' quality, capitalizing on mood and ordinary conversation. At one point the siblings assigned the scripts to someone else for a brief period; *Variety* said the tale improved noticeably, becoming more realistic upon their return. *1940–1943, 1946, NBC; 1946–1947, CBS; 1951–1952, ABC.*

Lonely Women — (*Soap Opera*). Pining secretary Judith Clark and stunning model Marilyn Larimore are central figures in a drama about gals whose men defend the nation on the World War II battlefields. They reside at the Towers Hotel for Women as their encounters with isolation and depression contribute to their ordeal of unfortunate circumstances. Two gentlemen are added to the mix to stir up the story line. *1942–1943, NBC.*

Lora Lawton —(*Soap Opera*). A simple widowed lass from the sticks marries great wealth and spends her days fending off the vixens who tempt her spouse—a hackneyed Hummert theme. Handsome shipping magnate Peter Carver, easily one of the East Coast's most eligible bachelors, weds Lawton, his housekeeper, who soon starts her own career as a fashion designer. Operating a boutique, she constantly rises above the tramps that have her hubby on their minds. *1943–1950, NBC.*

Lorenzo Jones —(*Soap Opera*). The Hummerts interrupted the pathos of matinee misery to focus on a story that dwells on humorous absurdities. The protagonist (a daytime version of primetime's zany Fibber McGee), whose stability is firmly rooted in *his* spouse, Molly, concocts all sorts of idiotic devices. The epigraph tells what to expect: "We all know couples like lovable, impractical Lorenzo Jones and his devoted wife, Belle. Lorenzo's inventions have made him a character to the town—but not to Belle, who loves him. Their struggle for security is anybody's story. But somehow with Lorenzo, it has more smiles than tears." That is, until the final three years of the run when the ratings plunge. Lorenzo becomes an amnesiac, wanders for three years in New York, almost becomes a bigamist and regains his memory as the show is canceled. Perfect timing! *1937–1855, NBC.*

Love Song —(*Soap Opera*). Apparently no details of the story line survive. *Inaugurated as a dual-station feature over Chicago's WGN and Cincinnati's WLW, 1936; 1936–1937, MBS.*

Ma Perkins —(*Soap Opera*). An affable widow blessed with the wisdom of Solomon characterizes America's "mother of the airwaves" on one of the most heartwarming and enduring series ever to air. Ma's convivial spirit, love for humanity and concern that decency prevail are hallmarks that endear her to millions. As the unassuming conscience of Rushville Center (and perhaps the nation), she's sought for advice in response to moral and ethical issues. Ma's family surrounds her: two daughters and a son (he dies in the Second World War), grandkids, son-in-law and a business partner–confidante who assists in running her late husband's lumberyard. *1933–1949, NBC; 1936–1937,*

MBS (concurrent); 1937, *NBC Blue (concurrent);* 1938, *CBS (concurrent);* 1938, *NBC Blue (concurrent);* 1942–1960, *CBS (concurrent, 1942–1949).*

The Man I Married—(*Soap Opera*). A millionaire's dispossessed son, Adam Waring, appears in a familiar Hummert theme. He and his wife Evelyn attempt a fresh start in a tiny burg. They're burdened with his addiction to alcohol, however, as well as a lack of persistence and discipline. This gives Evelyn plenty to fret over as she tries to uphold fidelity in their home. 1939–1941, NBC; 1941–1942, CBS.

Manhattan Merry-Go-Round—(*Musical*). The premise offers mythical visits to famous New York nightspots. Debuting as a musical-variety series, in its formative years well-known comedians are mixed with vocalists Rachel Carlay, Conrad Thibault and others. The funny business vanishes by the early 1940s. Baritone Thomas L. Thomas, "beloved singer of stage and radio," is the new star, complemented by soloists Glenn Cross, Rodney McClennan, Marian McManus, Lucy Monroe, Dick O'Connor, Barry Roberts and Dennis Ryan. Choral groups and an orchestra led by Victor Arden and Andy Sannella accompany. *1932–1933, NBC Blue;* 1933–1949, NBC.

Marie, the Little French Princess—(*Soap Opera*). A young woman of noble birth finds love and contentment as an American commoner, married to Richard Collins. Scarcely recalled today, the drama premiers in a Depression-worn era when riches-to-rags isn't nearly as popular as a rags-to-riches motif. *1933–1935, CBS.*

Mark Sabre—(*Mystery*). This is one of two spinoffs of *Mystery Theater,* and it also appeared under the title *Inspector Mark Sabre.* The namesake character is a rather charming sophisticate, a homicide detective employed by the Los Angeles Police Department. Assisting Sabre with his investigations is Sergeant Tim Maloney, who clearly springs from the Hummert consortium of inept sidekicks. The narrative runs along traditional murder-solving patterns witnessed in several other Hummert crime dramas. Possibly due to the setting, however, this one comes across just a wee bit more urbane. *1951–1954, ABC.*

Mary Kay and Johnny—(*Situation Comedy*). A domestic farce starring Mary Kay and Johnny Stearns, presented live. It's the only television series for which there is solid evidence of a Hummert connection, most likely in packaging the commercials. *1947–1948, Dumont TV; 1948–1949, NBC-TV; 1949, CBS-TV; 1949–1950, NBC-TV.*

Matinee Melodies — (*Musical*). It's one of numerous tune-filled features whose details haven't been preserved. *c1942.*

Melodiana — (*Musical*). Abe Lyman's Orchestra is featured along with guest artists. *1934–1936, CBS; 1936, NBC Blue.*

MGM Radio Movie Club — (*Musical*). A musical-variety feature that plugs songs controlled by Metro-Goldwyn-Mayer's music publishing companies. The realistic setting of this miniscule movierama includes a grinding camera, cameraman, shouting director and actors performing with music. *1927–1936, WHN, New York City.*

Mr. Chameleon — (*Mystery*). "The man of many faces" is "the famous and dreaded detective" who works in the police homicide bureau. He applies an unusual device, appearing in a disguise that "at all times is recognized by the audience" as he tries to trap killers with unplanned confessions and other giveaways. A knuckle-headed Detective Dave Arnold, personifying the dumbbells that turn up as partners on Hummert crime dramas, assists the sleuth, usually offering dim-witted observations. *1948–1953, CBS.*

Mr. Gallagher and Mr. Shean — (*Musical*). A comedy-singing duo, the pair had already achieved some notoriety for their early phonograph recordings. *c1933.*

Mr. Keen, Tracer of Lost Persons — (*Mystery*). Actually this is two shows with a single moniker. In the first half-dozen years private detective Keen searches relentlessly for folks who've vanished. Some disappear of their own volition; others have help, victims of foul play. When a metamorphosis occurs, "the kindly old tracer" drops his rather easygoing demeanor to take on a stern quality, tracking and exposing at least one murderer per case. A buffoon bearing an Irish brogue, Mike Clancy, assists him; he's called Keen's partner, but in no way is he equal to "the great investigator." This longest running broadcast sleuthing series (18 years on radio) sets the pattern for all subsequent Hummert detective thrillers: a murder is committed in the first few seconds and the hero is tapped to finger a cold-blooded killer. It's highly addictive. The audience, closely attuned, eliminates suspects until the culprit is revealed. *1937–1942, NBC Blue*; *1942–1951, CBS*; *1951–1952, NBC*; *1952–1955, CBS*.

Modern Cinderella — (*Soap Opera*). Hope Carter, Larry Burton and Jimmy Gale are the principals in a romantic tease in which Carter attempts to improve her social status and discover the man of her dreams. It's a child's fairy tale brought to life. *1936–1937, CBS*.

Molly of the Movies — (*Soap Opera*). A young girl attempts to launch a career in the motion picture industry. Her frustrations, disappointments and achievements form the basis for the story. *1935–1937, MBS*.

Monday Merry-Go-Round — (*Musical*). A celebrated long-running Sunday night standard, *Manhattan Merry-Go-Round*, is spun off for a Monday night insertion. Singers Phil Duey and Bea Wain, backed by Victor Arden's Orchestra, are featured. *1941–1942, NBC Blue*.

Mrs. Wiggs of the Cabbage Patch — (*Soap Opera*). This first network washboard weeper purportedly based on a novel; a variation of a mythical tale by Alice Hegan Rice about life in an urban ghetto in Louisville, Kentucky. The Cabbage Patch is a respectful term for a shantytown outside a bustling city in the early twentieth century. The Wiggs family, including Elvira and Hiram and their son Billy, is on poverty row. Their struggles to improve their circumstances are highlighted. *1935–1936, CBS*; *1936–38, NBC*.

The Musical Revue — (*Musical*). This is one of numerous poorly remembered series, all bearing similar appellations, that feature songs and artists of the day. *c1933–1935*.

The Mystery Chef — (*Advice*). John MacPherson is the culinary connoisseur offering recipes and kitchen hints for the ladies. One authority suggests MacPherson's radio career spanned nearly two decades, 1929–1948, debuting in Boston, although the network run appears to have been briefer. *1931–1932, 1934, NBC Blue*; *1932, 1933–1934, CBS*; *1932–1934, 1935–1938, 1941, NBC*; *1942–1944, ABC*.

Mystery Theater — (*Mystery*). This program sports a name adopted by the Hummerts from the *Molle Mystery Theater* when the couple inherited that show's timeslot after the sponsor bowed out. They introduce Inspector Hearthstone and his sidekick, Detective Sam Cook, the latter as dimwitted as the assistants on other Hummert crime shows. The pair work out of London's metropolitan police department, and Hearthstone, the "impeccable manhunter," comes complete with a distinctly British dialect. He never minces words, seems suspicious of everyone connected with a case, and appears to revel in fastening his grip on the murderers he seeks. The show spins off under his own name for an added year after the present series departs. *1948–1951, CBS.*

Night Club of the Air — (*Musical*). Bands and crooners of the day are featured in one of many such radio cabaret–style venues. c1936–1937.

Nona from Nowhere — (*Soap Opera*). Nona Dutell, adopted as a child, is a 23-year-old Hollywood actress who tries to find her real parents, feeling she was denied her true identity. Her dad once saved the life of a famous tinseltown producer, then asked the man to help his child. But the producer falls in love with Nona, significantly complicating his mission. Unfortunately, Nona arrives on the air just as many fans are switching their radios off or she might have been looking for her folks for a long, long time. *1950–1951, CBS.*

Old Doctor Jim — (*Soap Opera*). The series obviously appeared briefly, although no details are known to have survived. *c1936.*

Orphans of Divorce — (*Soap Opera*). Starting with an evening run, the series is soon transferred to daytime. The story concerns the obstacles faced by a middle-aged wife, Nora Worthington. Upon her divorce and her ex-husband Cyril's remarriage to a younger woman, Nora relinquishes custody of several kids so they may be raised in an affluent setting. She opens a small shop to support herself. Having been there and done that, she's consulted when her own daughter experiences marital discord. *1939–1942, NBC Blue.*

Our Gal Sunday (*Soap Opera*). Here's the ultimate example of the repetitious Hummert formula of the penniless waif marrying into money. An interlocutor sets the stage each day: "Once again, we present *Our Gal Sunday*, the story of an orphan girl named Sunday from the little mining town of Silver Creek, Colorado, who in young womanhood married England's richest, most handsome lord, Lord Henry Brinthrope. The story that asks the question: Can this girl from the little mining town in the West find happiness as the wife of a wealthy and titled Englishman?" She would find far more joy in her marriage, of course, if the Hummerts didn't throw dozens of wily vixens at her, each more determined than the previous ones to snare her wealthy spouse. To his credit, he remains as chaste as possible under such pressuring circumstances. Lady Brinthrope is exceedingly fearful that one of the tramps will actually become "the next mistress of Black Swan Hall," the Brinthropes' "lovely Virginia estate." Could there be a more beleaguered heroine? *1937–1959, CBS.*

Painted Dreams — (*Soap Opera*). The first of the breed, this serial's creator was a soon-to-be rival of the Hummerts, Irna Phillips, who would become broadcasting's second-most prolific originator of daytime drama. It's one of only two narratives on which both camps are known to have collaborated. The story develops around Mother Moynihan, an elderly, widowed woman. She's a kindly, philosophical, all-wise protagonist who is capable of coping with the realities of the Depression epoch. Her single goal in life is to ensure the ultimate happiness of her grown offspring. The simple message is that marriage, love and motherhood offer the greatest achievement and destiny any female could hope to experience. Most of the action occurs in an urban Chicago neighborhood where the Moynihans live. When a legal dispute erupts over the program's ownership, Irna Phillips reintroduces it with similar characters, setting and premise under the banner *Today's Children*. *1930–1933, WGN, Chicago; 1933–1934, CBS; 1935–1936, MBS (Midwest region only); 1940, NBC Blue.*

Paris Night Life — (*Musical*). This is one of a handful of Hummert musical creations bearing French themes and settings. It features the instruments of Bertram Hirsch's Orchestra. *1931–1932, 1933, 1936, NBC Blue.*

Penrod and Sam — (*Juvenile Adventure*). Booth Tarkington's comic novel forms the basis for this serialized adaptation. Because it airs in the early evening hours, the audience likely consists of people of all ages. *1934, NBC.*

Appendix B

Popeye the Sailor — (*Juvenile Adventure*). A cartoon comes to life. The gravelly-voiced character taken from Elzie Crisler Segar's comic strip (and fondly recalled by cinema audiences) is the star. Similar predicaments to those seen on the screen — like Olive Oyl's incessant kidnapping by a no-account and her dramatic rescue by Popeye — abound. Some of the adventures are based on familiar fairy tales. It's all pointed strictly at the younger set. *1935–1936, NBC; 1936–1937, 1938, CBS.*

Rainbow Trail — (*Soap Opera*). No further details available. *c1941–42.*

Real Stories from Real Life — (*Soap Opera*). Applying flashback techniques, each of the narratives in this composite of closed-ended tales focuses on a central figure. That person relates his story in his own words. A new cast is usually offered each week. Not to be confused with NBC's *Real Life Stories* in 1958–1959. *1944–1947, MBS.*

Rich Man's Darling — (*Soap Opera*). If there's such a thing as a practice run for a soap opera, this may be it. It's the precursor of an eminently more successful *Our Gal Sunday*. Peggy Burchard marries a thriving middle-aged businessman, Gregory Alden, a revision of yet another incarnation that debuted in 1935 over Chicago's WGN. By the time *Sunday* arrives, the motif is totally refined, and there's a polish that makes that poor waif who marries into royalty an erudite, cultured sophisticate. *1936–1937, CBS.*

The Romance of Helen Trent — (*Soap Opera*). Widowed Hollywood fashion designer Helen Trent "interfered with more housework than any other serial queen on the air," one pundit noted. For 27 years she led men on a merry chase — they sought her, not the other way around — and she was betrothed to several. Most were lecherous gents with diabolical plans — save one, longtime suitor-lawyer Gil Whitney. But, alas, she couldn't marry him; she had to protect the show's premise. Her soul-mate, Hummert heroine Ellen Brown, the infamous *Young Widder Brown*, couldn't marry her suitors for the same reason, keeping them at bay for an 18-year run, lest the theme evaporate. Helen's epigraph enumerates her troubles: "And now *The Romance of Helen Trent*, the real-life drama of Helen Trent who, when life mocks her, breaks her hopes, dashes her against the rocks of despair, fights back bravely, successfully, to prove what so many women long to prove in their own lives: that because a woman is 35, or more, romance in life need not be over; that the romance of youth can extend into middle life, and even beyond." *1933–1960, CBS.*

Rose of My Dreams — (*Soap Opera*). Sibling rivalry comes to the forefront with the good sister, Rose, sweet and kind, and the bad sister, Sarah, devious and scheming, involved in an ongoing clash. They're vying for the affections of the same Englishman, who finds them both intriguing. *1946–1948, CBS.*

Roxy Symphony Theater of the Stars — (*Musical*). One of many similarly titled musical revues emanating from New York City's infamous Roxy Theater during the early 1930s. *c1932–1933.*

Russ Lamb — (*Sports-Fitness*). A prominent sportscaster offers comments. *c1941.*

Scramby Amby — (*Game*). "Listening clubs" all over America are spawned by this radio anagram conducted by Perry Ward and Larry Keating. Tossing scrambled words at studio contestants, a host offers hints for prize money — the fewer hints given, the larger the prize. Musical suggestions, silly rhymes and dictionary definitions generate clues. Listeners at home suggest thousands of scrambled terms weekly. The parlor game played in home parties pits guests against each other as they vie for a pot to which all have contributed. *1941–1943, WLW, Cincinnati; 1943–1944, NBC West Coast; 1944–1945, NBC Blue; 1946–1947, MBS.*

Second Husband — (*Soap Opera*). When Brenda, a widowed mother of two, marries wealthy Grant Cummings, all manner of conflicts arise within the family. Her hands are full trying to persuade her son and daughter to accept their new father. Then she runs headlong into marital discord when she succeeds as an acting neophyte and hopes for a permanent career in films, something her spouse bitterly opposes. The drama begins as an evening series, switching to daytime in 1942. *1936–1937, NBC Blue; 1937, NBC; 1937–1942, CBS; 1942, NBC Blue; 1942–1946, CBS.*

Showland Memories — (*Musical*). This is one of several musical productions for which no further information has surfaced. *c1934–1939.*

Skippy—(*Juvenile Adventure*). Based on Percy Crosby's animated newspaper strip, the serial focuses on Skippy Skinner and his young friends. Skippy's physical and ethical traits magnify the wisdom and courage he exhibits as their leader. Trouble finds these kids, although it usually overtakes them in humorous fashion. *1932, NBC; 1932–1935, CBS.*

Stella Dallas—(*Soap Opera*). The epigraph reads: "We give you now— *Stella Dallas!*—a continuation on the air of the true-to-life story of mother love and sacrifice in which Stella Dallas saw her beloved daughter Laurel marry into wealth and society and, realizing the difference in their tastes and worlds, went out of Laurel's life. These episodes in the later life of Stella Dallas are based on the famous novel of that name by Olive Higgins Prouty and are written by Anne Hummert." Well, not quite. Stella never leaves her precious "Lolly-Baby's" side. If she did, the plot would evaporate. She's there to fend off lecherous sheiks and other no-accounts who would destroy Lolly's happiness, since it's obvious the poor girl can do nothing for herself. Nor is Anne Hummert the writer. She takes the scripts off the assembly line and adds her name as author. It's sometimes nice to own the company. *1937–1938, WEAF, New York; 1938–1955, NBC.*

Stevens and Son of Scotland Yard—(*Mystery*). No details preserved. *c1932.*

The Stolen Husband—(*Soap Opera*). The Hummerts' initial attempt could scarcely be termed a drama. At its inception, one actor reads the narrative, altering voice and tone to suggest different characters. But the audience turns away, and other actors are thrown into the breach to perform the final chapters. Husband hijacking is the theme, one the Hummerts would repeat many times over the years. The plot concerns a good-looking businessman, a striking secretary eager to advance her boss's career and a dense spouse who discovers a bit late that a man spending nights at the office with a voluptuous dame may be preoccupied beyond his occupation. While unsuccessful, the series helps the Hummerts acquire techniques that they would employ for decades. *1931.*

The Strange Romance of Evelyn Winters—(*Soap Opera*). "The story of Gary Bennett, playwright, who suddenly and unexpectedly finds himself the guardian of lovely Evelyn Winters" sets the stage for this romantic tale. Bennett, 38, doesn't know of his obligation concerning the daughter of his former colonel, killed in battle, until his medical discharge from World War II. At 23, she's just out of finishing school. While significantly older than his ward, Bennett and the girl fall in love, try to deny it for a while and prompt a myriad of reactions when it becomes public. *1944–1948, CBS; 1951–1952, ABC.*

Sweetest Love Songs Ever Sung –(*Musical*). Frank Munn stars, along with Metropolitan Opera soprano Natalie Bodanya. *NBC Blue, 1936– 1937.*

Terry and Mary—(*Juvenile Adventure*). Details of this early children's drama, penned by the Hummerts' most prolific author, Robert Hardy Andrews, regrettably have not been preserved.

Terry and the Pirates—(*Juvenile Adventure*). U.S. Air Corps Colonel Terry Lee and his buddies battle the archenemies of the nation, including his nemesis, the Dragon Lady. They fight Axis powers during World War II, and other global villains and crime cartels before and after that period. Milton Caniff's popular comic strip is the basis for the serial. *1937–1938, NBC; 1938–1939, NBC Blue; 1941–1942, WGN, Chicago; 1943–1948, NBC Blue/ABC.*

This Day Is Ours—(*Soap Opera*). In the earliest days of World War II, Eleanor MacDonald, a missionary's daughter, tries to relieve the plight of unfortunates in a ravaged China. Assisting her is missionary Curt Curtis. *1938–1940, CBS; 1940, NBC Blue.*

Those Happy Gilmans—(*Soap Opera*). This lighthearted and all-too-brief respite from habitual pathos and spousal worship (of someone else's spouse) reflects the lives of average Americans trying to make ends meet while upholding traditional values. Ethel Gilman is wise; her husband, Gordon, is a dedicated provider. The older kids echo the pleasures and pain of late adolescence while the youngest is usually in trouble with everybody. "A refreshing departure for the Hummerts," said one reviewer. *1938, NBC Blue; 1938–1939, NBC.*

The Trouble with Marriage—(*Soap Opera*). The theme song of this brief feature, "Jealousy," probably says it all. *1939, NBC Blue.*

Valiant Lady — (*Soap Opera*). When actress Joan Blake relinquishes her career to marry her childhood sweetheart, plastic surgeon Truman (Tubby) Scott, she makes a vow that often leaves her audience doubting. He's an insanely jealous man who becomes even more unstable when a blood clot enters his brain. She earns empathy from her father, Jim Barrett, and from a single, attractive artist, Paul Morrison. But she's basically engaged in misery, fighting bravely against the odds. As so many serials do, this one purports to be "the story of her struggle to keep his feet planted firmly upon the pathway to success." It's doubtful he'll ever arrive, making her one of the most beleaguered women of the genre. *1938, CBS; 1938–1942, NBC; 1942–1946, CBS; 1951–1952, ABC.*

Waltz Time — (*Musical*). Introduced with "it's dance time on the air," *Waltz Time* is initially headlined by "the golden voice of radio," tenor Frank Munn. In the early 1940s contralto Evelyn MacGregor joins him as costar. When Munn retires in 1945, Bob Hannon becomes his replacement. Other vocalists include Lois Bennett, Bernice Claire, Mary Eastman, Lucy Monroe and Vivienne Segal. Abe Lyman conducts the orchestra's memorable tunes. *1933–1948, NBC.*

Waves of Melody — (*Musical*). Tenor Tom Brown is featured in a tune-filled fest accompanied by Vic Arden's orchestra. *1931–1932, NBC Blue.*

Way Down East — (*Soap Opera*). Based on Lottie Blair Parker's 1889 play and a subsequent 1935 movie, this is "the sequel, as written by us, to the great stage and screen melodrama." It's the story of Anna and David Bartlett and it takes place in the Northeastern U.S. *1936–1937, MBS.*

Who's Who in the News — (News). A current events feature purporting to introduce youngsters to the day's major public figures. *c1937.*

Wife vs. Secretary — (*Soap Opera*). While this serial is cited in several references, including Mary Jane Higby's and Gerald Nachman's perceptive works, no specific details about it have come to light. *c1937.*

Young Widder Brown — (*Soap Opera*). Ellen Brown, a widow and single mom, operates a tearoom while fending off legions of suitors in an attempt to remain faithful to her true love, Dr. Anthony Loring.

Incalculable obstacles prevent them from marching down the aisle, some of them quite trivial. Her problem is the same as Helen Trent's on *her* soap opera: if she married, there would be no story. The epigraph sums up her plight: "Again we present the moving human drama of a woman's heart and a mother's love — *Young Widder Brown*. In the little town of Simpsonville, attractive Ellen Brown, with two children to support, faces the question of what she owes to them and what she owes to herself. Here's the story of life and love as we all know it." In reality, probably not very many did — or do. *1938, MBS (as Young Widder Jones)*; *1938–1956, NBC*.

Your Song and Mine — (*Musical*). Baritone Thomas L. Thomas, a Hummert favorite, stars in a midweek musical feature. *1948, CBS*.

Appendix C

IN THEIR
OWN WORDS

Some of the most characteristic statements attributed to Frank or Anne Hummert embody their philosophy of broadcast programming development and design. In capsulated form, a few of their declarations follow.

I shall only call you once. That will be to tell you that I no longer need your services.— Anne to new writers for Air Features upon their hiring.

We had one writer who lasted for seven years.— Anne, giving a *Newsweek* reporter some inside information.

I have listened to the show today, and I think that it is in a deplorable state.— Anne, in an inter-office memorandum, assessing her opinion of one of the daytime serials before enumerating specific faults of the various cast members.

It is not money and high position that count, but what you do for others— what's in your heart.— A summation in a characterization outline given to those who were enlisted to write Air Features serial scripts.

If there is anything I hate, it's lawyers. If lawyers get involved in a thing, it poisons the whole business.— Frank's revelation, when confronted by Radio Writers Guild officials over Air Features' low compensation to its scribes.

Include God on every page of every script.— Anne's directive to one of her nameless hacks.

It would spoil the illusion ... [for] our listeners believe these stories are real.— A Hummert justification for not recognizing the contributions of most of their dialoguers by having their names announced on the air.

Ours is a religious country, so we try to embody the idea of right. Crime may appear, but either the annihilation or change of heart of the unerring one must follow. Divorce is not unknown among our characters, but it is deplored and does nothing to make the participants happier.— Anne, delineating their stance to an interviewer on a couple of thorny issues.

For God's sake, leave something to the imagination!— Frank's appeal to producers who exploit sex in the media.

We produce successful stories about unsuccessful people. By "unsuccessful" I mean only that our characters aren't wealthy people. In other than a material sense, they are by no means failures. They may be very successful in their family life or in the way they manage to help their neighbors and their friends. Our stories are about the everyday doings of plain, everyday people — stories that can be understood and appreciated on Park Avenue and on the prairie.— Frank, delineating the intrinsic values of their serials.

Does Mr. Toscanini give me credit on his programs?— Frank's retort to a minion when pressed to hype one of his regular singers' radio appearances with the NBC Symphony Orchestra under the baton of Arturo Toscanini.

What's to become of all my actors?— Anne's inquiry when whole programming blocks were deleted from daytime and nighttime schedules as radio audiences sharply declined in the 1950s.

Everyone said I couldn't retire, but when Frank died I was ravaged. I was knocked for a loop. I thought I had worked enough. I didn't slow down; I simply stopped. — Anne's recollections to a reporter sometime after Frank's passing.

A beautiful swan song … one of the happiest experiences of my later life. — Anne's reaction upon being named first artist-in-residence at her alma mater in 1978.

Appendix D

A Hummert Chronology

Some defining milestones in the personal and professional lives of Frank and Anne Hummert

June 2, 1884	Frank is born in St. Louis, Missouri.
1904	Frank's developing interest in journalism leads him to a reporting position with *The St. Louis Post-Dispatch* at about this juncture.
January 19, 1905	Anne Schumacher is born in Baltimore, Maryland.
1908	Frank marries Adeline E. Woodlock of St. Louis and lives at various times at the residences of both sets of parents.
1911	By now Frank has formed Hummert Advertising Agency, Inc., St. Louis, naming himself president.
1920	Frank is named chief copywriter for Lord & Thomas Advertising Agency, New York City.
1925	Anne Schumacher graduates Goucher College magna cum laude and joins *The Baltimore Sun* as a full time reporter.

1926	Anne accompanies John W. Ashenhurst to Paris for reportorial assignments.
July 26, 1926	Anne marries John Ashenhurst in Paris.
1927	Frank joins the Blackett & Sample agency in Chicago as vice president; his name will be added to the firm's masthead in the early 1930s.
April 26, 1927	John (Johnny) Randle Ashenhurst is born in the United States.
1929	John and Anne Ashenhurst separate and are later divorced.
1930	Frank is beginning to wonder if American housewives might be interested in serialized drama via radio.
1931	Anne becomes editorial assistant to Frank Hummert at Blackett and Sample, Inc.
1930–1934	Adeline Hummert dies of an unknown cause on an unconfirmed date.
1931	Frank and Anne put his idea to a test by hiring Robert Hardy Andrews to write a drama-by-installment; *The Stolen Husband* debuts on the air but quickly fades.
October 11, 1931	Frank and Anne launch their most prestigious and durable musical show, *The American Album of Familiar Music*, opening a new niche for which they will create several well-received entries.
September 19, 1932	After multiple tries at launching radio serials with only mediocre results, Frank and Anne premiere *Just Plain Bill*; it becomes an overnight success and the inspiration for a broadcast empire.

July 31, 1933   Frank and Anne's most important juvenile adventure creation, *Jack Armstrong, the All-American Boy*, premiers; including a spin-off, it will run for 18 years.

October 30, 1933   *The Romance of Helen Trent*, destined to be Frank and Anne's longest-running program, appears on the ether for the first time.

December 4, 1933   Frank and Anne assume production of what many consider to be America's most beloved soap opera, *Ma Perkins*, the second longest running of the breed (7,065 broadcasts); it confirms their unrivaled authority in developing matinee melodrama.

1935   Frank marries Anne S. Ashenhurst.

1937   Frank is cited as advertising's highest paid executive.

October 12, 1937   *Mr. Keen, Tracer of Lost Persons*, the couple's most memorable crime detective series, is introduced on the air.

1938   Frank and Anne move to the New York City area to be nearer broadcast, advertising and talent centers; they later buy property at Greenwich, Connecticut, for a magnificent personal estate.

1938–1939   Anne's only known public speaking appearance, given before a Columbia University class in broadcasting.

Early Mid–1940s   Frank and Anne transfer most of their Chicago-based shows to New York, allegedly to take advantage of a larger talent supply culled from radio and theater venues

Early to Mid–1940s   Anne becomes a special consultant to the U. S. War and Treasury departments, and the pair include homefront issues in some of their programming.

| December 31, 1943 | Blackett-Sample-Hummert, Inc. is dissolved. |

January 1, 1944   Frank and Anne form Air Features, Inc. to produce their radio programs, and Featured Artist Service, Inc. to furnish talent for those shows.

June 17, 1951   Their most impressive and durable musical feature, *The American Album of Familiar Music*, broadcasts for the last time, after playing for 20 years.

September 26, 1955   *Mr. Keen, Tracer of Lost Persons*, leaves the air after 1,693 chapters (18 years), the Hummerts' most important crime detective series and the longest running in the history of broadcasting (including television).

January 2, 1959   In the national networks' final inglorious sweep of daytime dramatic programming before abandoning it in late 1960, four soap operas are discharged, including two—*Backstage Wife* (23 years) and *Our Gal Sunday* (22 years)—Hummert properties, leaving the couple with but one series remaining on the air.

June 24, 1960   *The Romance of Helen Trent* departs after airing 7,222 episodes—the longest running drama in the history of radio; upon its demise, all Hummert-produced series still under their control are permanently off the air, signifying the end of an era.

Early 1960s   Frank and Anne sell their Greenwich mansion and move to a Park Avenue triplex apartment overlooking New York's Central Park; they pursue a life of international travel and leisure.

March 12, 1966   Frank dies in New York; afterward, Anne moves to a smaller Fifth Avenue apartment, also overlooking Central Park.

1978   Anne is celebrated as the first artist-in-residence by Goucher College's communication program.

1989   Anne agrees to transfer the Hummerts' script and personal papers collection to the American Heritage Center at the University of Wyoming.

July 5, 1996   Anne dies in New York.

Appendix E

TYPICAL AIR
FEATURES SCHEDULES

These tables will be helpful in giving the reader a more inclusive perspective of the involvement of Frank and Anne Hummert in producing programming during radio's golden age. Three sample schedules are offered, drawn from widely differing eras, each of them separated by a decade: the more heavily weighted, frenetic schedule of 1939; the average agenda of 1949, shortly before television became a major competitor for radio audiences; and the sparse schedule of 1959, reflecting the near-abandonment of the medium as the 1950s drew to a close. Of note is the Hummerts' reliance upon certain national chains that carried their programs, and especially their heavy involvement with a handful of major recognized firms that purchased the time to advertise their commodities.

1939

The following data was adapted from *Radio Guide* for the week of February 26 to March 4, 1939.

Sunday, February 26, 1939
9:00–9:30 P.M. NBC —*Manhattan Merry-Go-Round* (Sterling Drugs, Inc.)
9:30–10:00 P.M. NBC —*The American Album of Familiar Music* (Sterling Drugs, Inc.)

Weekdays, February 27–March 3, 1939

10:00–10:15 A.M. NBC—*Central City* (Procter & Gamble Co.)

10:15–10:30 A.M. NBC—*John's Other Wife* (Monday-Wednesday: Philippe Cosmetics; Thursday-Friday: American Home Products Corp.)

10:30–10:45 A.M. NBC—*Just Plain Bill* (Monday-Wednesday: American Home Products Corp.)

10:45–11:00 A.M. NBC—*Houseboat Hannah* (Procter & Gamble Co.)

11:00–11:15 A.M. NBC—*David Harum* (B.T. Babbitt)

11:15–11:30 A.M. NBC—*Lorenzo Jones* (Sterling Drugs, Inc.)

ll:30–11:45 A.M. NBC—*Young Widder Brown* (Sterling Drugs, Inc.)

11:45–12:00 noon NBC Blue—*Kitty Keene, Inc.* (Procter & Gamble Co.)

12:00–12:15 P.M. NBC—*The Carters of Elm Street* (Ovaltine)

12:30–12:45 P.M. CBS—*The Romance of Helen Trent* (Monday-Wednesday: Edna Wallace Hopper Cosmetics; Thursday-Friday: American Home Products Corp.)

12:45–1:00 P.M. CBS—*Our Gal Sunday* (American Home Products Corp.)

1:45–2:00 P.M. NBC—*Those Happy Gilmans* (General Mills, Inc.)

l:45–2:00 P.M. CBS—*This Day Is Ours* (Procter & Gamble Co.)

2:00–2:15 P.M. NBC—*Betty and Bob* (General Mills, Inc.)

2:00–2:15 P.M. CBS—*Doc Barclay's Daughters* (Personal Finance Corp.)

2:15–2:30 P.M. NBC—*Arnold Grimm's Daughter* (General Mills, Inc.)

2:30–2:45 P.M. NBC—*Valiant Lady* (General Mills, Inc.)

3:15–3:30 P.M. NBC—*Ma Perkins* (Procter & Gamble Co.)

4:00–4:15 P.M. NBC—*Backstage Wife* (Sterling Drugs, Inc.)

4:15–4:30 P.M. NBC—*Stella Dallas* (Sterling Drugs, Inc.)

5:15–5:30 P.M. NBC—*Terry and the Pirates* (Dari-Rich, Inc.)

5:30–5:45 P.M. NBC—*Jack Armstrong, the All-American Boy* (General Mills, Inc.)

5:45–6:00 P.M. NBC—*Little Orphan Annie* (Ovaltine)

Monday Evening, February 27, 1939

7:00–7:30 P.M. NBC Blue—*Orphans of Divorce* (Sterling Drugs, Inc.)

Tuesday Evening, February 28, 1939

7:00–7:15 P.M. NBC Blue—*Easy Aces* (American Home Products Corp.)

7:15–7:30 P.M. NBC Blue —*Mr. Keen, Tracer of Lost Persons* (American Home Products Corp.)
7:30–8:00 P.M. CBS —*Second Husband* (Sterling Drugs, Inc.)

Wednesday Evening, March 1, 1939
7:00–7:15 P.M. NBC Blue —*Easy Aces* (American Home Products Corp.)
7:15–7:30 P.M. NBC Blue —*Mr. Keen, Tracer of Lost Persons* (American Home Products Corp.)

Thursday Evening, March 2, 1939
7:00–7:15 P.M. NBC Blue —*Easy Aces* (American Home Products Corp.)
7:15–7:30 P.M. NBC Blue —*Mr. Keen, Tracer of Lost Persons* (American Home Products Corp.)

Friday Evening, March 3, 1939
9:00–9:30 P.M. NBC —*Waltz Time* (Sterling Drugs, Inc.)

Saturday, March 4, 1939
No broadcast series scheduled

1949

The following data was adapted from *Radio Mirror* for April 1949.

Sunday
9:00–9:30 P.M. NBC —*Manhattan Merry-Go-Round* (Sterling Drugs, Inc.)
9:30–10:00 P.M. NBC —*The American Album of Familiar Music* (Sterling Drugs, Inc.)

Weekdays
11:45–12:00 noon NBC —*Lora Lawton* (B.T. Babbitt)
12:30–12:45 P.M. CBS —*The Romance of Helen Trent* (American Home Products Corp.)
12:45–1:00 P.M. CBS —*Our Gal Sunday* (American Home Products Corp.)
1:15–1:30 P.M. CBS —*Ma Perkins** (Procter & Gamble Co.)
2:45–3:00 P.M. NBC —*The Light of the World* (General Mills, Inc.)
3:00–3:15 P.M. CBS —*David Harum* (B. T. Babbitt)
3:15–3:30 P.M. NBC —*Ma Perkins** (Procter & Gamble Co.)

4:00–4:15 P.M. NBC—*Backstage Wife* (Sterling Drugs, Inc.)
4:15–4:30 P.M. NBC—*Stella Dallas* (Sterling Drugs, Inc.)
4:30–4:45 P.M. NBC—*Lorenzo Jones* (Sterling Drugs, Inc.)
4:45–5:00 P.M. NBC—*Young Widder Brown* (Sterling Drugs, Inc.)
5:30–6:00 P.M. ABC (Monday-Wednesday-Friday)—*Jack Armstrong, the All-American Boy** (General Mills, Inc.)
5:30–5:45 P.M. NBC—*Just Plain Bill* (American Home Products Corp.)
5:45–6:00 P.M. NBC—*Front Page Farrell* (American Home Products Corp.)

Monday Evening
No broadcast series scheduled

Tuesday Evening
8:00–8:30 P.M. CBS—*Mystery Theater* (Sterling Drugs, Inc.)

Wednesday Evening
8:00–8:30 P.M. CBS—*Mr. Chameleon* (Sterling Drugs, Inc.)
9:00–9:30 P.M. CBS—*Your Song and Mine* (Borden Co.)

Thursday Evening
8:30–9:00 P.M. CBS—*Mr. Keen, Tracer of Lost Persons* (American Home Products Corp.)

Friday Evening
No broadcast series scheduled

Saturday Evening
No broadcast series scheduled
**These series may have been transferred to other producers by this time.*

1959

The following data was adapted from several sources, including *The Great Radio Soap Operas* by Jim Cox, *On the Air* by John Dunning, and *The Second Revised Ultimate History of Network Radio Programming and Guide to All Circulating Shows* by Jay Hickerson, reflecting programming in the spring of 1959.

Weekdays

12:30–12:45 P.M. CBS — *The Romance of Helen Trent* (participating sponsors)

Final broadcast: June 24, 1960

Note: Two former Hummert series that continued until the generally accepted finale of radio's golden age, November 25, 1960 — *The Couple Next Door* and *Ma Perkins* — had been shifted to other program producers many years earlier.

NOTES

Chapter 1

1. Nachman, Gerald. *Raised on Radio: In Quest of The Lone Ranger, Jack Benny, Amos 'n' Andy, The Shadow, Mary Noble, The Great Gildersleeve, Fibber McGee and Molly, Bill Stern, Our Miss Brooks, Henry Aldrich, The Quiz Kids, Mr. First Nighter, Fred Allen, Vic and Sade, The Cisco Kid, Jack Armstrong, Arthur Godfrey, Bob and Ray, The Barbour Family, Henry Morgan, Joe Friday and Other Lost Heroes from Radio's Heyday.* New York: Pantheon Books, 1998, p. 380.

2. Stedman, Raymond William. *The Serials: Suspense and Drama by Installment.* Norman: University of Oklahoma Press, 1971, p. 233.

3. MacDonald, J. Fred. *Don't Touch That Dial! Radio Programming in American Life from 1920 to 1960.* Chicago: Nelson-Hall, 1991, p. 250.

4. Whiteside, Thomas. "Life Can Be Terrible." *New Republic,* July 14, 1947, p. 22.

Chapter 2

1. Gould, Jack. "Soap Factory: Something About the Hummerts, Frank and Anne, and 6,000,000 Words a Year." *The New York Times,* February 14, 1943, Sec. X, p. 9.

2. At least one source claims Frank Hummert was a native of New Orleans, although no evidence supporting that allegation has been produced. A preponderance of published authorities, including records of the U.S. Census Bureau, provide a compelling argument that the family lived in Missouri, not Louisiana, at the time of Frank's birth.

3. Edmondson, Madeleine, and David Rounds. *The Soaps: Daytime Serials of Radio and TV.* New York: Stein and Day, 1973, p. 53; also, Nachman Gerald. *Raised on Radio: In Quest of The Lone Ranger, Jack Benny, Amos 'n' Andy,*

197

The Shadow, Mary Noble, The Great Gildersleeve, Fibber McGee and Molly, Bill Stern, Our Miss Brooks, Henry Aldrich, The Quiz Kids, Mr. First Nighter, Fred Allen, Vic and Sade, The Cisco Kid, Jack Armstrong, Arthur Godfrey, Bob and Ray, The Barbour Family, Henry Morgan, Joe Friday and Other Lost Heroes from Radio's Heyday. New York: Pantheon Books, 1998, p. 376.

4. Clark, Rocky. "They Started Radio Serials—Can You Blame Them?" *The Bridgeport Sunday Post*, Bridgeport, Conn., October 8, 1939, Sec. 3, p. 1.

5. *Time*, January 23, 1939, p. 30.

6. Horwell, Veronica. "Empress of the Radio Soaps." An obituary appearing in *The Guardian*, published in London, England, July 27, 1996, p. 28.

7. Thomas, Robert M., Jr. "Anne Hummert, 91, Dies; Creator of Soap Operas." An obituary appearing in *The New York Times*, July 21, 1996.

8. *Ibid.*

9. Duncan, Jacci, ed. *Making Waves: The 50 Greatest Women in Radio and Television as Selected by American Women in Radio and Television, Inc.* Kansas City, Mo.: Andrews McMeel, 2001, p. 138.

10. Abelson, Joan S. "Mother of the Soaps." Goucher *Quarterly*, Vol. 63, No. 3, Spring 1985, p. 5.

11. Personal communication to the author from Jim Ashenhurst, May 18, 2002. Used by permission.

12. *Ibid.*

13. *Ibid.*

14. *Ibid.*

15. Edmondson and Rounds, p. 235.

16. Sterling, Christopher H., editor. *Telecommunications: Special Reports on American Broadcasting, 1932–1947.* New York: Arno Press, 1974, p. 167.

17. Sterling, p. 168.

18. MacDonald, J. Fred. *Don't Touch That Dial! Radio Programming in American Life from 1920 to 1960.* Chicago: Nelson-Hall, 1979, p. 250.

19. Web site of *Advertising Age* industry publication.

20. Landry, Robert J. "Pioneer Soaper Frank Hummert, Ever the Hermit, Almost 'Sneaks' His Obit." *Variety*, April 27, 1966.

21. *Ibid.*

22. Blue, Howard. *Words at War: World War II Era Radio Drama and the Postwar Broadcasting Industry Blacklist.* Lanham, Md.: Scarecrow Press, 2002, pp. 187–188.

23. Personal communication with author from Nick Ryan, January 11, 2002. Used by permission.

24. Web site operated by *Advertising Age*, May 18, 2002.

25. Barnouw, Erik. "Frank and Ann [*sic*] Hummert." *Media Marathon.* Durham, N.C.: Duke University Press, 1996, pp. 117–118.

26. Cox, Jim. *The Great Radio Soap Operas.* Jefferson, N.C.: McFarland, 1999, p. 82.

27. Barnouw, p. 118.

28. *Ibid.*
29. *Newsweek*, Jan. 10, 1944, p. 81.
30. Whiteside, Thomas. "Life Can Be Terrible." *New Republic*, July 14, 1947, p. 19.
31. Higby, Mary Jane. *Tune in Tomorrow: or How I Found The Right to Happiness with Our Gal Sunday, Stella Dallas, John's Other Wife, and Other Sudsy Radio Serials.* New York: Cowles Education Corp., 1968, p. 130.
32. Duncan, p. 141.
33. Landry, *op cit.*
34. Whiteside, p. 19
35. Whiteside, p. 22.
36. Clark, p. 1.
37. *Ibid.*
38. Landry, *op cit.*
39. *Ibid.*
40. *Ibid.*
41. Duncan, p. 140.
42. Higby, p. 129.
43. Thomas, *op cit.*
44. *Ibid.*
45. Higby, p. 129.
46. Thurber, James. "O Pioneers!" *Worlds Without End: The Art and History of the Soap Opera.* New York: Harry N. Abrams, Inc., 1997, p. 48.
47. Personal communication with the author from Jim Ashenhurst, May 18, 2002. Used by permission.
48. DeLong, Thomas A. *The Mighty Music Box: The Golden Age of Musical Radio.* Los Angeles: Amber Crest Books, 1980, p. 193.
49. Higby, p. 129.
50. Nachman, p. 376.
51. Kamen-Kaye, Dorothy Allers. "Romance in the Air," *Goucher Alumnae Quarterly*, Spring 1957, p. 13.
52. *Ibid.*
53. LaGuardia, Robert. *From Ma Perkins to Mary Hartman: The Illustrated History of Soap Operas.* New York: Ballantine Books, 1977, p. 13.
54. Smith, Sally Bedell. *In All His Glory: The Life of William S. Paley, the Legendary Tycoon and His Brilliant Circle.* New York: Simon and Schuster, 1990, p. 93.
55. Lyons, Eugene. *David Sarnoff: A Biography.* New York: Harper & Row, 1966.
56. Whiteside, p. 13.
57. Landry, *op cit.*
58. Edmondson and Rounds, p. 57.
59. LaGuardia, p. 13.
60. Higby, p. 130.
61. Nachman, p. 475.

62. Whiteside, p. 21.
63. *Variety*, May 11, 1938, p. 27, and December 30, 1936, p. 33.
64. LaGuardia, p. 14.
65. Whiteside, p. 22.
66. Barnouw, p. 118.
67. Whiteside, p. 23.
68. Dunning, p. 58.
69. Barnouw, pp. 114–115.
70. Barnouw, p. 118.
71. Barnouw, pp. 118–119.
72. Barnouw, pp. 119–120.
73. Harvey, Rita Morley. *Those Wonderful, Terrible Years: George Heller and the American Federation of Television and Radio Artists.* Carbondale: Southern Illinois University Press, 1996, p. 19.
74. *Ibid.*
75. Thomas, *op cit.*
76. Landry, *op cit.*
77. Edmondson and Rounds, pp. 56–57.
78. Dunning, p. 59.
79. Nachman, p. 371; Edmondson and Rounds, p. 61.
80. Blue, p. 187.
81. Barnouw, p. 114.
82. Landry, *op cit.*
83. Abelson, *op cit.*
84. *Ibid.*
85. Andrews, Robert Hardy. *Legend of a Lady: The Story of Rita Martin.* New York: Coward-McCann, 1949.
86. Stedman, p. 236.
87. *Ibid.*, pp. 236–237.

Chapter 3

1. DeLong, Thomas A. *The Mighty Music Box: The Golden Age of Musical Radio.* Los Angeles: Amber Crest Books, 1980, p. 193.
2. Landry, Robert J. "Pioneer Soaper Frank Hummert, Ever the Hermit, Almost 'Sneaks' His Obit." *Variety*, April 27, 1966.
3. *Ibid.*
4. Nachman, Gerald. *Raised on Radio: In Quest of The Lone Ranger, Jack Benny, Amos 'n' Andy, The Shadow, Mary Noble, The Great Gildersleeve, Fibber McGee and Molly, Bill Stern, Our Miss Brooks, Henry Aldrich, The Quiz Kids, Mr. First Nighter, Fred Allen, Vic and Sade, The Cisco Kid, Jack Armstrong, Arthur Godfrey, Bob and Ray, The Barbour Family, Henry Morgan, Joe Friday*

and Other Lost Heroes from Radio's Heyday. New York: Pantheon Books, 1998, p. 156.

5. Cox, Jim. *The Great Radio Soap Operas.* Jefferson, N.C.: McFarland, 1999, pp. 99–101.

6. Dunning, John. *Tune In Yesterday: The Ultimate Encyclopedia of Old-Time Radio, 1925–1976.* Englewood Cliffs, N.J.: Prentice Hall, 1976, p. 55.

7. Whiteside, Thomas. "Life Can Be Terrible." *New Republic,* July 14, 1947, p. 21.

8. DeLong, *The Mighty Music Box,* p. 380.

9. Clark, Rocky. "They Started Radio Serials—Can You Blame Them?" *The Bridgeport Sunday Post,* October 8, 1939, Sec. 3, p. 1.

10. DeLong, *The Mighty Music Box,* p. 215.

11. DeLong, Thomas A. *Radio Stars: An Illustrated Biographical Dictionary of 953 Performers, 1920 through 1960.* Jefferson, N.C.: McFarland, 1996, p. 198.

12. DeLong, *The Mighty Music Box,* p. 216.

13. DeLong, *Mighty,* p. 218.

14. DeLong, *Mighty,* pp. 57–58.

15. DeLong, *Radio Stars,* p. 262.

16. Dunning, *On the Air,* p. 457.

17. Dunning, *On the Air,* p. 458.

18. DeLong, *The Mighty Music Box,* p. 131.

19. Dunning, John. *On the Air: The Encyclopedia of Old-Time Radio.* New York: Oxford University Press, 1998, p. 433.

20. Buxton, Frank, and Bill Owen. *The Big Broadcast, 1920–1950,* 2nd ed. Lanham, Md.: Scarecrow Press, 1997, p. 145.

21. Dunning, *On the Air,* p. 433.

22. DeLong, *The Mighty Music Box,* p. 194.

23. DeLong, *Mighty,* p. 193.

24. DeLong, *Mighty,* pp. 193–194.

25. DeLong, *Mighty,* p. 194.

26. Whiteside, p. 21.

Chapter 4

1. Wolfe, Charles Hull. *Modern Radio Advertising.* New York: Printers' Ink Publishing Co., 1949, p. 277.

2. MacDonald, J. Fred. *Don't Touch That Dial! Radio Programming in American Life from 1920 to 1960.* Chicago: Nelson-Hall, 1991, p. 158.

3. *Ibid.*

4. Abelson, Joan S. "Mother of the Soaps." Goucher *Quarterly,* Vol. 63, No. 3, Spring 1985, p. 5.

5. For further exploration, see Cox, Jim. *Radio Crime Fighters: Over 300 Programs from the Golden Age.* Jefferson, N.C.: McFarland, 2002.

6. Private communication with the author, April 27, 2002. Used by permission.

7. Chambers, Robert W. *The Tracer of Lost Persons*. New York: D. Appleton and Co., 1906.

8. MegaWeb Internet site, reference to *The King in Yellow* by Robert W. Chambers, December 24, 2001.

9. Memo from Frank and Anne Hummert to Richard Leonard, July 17, 1953.

10. Dunning, John. *On the Air: The Encyclopedia of Old-Time Radio*. New York: Oxford University Press, 1998, p. 467.

11. Dunning, John. *Tune In Yesterday: The Ultimate Encyclopedia of Old-Time Radio, 1925–1976*. Englewood Cliffs, N.J.: Prentice-Hall, 1976, p. 419.

12. Dunning, *Tune In*, p. 422.

Chapter 5

1. Harmon, Jim. *The Great Radio Heroes*. Garden City, N.Y.: Doubleday, 1967, p. 11.

2. Wolfe, Charles Hull. *Modern Radio Advertising*. New York: Printers' Ink Publishing Co., 1949, pp. 175–176.

3. Hickerson, Jay. *The Second, Revised Ultimate History of Network Programming and Guide to All Circulating Shows*. Hamden, Conn.: Jay Hickerson, 2001, p. 422.

4. Dunning, John. *On the Air: The Encyclopedia of Old-Time Radio*. New York: Oxford University Press, 1998, p. 402.

5. Stedman, Raymond William. *The Serials: Suspense and Drama by Installment*. Norman: University of Oklahoma Press, 1971, p. 183.

6. Harmon, *op cit.*

7. Nachman, Gerald. *Raised on Radio: In Quest of The Lone Ranger, Jack Benny, Amos 'n' Andy, The Shadow, Mary Noble, The Great Gildersleeve, Fibber McGee and Molly, Bill Stern, Our Miss Brooks, Henry Aldrich, The Quiz Kids, Mr. First Nighter, Fred Allen, Vic and Sade, The Cisco Kid, Jack Armstrong, Arthur Godfrey, Bob and Ray, The Barbour Family, Henry Morgan, Joe Friday, and Other Lost Heroes from Radio's Heyday*. New York: Pantheon Books, 1998, p. 182.

8. Nachman, p. 207.

9. Stedman, *op cit.*

10. Harmon, p. 103.

11. Nachman, p. 380.

12. Dunning, *On the Air*, p. 619.

13. *Radio Digest*, April 1932, p. 63.

14. Swartz, Jon D., and Robert C. Reinehr. *Handbook of Old-Time Radio: A Comprehensive Guide to Golden Age Radio Listening and Collecting*. Metuchen, N.J.: Scarecrow Press, 1993, p. 545.

15. Thurber, James. "O Pioneers!" *Worlds without End: The Art and History of the Soap Opera*. New York: Harry N. Abrams, 1997, p. 49.
16. Stedman, p. 189.
17. Duncan, Jacci, ed. *Making Waves: The 50 Greatest Women in Radio and Television As Selected by American Women in Radio and Television, Inc.* Kansas City, Mo.: Andrews McMeel, 2001, p. 139.
18. Stedman, p. 186.
19. Stedman, p. 185.

Chapter 6

1. Best, Katherine. "'Literature' of the Air: Radio's Perpetual Emotion." *The Saturday Review of Literature*, April 20, 1940, pp. 11–12.
2. The term "soap opera" was probably instigated in the entertainment trade press of the late 1930s.... *Variety*, a bible of the industry, may have coined the term. By 1939 *Newsweek* and other national publications were referring to the "daytime dramatic serial" with easier-to-understand handles. Journalists preferred simpler names like "soap opera" and "washboard weeper." "Soap" in the term "soap opera" was derived from the fact that manufacturers of household and personal cleaning products took great interest in sponsoring serialized dramas. Foremost among them were Procter & Gamble, Lever Brothers, Colgate-Palmolive-Peet, B.T. Babbitt and Manhattan Soap. (Adapted from *The Great Radio Soap Operas* by Jim Cox; McFarland, 1999, p. 172.)
3. Siepmann, Charles A. *Radio's Second Chance*. Boston: Little, Brown, 1947, p. 56.
4. Siepmann, *Radio's Second*, pp. 56–57.
5. Siepmann, *Radio's Second*, pp. 58–59.
6. Morton, Robert, editor. *Worlds Without End: The Art and History of the Soap Opera*. New York: Harry N. Abrams, 1997, p. 20.
7. Arnheim, Rudolph. "The World of the Daytime Serial." *Radio Research 1942–43*. New York: Duell, Sloan and Pearce, 1944, p. 60.
8. Morton, p. 20.
9. Siepmann, *Radio's Second*, pp. 55–56.
10. Best, pp. 11–12.
11. Best, p. 13.
12. Best, p. 16.
13. In 1958 Hummert recalled: "As I remember it now the idea for a daytime serial was predicated upon the success of serial fiction in newspapers and magazines. It occurred to me that what people were reading might appeal to them in the form of radio drama. It was as simple as that. And results prove that my guess was right." Stedman, Raymond William. *The Serials: Suspense and Drama by Installment*. Norman: University of Oklahoma Press, 1971, pp. 235, 283.
14. Smulyan, Susan. *Selling Radio: The Commercialization of American*

Notes — Chapter 6

Broadcasting, 1920–1934. Washington, D.C.: Smithsonian Institution Press, 1994, p. 87.

15. LaGuardia, Robert. *From Ma Perkins to Mary Hartman: The Illustrated History of Soap Operas*. New York: Ballantine, 1977, p. 12.

16. For a provocative, introspective examination of the history and development of the daytime melodrama, the reader is referred to Robert C. Allen's scholarly work, *Speaking of Soap Operas* (University of North Carolina Press, 1985).

17. Andrews, Robert Hardy. "A Voice in the Room," adapted from *Legend of a Lady: The Story of Rita Martin*. New York: Coward-McCann, 1949, pp. 111–112.

18. Buxton, Frank, and Bill Owen. *The Big Broadcast*. New York: Avon Books, 1972, p. 183; Buxton, Frank, and Bill Owen. *The Big Broadcast, 1920–1950*, 2nd ed. Lanham, Md.: Scarecrow Press, 1997, p. 175; Buxton, Frank, and Bill Owen. *Radio's Golden Age: The Programs and the Personalities*. New York: Easton Valley Press, 1967, p. 271; Stumpf, Charles K. *Ma Perkins, Little Orphan Annie and Heigh Ho, Silver!* New York: Carlton Press, 1971, pp. 16–17.

19. Ironically, Irna Phillips and Frank and Anne Hummert were destined to collaborate on yet another Phillips-originated serial, an outgrowth of *Painted Dreams*. The Hummerts supervised *Lonely Women* for Blackett-Sample-Hummert on behalf of General Mills (1942–1943). *The Great Radio Soap Operas* by Jim Cox (McFarland, 1999), pp. 251–255, provides further detail on these dual dramas' intertwining and incredibly fascinating histories.

20. Horwell, Veronica. "Empress of the Radio Soaps." An obituary for Anne S. Hummert appearing in *The Guardian*, published in London, England, July 27, 1996, p. 28.

21. Morton, p. 70.

22. Thurber, James. "O Pioneers!" *Worlds Without End: The Art and History of the Soap Opera*. New York: Harry N. Abrams, Inc., 1997, p. 48.

23. *Ibid.*

24. LaGuardia, p. 20.

25. Higby, Mary Jane. *Tune in Tomorrow; or, How I Found The Right to Happiness with Our Gal Sunday, Stella Dallas, John's Other Wife, and Other Sudsy Radio Serials*. New York: Cowles Education Corporation, 1968, p. 129.

26. Harmon, Jim. *The Great Radio Heroes*. Garden City, N.Y.: Doubleday, 1970, p. 176.

27. Dunning, John. *Tune In Yesterday: The Ultimate Encyclopedia of Old-Time Radio, 1925–1976*. Englewood Cliffs, N.J.: Prentice Hall, 1976, p. 339.

28. Thomas, Robert M., Jr. "Anne Hummert, 91, Dies; Creator of Soap Operas." An obituary appearing in *The New York Times*, July 21, 1996.

29. Horwell, p. 2.

30. It was inevitable that comparisons were made between two of the Hummerts' initial trio of successful soap operas, *Just Plain Bill* and *Ma Perkins*. Each was widowed and a tenderhearted, respectable figure set in a small hamlet. "Both could hold their own," commented James Thurber, "with a series of spite-

ful women, deceitful men, powerful bankers, and tough gangsters." He noted further: "Hummert and Mrs. Ashenhurst had found a formula that worked." (Adapted from "O Pioneers!")

31. Personal communication with the author from Jim Ashenhurst, May 18, 2002. Used by permission.

32. Rothel, David. *Who Was That Masked Man?: The Story of the Lone Ranger.* New York: A.S. Barnes, 1976, p. 40.

33. Stedman, p. 247.

34. Clark, Rocky. "They Started Radio Serials—Can You Blame Them?" *The Bridgeport Sunday Post,* Oct. 8, 1939, Sec. 3, p. 1.

35. Duncan, Jacci, ed. *Making Waves: The 50 Greatest Women in Radio and Television as Selected by American Women in Radio and Television, Inc.* Kansas City, Mo.: Andrews McMeel, 2001, p. 139.

36. Higby, p. 133.

37. Ansbro, George. *I Have a Lady in the Balcony: Memoirs of a Broadcaster.* Jefferson, N. C.: McFarland, 2000, p. 110.

38. Wolfe, Charles Hull. *Modern Radio Advertising.* New York: Printers' Ink Publishing Co., 1949, p. 192.

39. Wolfe, pp. 192–193.

40. Dunning, *On the Air,* p. 59.

41. *Ibid.*

42. Stedman, p. 267.

43. Dunning, *On the Air,* p. 58.

44. Nachman, Gerald. *Raised on Radio: In Quest of The Lone Ranger, Jack Benny, Amos 'n' Andy, The Shadow, Mary Noble, The Great Gildersleeve, Fibber McGee and Molly, Bill Stern, Our Miss Brooks, Henry Aldrich, The Quiz Kids, Mr. First Nighter, Fred Allen, Vic and Sade, The Cisco Kid, Jack Armstrong, Arthur Godfrey, Bob and Ray, The Barbour Family, Henry Morgan, Joe Friday and Other Lost Heroes from Radio's Heyday.* New York: Pantheon Books, 1998, p. 376.

45. Nachman, p. 371.

46. Dunning, John. *Tune In Yesterday: The Ultimate Encyclopedia of Old-Time Radio, 1925–1976.* Englewood Cliffs, N.J.: Prentice Hall, 1976, p. 56.

47. Nachman, p. 371.

48. Edmondson, Madeleine, and David Rounds. *The Soaps: Daytime Serials of Radio and TV.* New York: Stein and Day, 1973, p. 56.

49. This is the assessment of numerous published authors and not that of this writer alone.

50. Stedman, *Ibid.*

51. *Ibid.*

52. Higby, pp. 129–130.

53. Lackmann, Ron. *Same Time ... Same Station: An A–Z Guide to Radio from Jack Benny to Howard Stern.* New York: Facts on File, 1996, p. 138.

54. Stedman, p. 327.

55. Abelson, Joan S. "Mother of the Soaps." Goucher *Quarterly*, Vol. 63, No. 3, Spring 1985, p. 5.
56. Whiteside, Thomas. "Life Can Be Terrible." *New Republic*, July 14, 1947, p. 22.
57. Stedman, p. 283.
58. Whiteside, p. 22.
59. Ansbro, p. 107.
60. Ansbro, p. 109.
61. *Ibid.*
62. Nachman, p. 475.
63. Abelson, p. 5.
64. Higby, p. 139.
65. *Ibid.*
66. Nachman, pp. 380–381.
67. Nachman, p. 381.
68. LaGuardia, p. 12.
69. Sies, Luther F. *Encyclopedia of American Radio, 1920–1960.* Jefferson, N.C.: McFarland, 2000, p. 621.
70. Blue, Howard. *Words at War: World War II Era Radio Drama and the Postwar Broadcasting Industry Blacklist.* Lanham, Md.: Scarecrow Press, 2002, p. 187.
71. The Hummerts influenced all of these programs through their full runs with the exception of *Ma Perkins.*
72. LaGuardia, pp. 16–17.

Chapter 7

1. Nachman, Gerald. *Raised on Radio: In Quest of The Lone Ranger, Jack Benny, Amos 'n' Andy, the Shadow, Mary Noble, the Great Gildersleeve, Fibber McGee and Molly, Bill Stern, Our Miss Brooks, Henry Aldrich, the Quiz Kids, Mr. First Nighter, Fred Allen, Vic and Sade, the Cisco Kid, Jack Armstrong, Arthur Godfrey, Bob and Ray, the Barbour Family, Henry Morgan, Joe Friday and Other Lost Heroes from Radio's Heyday.* New York: Pantheon Books, 1998, p. 378.
2. For an absorbing account of the birth of this serial and, of course, an entire genre, the reader may wish to peruse *The Great Radio Soap Operas* by Jim Cox (McFarland, 1999), noting especially pp. 251–255. For a fuller biography of Phillips, see pp. 38–40.
3. Since Phillips maintained ownership of the serials she created, the ad agencies, sponsors and networks had little control over them. She appointed Carl Wester and Company to produce her programs, allowing that firm the privilege of selecting the announcers and casts. The Phillips dramas were sold to sponsors individually, and offered to networks as complete packages, similar to the Hummert plan.

4. Allen, Robert C. *Speaking of Soap Operas*. Chapel Hill: University of North Carolina Press, 1985, p. i.

5. "The major difference between Phillips and the Hummerts (aside from the considerable differences in style) was that Phillips wrote her own material," declared incisive media observer John Dunning. His statement is further applicable to the disparities between the Hummerts and Elaine Carrington, yet another prolific contributor to daytime melodrama. (Dunning, p. 531.)

6. *The Great Radio Soap Operas*, p. 62; and Dunning, John. *On the Air: The Encyclopedia of Old-Time Radio*. New York: Oxford University Press, 1998, p. 301.

7. LaGuardia, Robert. *From Ma Perkins to Mary Hartman: The Illustrated History of Soap Operas*. New York: Ballantine, 1977, p. 23.

8. Stedman, Raymond William. *The Serials: Suspense and Drama by Installment*. Norman: University of Oklahoma Press, 1971, p. 297.

9. DeLong, Thomas A. *Radio Stars: An Illustrated Biographical Dictionary of 953 Performers, 1920 through 1960*. Jefferson, N.C.: McFarland, 1996, p. 5.

10. MacDonald, J. Fred. *Don't Touch That Dial! Radio Programming in American Life from 1920 to 1960*. Chicago: Nelson-Hall, 1991, p. 252.

11. Dunning, *On the Air*, p. 58.

12. Dunning, *On the Air*, p. 300.

13. Higby, Mary Jane. *Tune in Tomorrow: Or How I Found The Right to Happiness with Our Gal Sunday, Stella Dallas, John's Other Wife, and Other Sudsy Radio Serials*. New York: Cowles Education Corp., 1968, p. 139.

14. Stedman, p. 389.

15. MacDonald, p. 251.

16. Said historiographer John Dunning: "*Road of Life* was the first major soap opera to be set in the world of doctors and nurses. It departed significantly from the 'common hero' so favored by Frank and Anne Hummert, and launched writer Irna Phillips to the top of daytime drama." (Dunning, *On the Air*, p. 579.)

17. Edmondson, Madeleine, and David Rounds. *The Soaps: Daytime Serials of Radio and TV*. New York: Stein and Day, 1973, p. 46.

18. MacDonald, p. 252.

19. LaGuardia, p. 15.

20. Siepmann, *Radio's Second Chance*, pp. 54–55.

21. Morrison, Hobe. *Variety*, August 18, 1943.

22. Morton, Robert, editor. *Worlds Without End: The Art and History of the Soap Opera*. New York: Harry N. Abrams, 1997, p. 46.

23. Stedman, p. 297.

24. *Ibid.*

25. Lackmann, Ron. *Same Time ... Same Station: An A–Z Guide to Radio from Jack Benny to Howard Stern*. New York: Facts on File, 1996, p. 59.

26. Carrington, Elaine. "Writing the Radio Serial." Cuthbert, Margaret, Editor. *Adventure in Radio*. New York: Howell, Soskin, 1945, p. 111.

27. *Ibid.*
28. Edmondson and Rounds, pp. 54–55.
29. Edmondson and Rounds, p. 56.
30. Stedman later clarified that neither Frank Hummert nor Irna Phillips considered their work to be literary or dramatic masterpieces. Edmondson and Rounds, p. 427.
31. Edmondson and Rounds, p. 297.
32. Wylie, Max, Editor. *Best Broadcasts of 1939–40.* New York: Whittlesey House, 1940, pp. 301–302.
33. *Ibid.*
34. Stedman, p. 269.
35. MacDonald, p. 253.
36. Morton, p. 68.
37. Allen, pp. 128–129.
38. Private communication with author from John Leasure, July 14, 2002. Used by permission.
39. Despite this, Frank Hummert staunchly defended his serials right along as in this communiqué penned in the summer of 1958, only a couple of years before the aural soaps vanished altogether: "From the great number of letters— fantastic in fact — that listeners write to these shows over the years, they seemed to fill a void in the lives of many people in all walks of life. So they are probably not as horrible as they have been said to be." (Stedman, p. 389.)

Chapter 8

1. McNeil, Alex. *Total Television: The Comprehensive Guide to Programming from 1948 to the Present,* 4th ed. New York: Penguin Books, 1996, p. 524.
2. Brooks, Tim, and Earle Marsh. *The Complete Directory to Prime Time Network TV Shows, 1946–Present,* 4th ed. New York: Ballantine Books, 1988, p. 493.

BIBLIOGRAPHY

Abelson, Joan S. "Mother of the Soaps." Goucher *Quarterly*, Spring 1985.

Advertising Age web site, May 18, 2002.

Allen, Robert C. *Speaking of Soap Operas*. Chapel Hill: University of North Carolina Press, 1985.

Anderson, Arthur. *Let's Pretend: A History of Radio's Best Loved Children's Show by a Longtime Cast Member*. Jefferson, N.C.: McFarland, 1994.

Andrews, Robert Hardy. *Legend of a Lady: The Story of Rita Martin*. New York: Coward-McCann, 1949.

Ansbro, George. *I Have a Lady in the Balcony: Memoirs of a Broadcaster*. Jefferson, N.C.: McFarland, 2000.

Arnheim, Rudolph. "The World of the Daytime Serial." *Radio Research 1942–43*. New York: Duell, Sloan and Pearce, 1944.

Ashenhurst, Jim. Numerous personal communications with the author in 2001 and 2002. Used by permission.

Barnouw, Erik. "Frank and Ann [*sic*] Hummert." *Media Marathon*. Durham, N.C.: Duke University Press, 1996.

Best, Katherine. "'Literature' of the Air: Radio's Perpetual Emotion." *The Saturday Review of Literature*, April 20, 1940.

Blue, Howard. *Words at War: World War II Era Radio Drama and the Postwar Broadcasting Industry Blacklist*. Lanham, Md.: Scarecrow Press, 2002.

Brooks, Tim, and Earle Marsh. *The Complete Directory to Prime Time Network TV Shows, 1946–Present*, 4th ed. New York: Ballantine Books, 1988.

Buxton, Frank, and Bill Owen. *The Big Broadcast, 1920–1950: A New, Revised, and Greatly Expanded Edition of Radio's Golden Age — The Complete Reference Work*. New York: Viking Press, 1972.

_____. *The Big Broadcast, 1920–1950*, 2nd ed. Lanham, Md.: Scarecrow Press, 1997.

_____. *Radio's Golden Age: The Programs and the Personalities*. New York: Easton Valley Press, 1967.

Bibliography

Chambers, R.W. *The Tracer of Lost Persons*. New York: D. Appleton, 1906.

Clark, Rocky. "They Started Radio Serials— Can You Blame Them?" *The Bridgeport Sunday Post*, October 8, 1939.

Cox, Jim. *The Great Radio Audience Participation Shows*. Jefferson, N.C.: McFarland, 2001.

_____. *The Great Radio Soap Operas*. Jefferson, N.C.: McFarland, 1999.

_____. *Radio Crime Fighters: Over 300 Programs from the Golden Age*. Jefferson, N.C.: McFarland, 2002.

_____. *Say Goodnight, Gracie: The Last Years of Network Radio*. Jefferson, N.C.: McFarland, 2002.

Cuthbert, Margaret, editor. *Adventure in Radio*. New York: Howell, Soskin, 1945.

DeLong, Thomas A. *The Mighty Music Box: The Golden Age of Musical Radio*. Los Angeles: Amber Crest, 1980.

_____. *Quiz Craze: America's Infatuation with Game Shows*. New York: Praeger, 1991.

_____. *Radio Stars: An Illustrated Biographical Dictionary of 953 Performers, 1920 through 1960*. Jefferson, N.C.: McFarland, 1996.

Duncan, Jacci, editor. *Making Waves: The 50 Greatest Women in Radio and Television as Selected by American Women in Radio and Television, Inc*. Kansas City, Mo.: Andrews McMeel Publishing, 2001.

Dunning, John. *On the Air: The Encyclopedia of Old-Time Radio*. New York: Oxford University Press, 1998.

_____. *Tune In Yesterday: The Ultimate Encyclopedia of Old-Time Radio, 1925–1976*. Englewood Cliffs, N.J.: Prentice Hall, 1976.

Edmondson, Madeleine, and David Rounds. *The Soaps: Daytime Serials of Radio and TV*. New York: Stein and Day, 1973.

Gould, Jack. "Soap Factory: Something About the Hummerts, Frank and Anne, and 6,000,000 Words a Year." *The New York Times*, February 14, 1943.

Harmon, Jim. *The Great Radio Heroes*. Garden City, N.Y.: Doubleday, 1967. (Rev. ed., Jefferson, N.C.: McFarland, 2001.)

_____. *Radio Mystery and Adventure and Its Appearances in Film, Television and Other Media*. Jefferson, N.C.: McFarland, 1992.

Harvey, Rita Morley. *Those Wonderful, Terrible Years: George Heller and the American Federation of Television and Radio Artists*. Carbondale: Southern Illinois University Press, 1996.

Hickerson, Jay. *The Second, Revised Ultimate History of Network Programming and Guide to All Circulating Shows*. Hamden, Conn.: Jay Hickerson, 2001.

Higby, Mary Jane. *Tune in Tomorrow; or, How I Found the Right to Happiness with Our Gal Sunday, Stella Dallas, John's Other Wife and Other Sudsy Radio Serials*. New York: Cowles Education Corp., 1968.

Horwell, Veronica. "Empress of the Radio Soaps." *The Guardian*, July 27, 1996.

Hubin, Al. Personal communication with the author: April 27, 2002. Used by permission.

Bibliography

Lackmann, Ron. *Remember Radio*. New York: G.P. Putnam's Sons, 1970.

_____. *Same Time ... Same Station: An A–Z Guide to Radio from Jack Benny to Howard Stern*. New York: Facts on File, 1996.

LaGuardia, Robert. *From Ma Perkins to Mary Hartman: The Illustrated History of Soap Operas*. New York: Ballantine, 1977.

Landry, Robert J. "Pioneer Soaper Frank Hummert, Ever the Hermit, Almost 'Sneaks' His Obit." *Variety*, April 27, 1966.

Lyons, Eugene. *David Sarnoff: A Biography*. New York: Harper & Row, 1966.

MacDonald, J. Fred. *Don't Touch That Dial! Radio Programming in American Life from 1920 through 1960*. Chicago: Nelson-Hall, 1991.

McNeil, Alex. *Total Television: The Comprehensive Guide to Programming from 1948 to the Present*, 4th ed. New York: Penguin Books, 1996.

MegaWeb Internet site, December 24, 2001.

Morton, Robert, editor. *Worlds Without End: The Art and History of the Soap Opera*. New York: Harry N. Abrams, 1997.

Nachman, Gerald. *Raised on Radio: In Quest of The Lone Ranger, Jack Benny, Amos 'n' Andy, The Shadow, Mary Noble, The Great Gildersleeve, Fibber McGee and Molly, Bill Stern, Our Miss Brooks, Henry Aldrich, The Quiz Kids, Mr. First Nighter, Fred Allen, Vic and Sade, The Cisco Kid, Jack Armstrong, Arthur Godfrey, Bob and Ray, The Barbour Family, Henry Morgan, Joe Friday and Other Lost Heroes from Radio's Heyday*. New York: Pantheon Books, 1998.

Newsweek, January 10, 1944.

Old Time Radio Digest web site (as of spring 2003) at *old.time.radio-request@oldradio.net*.

Radio Digest, April 1932.

Radio Guide, February 26–March 4, 1939.

Radio Mirror, April 1949.

Recordings, transcriptions and tapes of random samplings of most of the Hummert series from the multiple genres featured in this volume.

Ryan, Nick. Personal communication with the author: January 11, 2002. Used by permission.

Siepmann, Charles A. *Radio, Television and Society*. New York: Oxford University Press, 1950.

_____. *Radio's Second Chance*. Boston: Little, Brown and Co., 1947.

Sies, Luther F. *Encyclopedia of American Radio, 1920–1960*. Jefferson, N.C.: McFarland, 2000.

Smith, Sally Bedell. *In All His Glory: The Life of William S. Paley, the Legendary Tycoon and His Brilliant Circle*. New York: Simon and Schuster, 1990.

Smulyan, Susan. *Selling Radio: The Commercialization of American Broadcasting, 1920–1934*. Washington, D.C.: Smithsonian Institution Press, 1994.

Stedman, Raymond William. *The Serials: Suspense and Drama by Installment*. Norman: University of Oklahoma Press, 1971.

Sterling, Christopher H., editor. *Telecommunications: Special Reports on American Broadcasting, 1932–1947*. New York: Arno Press, 1974.

Bibliography

Stumpf, Charles K. *Ma Perkins, Little Orphan Annie and Heigh Ho, Silver!* New York: Carlton Press, 1971.

Summers, Harrison B., editor. *A Thirty-Year History of Programs Carried on National Radio Networks in the United States, 1926–1956.* New York: Arno Press and the New York Times, 1971.

Swartz, Jon D., and Robert C. Reinehr. *Handbook of Old-Time Radio: A Comprehensive Guide to Golden Age Radio Listening and Collecting.* Metuchen, N.J.: Scarecrow Press, 1993.

Terrace, Vincent. *Radio Programs, 1924–1984: A Catalog of Over 1800 Shows.* Jefferson, N.C.: McFarland, 1999.

Thomas, Robert M., Jr. "Anne Hummert, 91, Dies; Creator of Soap Operas." *The New York Times*, July 21, 1996.

Variety, December 30, 1936; May 11, 1938; August 18, 1943.

Whiteside, Thomas. "Life Can Be Terrible." *New Republic*, July 14, 1947.

Widner, Jim, host. *Terry and the Pirates* web site, October 16, 2002.

Wolfe, Charles Hull. *Modern Radio Advertising.* New York: Printers' Ink Publishing Co., 1949.

Wylie, Max, ed. *Best Broadcasts of 1939–40.* New York: Whittlesey House, 1940.

INDEX

Index

Index

Index

Index

Index

Index

Index

Index

Index

Index